FrontPage® 2002 For Dummies®

Cheat Sheet

FrontPage Toolbars You'll Use Most Often

The Pictures toolbar

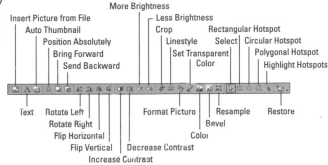

Insert Picture from File
Auto Thumbnail
Position Absolutely
Bring Forward
Send Backward

More Brightness
Less Brightness
Crop
Linestyle
Set Transparent Color

Rectangular Hotspot
Select
Circular Hotspot
Polygonal Hotspot
Highlight Hotspots

Text
Rotate Left
Rotate Right
Flip Horizontal
Flip Vertical
Increase Contrast
Decrease Contrast

Format Picture
Color

Resample
Bevel

Restore

The Views Bar

Click an icon on the Views bar to see your Web site in a whole new way.

Views
Page
Folders
Reports
Navigation
Hyperlinks
Tasks

The Formatting toolbar

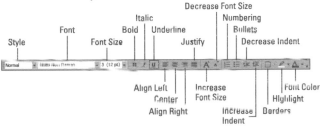

Style
Font
Font Size
Bold
Italic
Underline
Justify
Decrease Font Size
Numbering
Bullets
Decrease Indent

Align Left
Center
Align Right
Increase Font Size
Increase Indent
Borders
Highlight
Font Color

The Standard toolbar

Create New Normal page
Open
Save
Search
Spelling
Cut
Copy
Paste
Redo
Undo
Web Component
Insert Table
Stop
Drawing
Show All

Publish Web
Toggle Pane
Print
Format Painter
Preview in Browser
Insert Picture from File
Hyperlink
Refresh
Microsoft FrontPage Help

W9-BEZ-834

The Tables toolbar

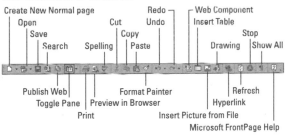

Draw Table
Insert Rows
Delete Cells
Split Cells
Center
Distribute Rows Evenly
Distribute Columns Evenly
AutoFit to Contents
Fill Color

Eraser
Insert Columns
Merge Cells
Align Top
Align Bottom
Table Auto Format Combo
Table Auto Format
Fill Down
Fill Right

FrontPage® 2002 For Dummies®

The FrontPage Buzzword Translator

FrontPage doesn't just come with a bucketful o' features; the program includes its very own set of obscure buzzwords! Check out the following terms:

- **FrontPage Web:** The FrontPage term for Web site, a collection of linked Web pages and files that's visible on the World Wide Web or an internal corporate network.

- **Web page:** An individual Web site file, written in HTML. Web pages (along with other types of files) make up the content of a Web site.

- **HTML:** Short for *HyperText Markup Language,* HTML is a set of simple text codes that defines the structure of a Web page. If you want to create Web pages, you need either to learn HTML or to use a program such as FrontPage, which cranks out the HTML for you.

- **URL:** Stands for *Uniform Resource Locator,* the technical name for an Internet site address. The URL for Microsoft's Web site is `www.microsoft.com`.

- **Web server:** A special type of program that knows how to deliver (serve) Web pages on request. The computer on which the Web server program is installed also is called a Web server.

- **Parent Web:** What FrontPage calls a top-level Web site. If you visit the Web site at `www.microsoft.com`, for example, you're looking at Microsoft's parent Web.

- **Subweb:** What FrontPage calls a second-level Web site, or a complete Web site that lives in a folder on the same server as the parent Web. If you visit the FrontPage Web site at `www.microsoft.com/frontpage`, for example, you're looking at the `frontpage` subweb.

- **Web components:** Unique FrontPage tools that you can add to your page. Web components simplify Web publishing tasks or add dynamic features to your Web site.

- **FrontPage Server Extensions:** A set of auxiliary programs, installed on the Web server, that enables certain FrontPage-specific features to work.

Where to Go for More Help

If you have a burning question this book doesn't answer, turn to the following resources for more help:

- **FrontPage Help system:** Sometimes you just can't beat the help that comes with FrontPage. To access Help, choose Help⇨Microsoft FrontPage Help.

- **The Microsoft FrontPage Web site:** This site contains lots of helpful articles, related links, and other tidbits. See `www.microsoft.com/frontpage`.

- **Microsoft Support Online:** Home of the mammoth Microsoft Knowledge Base, a searchable database of answers to all sorts of software-related questions. See `support.microsoft.com`.

- **Microsoft FrontPage Newsgroup:** People just like you are posting problems and sharing solutions on the FrontPage Usenet newsgroup. Point your news reader to `microsoft.public.frontpage.client` and join the fun!

- **Real, live tech support people:** Your licensed copy of FrontPage comes with access to Microsoft support engineers who can help you through persistent tough spots. Check the documentation that comes with FrontPage for contact information.

For Dummies: Bestselling Book Series for Beginners

FrontPage® 2002 FOR DUMMIES®

by Asha Dornfest

Hungry Minds™

HUNGRY MINDS, INC.

New York, NY ◆ Cleveland, OH ◆ Indianapolis, IN

FrontPage® 2002 For Dummies®

Published by
Hungry Minds, Inc.
909 Third Avenue
New York, NY 10022
www.hungryminds.com
www.dummies.com

Library of Congress Control Number: 2001086261

ISBN: 0-7645-0821-0

Printed in the United States of America

10 9 8 7 6 5 4 3 2

10/RQ/QV/QR/IN

Distributed in the United States by Hungry Minds, Inc.

Distributed by CDG Books Canada Inc. for Canada; by Transworld Publishers Limited in the United Kingdom; by IDG Norge Books for Norway; by IDG Sweden Books for Sweden; by IDG Books Australia Publishing Corporation Pty. Ltd. for Australia and New Zealand; by TransQuest Publishers Pte Ltd. for Singapore, Malaysia, Thailand, Indonesia, and Hong Kong; by Gotop Information Inc. for Taiwan; by ICG Muse, Inc. for Japan; by Intersoft for South Africa; by Eyrolles for France; by International Thomson Publishing for Germany, Austria and Switzerland; by Distribuidora Cuspide for Argentina; by LR International for Brazil; by Galileo Libros for Chile; by Ediciones ZETA S.C.R. Ltda. for Peru; by WS Computer Publishing Corporation, Inc., for the Philippines; by Contemporanea de Ediciones for Venezuela; by Express Computer Distributors for the Caribbean and West Indies; by Micronesia Media Distributor, Inc. for Micronesia; by Chips Computadoras S.A. de C.V. for Mexico; by Editorial Norma de Panama S.A. for Panama; by American Bookshops for Finland.

For general information on Hungry Minds' products and services please contact our Customer Care Department within the U.S. at 800-762-2974, outside the U.S. at 317-572-3993 or fax 317-572-4002.

For sales inquiries and reseller information, including discounts, premium and bulk quantity sales, and foreign-language translations, please contact our Customer Care Department at 800-434-3422, fax 317-572-4002, or write to Hungry Minds, Inc., Attn: Customer Care Department, 10475 Crosspoint Boulevard, Indianapolis, IN 46256.

For information on licensing foreign or domestic rights, please contact our Sub-Rights Customer Care Department at 212-884-5000.

For information on using Hungry Minds' products and services in the classroom or for ordering examination copies, please contact our Educational Sales Department at 800-434-2086 or fax 317-572-4005.

For press review copies, author interviews, or other publicity information, please contact our Public Relations department at 317-572-3168 or fax 317-572-4168.

For authorization to photocopy items for corporate, personal, or educational use, please contact Copyright Clearance Center, 222 Rosewood Drive, Danvers, MA 01923, or fax 978-750-4470.

Hungry Minds™ is a trademark of Hungry Minds, Inc.

About the Author

On her first day of college, **Asha Dornfest** took a bold step: She replaced her broken typewriter with a PC.

Asha did not consider herself a geek; her computer was simply a tool to help her write papers and reports — but by her senior year, she had defended her clunky PC against so many insults from Mac-loving roommates that she came to regard her computer with a sense of kinship.

After graduation, Asha trudged into the real world with a liberal arts degree and decent computer skills. (Which do you think got her a job?) She soon realized that she enjoyed showing people how computers could simplify their lives, when the things weren't making life more difficult, that is.

In 1994, Asha discovered the Internet. Soon after, she and her husband, Rael, started a Web design business in their dining room and began hawking their electronic wares. Mind you, this venture began during the Web-publishing Stone Age when many people had never even heard of the World Wide Web. A savvy friend quipped that *For Dummies* books about Web publishing may one day hit the shelves. Asha scoffed.

Today, Asha writes and teaches classes about Web publishing and other Internet-related topics. She welcomes visitors to her virtual home at www.ashaland.com.

Dedication

For Sam: my light, my inspiration.

Author's Acknowledgments

I'd like to thank the team of editors, software folks, family, friends, and other talented people who made this edition of *FrontPage 2002 For Dummies* run so smoothly. My thanks to Project Editor Shirley Jones, Acquisitions Editor Steve Hayes, Production Coordinators Emily Wichlinski and Regina Snyder, Technical Editor Mike Lerch, Senior Copy Editor Kim Darosett, Copy Editor Rebecca Huehls, and CD Production Guru Carmen Krikorian. Many more people helped put this book together than I can list here; thank you all.

The Microsoft FrontPage beta team was extremely helpful and responsive. This team really knows how to run a professional, efficient beta program, which is no small feat. I am especially grateful (as always) to Nancy Buchanan for her help and warm vibes.

My thanks to the folks at Studio B Productions for their advocacy and support. I'd also like to thank RCN/DNAI (www.dnai.com) for steady-as-a-rock Internet service.

As ever, the biggest Gratitude Prize goes to my family and friends. I am so lucky to be surrounded by such warm, loving, and intelligent people. Special thanks to Mom, Rael, and Aida Bjorklund for caring for Sam while I worked on this book.

Finally, to Rael . . . thank you for your never-ending support and love. You make it all possible.

Publisher's Acknowledgments

We're proud of this book; please send us your comments through our Hungry Minds Online Registration Form located at www.dummies.com.

Some of the people who helped bring this book to market include the following:

Acquisitions, Editorial, and Media Development

Project Editor: Shirley A. Jones

Acquisitions Editor: Steve Hayes

Senior Copy Editor: Kim Darosett

Copy Editor: Rebecca Huehls

Technical Editor: Mike Lerch

Editorial Manager: Leah Cameron

Media Development Manager: Laura Carpenter

Media Development Supervisor: Richard Graves

Media Development Coordinator: Marisa Pearman

Media Development Specialist: Brock Bigard

Editorial Assistants: Jean Rogers, Candace Nicholson

Production

Project Coordinators: Regina Snyder, Emily Wichlinski

Layout and Graphics: Joe Bucki, Gabriele McCann, Shelley Norris, Kristin Pickett, Heather Pope, Jacque Schneider, Jeremey Unger

Proofreaders: Laura Albert, John Bitter, John Greenough, TechBooks

Indexer: TechBooks

General and Administrative

Hungry Minds, Inc.: John Kilcullen, CEO; Bill Barry, President and COO; John Ball, Executive VP, Operations & Administration; John Harris, CFO

Hungry Minds Technology Publishing Group: Richard Swadley, Senior Vice President and Publisher; Mary Bednarek, Vice President and Publisher, Networking and Certification; Walter R. Bruce III, Vice President and Publisher, General User and Design Professional; Joseph Wikert, Vice President and Publisher, Programming; Mary C. Corder, Editorial Director, Branded Technology Editorial; Andy Cummings, Publishing Director, General User and Design Professional; Barry Pruett, Publishing Director, Visual

Hungry Minds Manufacturing: Ivor Parker, Vice President, Manufacturing

Hungry Minds Marketing: John Helmus, Assistant Vice President, Director of Marketing

Hungry Minds Production for Branded Press: Debbie Stailey, Production Director

Hungry Minds Sales: Roland Elgey, Senior Vice President, Sales and Marketing; Michael Violano, Vice President, International Sales and Sub Rights

◆

The publisher would like to give special thanks to Patrick J. McGovern, without whom this book would not have been possible.

◆

Contents at a Glance

Cartoons at a Glance

By Rich Tennant

page 7

page 277

page 323

page 45

page 333

"FRANKLY, I'M NOT SURE THIS IS THE WAY TO ENHANCE OUR COLOR GRAPHICS."

page 221

Cartoon Information:
Fax: 978-546-7747
E-Mail: richtennant@the5thwave.com
World Wide Web: www.the5thwave.com

Table of Contents

Part II: Creating Envy-Inducing Web Pages *45*

Chapter 3: Web Design Fundamentals 47

Chapter 4: Tweaking Your Text 57

Introduction

● ●

Not so long ago, geeks, academics, and soda-fueled computer jocks populated the Internet. Today, everyone, including CEOs, seventh-grade students, and weekend technology fiends, wants to get online. And people don't just want to surf. They each want to carve out a unique personal space: They want a Web site.

Until recently, only the technically gifted and artistically inclined attempted to publish sites on the Web. If you wanted to look good on the Web, you needed either techno-gusto or the bucks to commission someone who had it.

Not anymore. FrontPage 2002, the latest incarnation of Microsoft's popular Web site creation tool, brings new ease to Web publishing. Without any knowledge of HTML (the language used to create Web pages), you can use FrontPage to build and manage a beautiful and sophisticated Web site.

FrontPage is a hefty piece of software. And like a lot of powerful software, FrontPage is easy to use — *after* you figure out what all those buttons and menu items do.

Enter *FrontPage 2002 For Dummies*.

About This Book

You won't find lists of obscure technical terms or pages of unrelated details here. I concentrate on the practical information you need to build a well-designed, attractive, easy-to-navigate Web site. I figure you're not interested in becoming a FrontPage expert; you want to get up to speed with FrontPage quickly and easily so you can get your project underway *now*. And why not have a little fun while you're at it?

FrontPage 2002 For Dummies is a reference book, so you don't need to start at Chapter 1; just flip to the section of the book that tells you what you want to know. If you're new to Web publishing, you may want to skim the book first to get a sense of what building a Web site entails, and then read the stuff that looks particularly interesting. If you're the adventurous type, fire up FrontPage, push all the buttons, play with all the menu items, and refer to the book when you get stumped.

Conventions Used in This Book

I use a few text conventions throughout the book:

- ✔ A notation like "Choose File➪Open" is a condensed version of "from the File menu, choose the Open command."
- ✔ When I say, "Press Ctrl+N," I mean, "While holding down the Ctrl key on your keyboard, press the letter N."

FrontPage often gives you more than one way to tackle a particular task. For example, the following actions might all accomplish the same thing:

- ✔ Choosing a menu item
- ✔ Clicking a toolbar button
- ✔ Pressing a keyboard shortcut
- ✔ Right-clicking an item and then choosing an option from the pop-up menu that appears

In this book, I generally tell you the easiest way to carry out a particular task. If you prefer to use an alternate method, by all means, go ahead.

By the way, I wrote this book using Microsoft Windows 2000. If you use Windows 98 or NT, don't worry. The step-by-step instructions in this book still apply. Note, however, that some of the standard Windows dialog boxes look a little different in the book than they do on your screen. For the purposes of this book, the differences are only cosmetic; you can work through all the examples just fine.

This is a sidebar

Text tucked inside a gray-shaded box is called a *sidebar*. These sidebars highlight important information that's related to the topic being covered.

What You're Not to Read

For those of you who want a little more detail, I flag discussions about advanced or technical topics with the Technical Stuff icon. These discussions are purely optional; if you're not interested, feel free to pass up the information.

Foolish Assumptions

FrontPage 2002 For Dummies helps you jump right into using FrontPage. I therefore make a few assumptions about who you are and what you already know how to do

- ✔ **You've developed a cordial relationship with your computer and its associates: the mouse, keyboard, monitor, and modem.** You ask the computer nicely to do things by pressing keys and clicking the mouse, and it usually complies. You're comfortable with the basic workings of Windows such as using the Start menu, double-clicking items, getting around the Windows desktop, using Windows Explorer, clicking buttons on toolbars, and choosing commands from menu bars.

- ✔ **You have an Internet connection through your workplace, school, an Internet Service Provider (ISP), or an online service, and you've spent some time surfing the Web.** You don't necessarily understand how the Internet works, but you have a staff person at your ISP, company techie, or nerdy neighbor to call when you have a problem.

- ✔ **You have FrontPage sitting in a box in a highly visible location on your desk so that passersby can see it and think how technically savvy you are.** If you're brave, you've installed FrontPage on your computer (if not, I give you directions).

- ✔ **You've never tried your hand at Web publishing.** If you've tried Web publishing, you've never done it with FrontPage. If you have worked with FrontPage, you were perplexed after fiddling with the program, rushed to the bookstore, and are reading this book right now.

How This Book Is Organized

FrontPage 2002 For Dummies contains all the information you need to create great-looking Web sites with FrontPage 2002. FrontPage is no small topic, so I divide the subject into easily chewable parts.

Part I: Getting Friendly with FrontPage

Part I introduces you to FrontPage and helps you become comfortable with the program's interface and basic functions.

Part II: Creating Envy-Inducing Web Pages

Part II familiarizes you with the fundamentals of Web design and the page formatting and layout capabilities of FrontPage. You discover how to add and format text, create hyperlinks, insert graphics and image maps, and build tables (the electronic kind, not the wooden kind). You find out how to create interactive forms that let your visitors communicate with you. You also become acquainted with frames and how they can make your Web site easier to navigate.

Part III: Nifty Web Site Additions

Part III shows you how to add optional-but-impressive capabilities to your Web site. You become familiar with FrontPage themes (collections of colors and graphics that give your Web site style and polish). You find out how to pump up your Web site with multimedia, Dynamic HTML, and cascading style sheets. You get familiar with Web components, which are sets of ready-made tools you can plop into your Web site.

Part IV: Taking Your Web Site to a New Level

Part IV shows you how to take advantage of FrontPage's site management capabilities. You also find out how to control access to your Web site and use FrontPage workgroup and collaboration features. Finally, you discover how to make your Web site visible on the World Wide Web.

Part V: The Part of Tens

The Part of Tens is full of highly-useful-but-not-mandatory stuff. Read this part with your feet up on the desk, and a tall, cool drink in hand. Find out about ten things you can do with your Web site and ten Web spots you should visit in your spare time.

Part VI: Appendixes

Read Appendix A if you haven't yet installed FrontPage and you want more help than the documentation included in the box gives you.

Appendix B describes the goodies on the CD-ROM that is tucked away in the back of this book, including a bonus chapter.

Icons Used in This Book

Icon-studded paragraphs and sidebars highlight special information.

This icon points out important details you don't want to forget.

Here, you find a timesaving FrontPage shortcut. Or you may receive a design tip you can use to add oomph to your Web site.

Your computer doesn't explode when you see this icon. The icon alerts you to a potential FrontPage or Web publishing sticky spot.

The information flagged with this icon is for those of you who want to dig a little deeper into the technical aspects of Web publishing. If you just want to get that Web site published, skip this stuff.

The Web is a veritable cornucopia of Web publishing and FrontPage information. Throughout the book, I point to Web sites that offer additional help, free software tools, and information about related topics.

Some FrontPage and Web publishing effects are visible inside a page only if the visitor uses a particular kind of Web browser, or only if the site is stored on a particular type of Web server. (I explain all this in more detail later in the book.) I use this icon to point out features that require a certain type of Web browser or server program to be able to work.

Where to Go from Here

Enough preamble . . . it's time to get that Web site started! If you haven't already installed FrontPage and need help, turn to Appendix A.

If the instructions listed in the book don't exactly match what you see on your screen, check to see that your computer and Internet connection are working properly. If everything checks out, you may have stumbled upon a beta change. I wrote this book using a prerelease or *beta* version of FrontPage 2002. Although several editors and I tested all the examples in this book using the final beta version, the version of FrontPage 2002 you bought at the store may contain minor differences from the version I used to write the book.

I list all beta changes and errata on the Beta Changes and Errata page, located at `www.ashaland.com/webpub/errata.html`. Please check this page, and if you don't see what you need listed there, let me know. Your note helps me ensure that this book is as perfect as it can be; plus, I can integrate the bug fixes into future printings of *FrontPage 2002 For Dummies.*

My ultimate hope is that this book helps you develop the confidence and skills to create whatever Web site you envision. Onward, ho!

Part I
Getting Friendly with FrontPage

"Excuse me – is anyone here NOT talking about FrontPage?"

In this part . . .

Facing the task of mastering a new piece of software feels a little bit like walking into a party and not recognizing anyone. The scariest moment probably occurs after you launch the program for the first time and stare at all those unfamiliar buttons and menu items.

In this part, you get acquainted with FrontPage. I make some introductions, pass around a few refreshments, and pretty soon you'll feel right at home.

Chapter 1

Weaving a FrontPage Web

In This Chapter

▶ Understanding Web publishing

▶ Creating a new Web site

▶ Simplifying site creation with templates and wizards

▶ Using FrontPage to work with an existing Web site

▶ Creating a subweb

▶ Opening and closing an existing FrontPage Web site

▶ Deleting a Web site

▶ Exiting FrontPage

*W*ith so many people jumping on the Web publishing bandwagon, you can easily feel like you've been left in the dust. Just a few years ago, many of us used our computers as glorified typewriters and calculators. Today, regular folks are hitching the dusty, old desktop machine to a modem or network connection and are cranking out publications with worldwide distribution and impact. What happened?

The World Wide Web happened. Now that the Web has come into popular use, desktop computers are no longer isolated islands of correspondence, recipes, and personal finance records. Computers can now hook you into a world of information and communication possibilities. The writing's on the wall: The Web is here to stay, and everybody who's anybody wants to be a part of the excitement.

So where does that leave you? If you're edging your way into the dot-com world (or being dragged in, kicking and screaming, by your employer or your kids), you're in for a pleasant surprise: With a little help, creating a Web site with FrontPage 2002 is easy and fun.

In this chapter, you get your feet wet with FrontPage. You fire up the program and get started on your new Web site. You find out how to import an existing Web site into FrontPage, and how to open, close, and delete Web sites.

Exactly What Is Web Publishing?

Before you hang your shingle as a FrontPage Web publisher, it helps to understand what you're actually doing when you create and publish a Web site.

No doubt, you've already seen a Web site. Web sites are the places you visit as you make your way around the World Wide Web. Some folks refer to their Web sites as their *home pages*. FrontPage refers to Web sites simply as *Webs*. A FrontPage Web is a Web site that was created in or is maintained with FrontPage. A FrontPage Web is no different from any other Web site, aside from the capabilities FrontPage can add.

As a book is made up of individual pages, a Web site is made up of individual files called *Web pages*. Web pages contain the text, pictures, and other content you see when you visit a Web site.

As you construct a Web site, you create Web pages and then string the pages together with *hyperlinks*. Hyperlinks are the highlighted words and pictures inside the page that visitors can click to jump to a different location, page, or Web site.

After your site is complete, you *publish* it. In other words, you make the site visible to the rest of the world on the World Wide Web (or, if you're working on an internal company site, the company's *intranet*). This isn't automatic. For a Web site to be live, you must transfer the site's files from your computer to a host computer called a *Web server*.

If you're working on an intranet site, the publishing process is the same, except that the world at large won't be able to view your site; only those with password access to the intranet will have that privilege. An intranet, by the way, is an internal company network based on the same type of technology as the Internet, with access restricted to people within that company. Intranet sites generally contain information useful to company insiders, such as policies, collaborative tools, and department announcements.

Many people gain access to a host Web server by signing up for an account with an Internet service provider (or *ISP*) that makes Web server space available to its users. Others use a Web server maintained by their workplace or school. Yet another option is to sign up with one of the many hosting companies that offer server space for free (see Chapter 16 for pointers to some of these companies).

Creating Your First FrontPage Web Site

If you read the previous section of this chapter, you have a general idea about how Web publishing works. You don't need more than a fuzzy sense at this point — the process will become clearer as you become comfortable with FrontPage. You're now ready to get started with FrontPage by creating your first Web site.

If this feels like getting thrown into the deep end before learning to swim, relax. Creating your first Web site — even if you don't yet know what kind of information you want the Web site to contain — is the easiest way to become familiar with how FrontPage looks and acts. As you get acquainted with the program, you can change any aspect of the Web site or even delete the Web site and start over.

To create your first FrontPage Web site, follow these steps:

1. **Launch FrontPage by choosing Start⇨Programs⇨Microsoft FrontPage.**

   FrontPage launches. Your screen should look like Figure 1-1. A new, blank Web page named new_page_1.htm appears in the program's main window with its cursor blinking patiently.

2. **Insert some text into the page (that is, start typing).**

   Not sure what to say? How about "Welcome to My First Web Site" for starters? You can always change the text later.

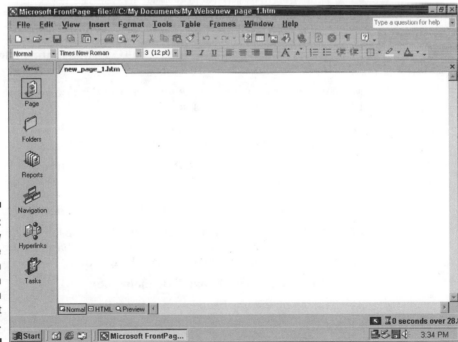

Figure 1-1:
How FrontPage looks when you launch the program for the first time.

3. **On the Standard toolbar near the top of the FrontPage window, click the Save button.**

   The Save As dialog box appears, as shown in Figure 1-2. The dialog box prompts you to save your new Web page in the My Webs folder (which is located inside the My Documents folder). When you installed FrontPage, the Setup program created the My Webs folder specifically to hold your first FrontPage Web site.

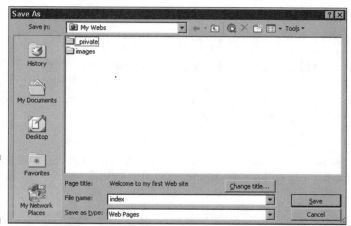

Figure 1-2:
The Save As
dialog box.

4. **Don't change the default filename (index) visible in the dialog box's File Name text box.**

   Most Web servers recognize the file named *index* as a Web site's initial page, also known as the site's *home page*.

   When you save the page, FrontPage automatically adds the .htm extension to the filename. I talk more about how to name Web pages in Chapter 2.

5. **To change the page title, click the Change Title button.**

   The Set Page Title dialog box appears.

6. **In the dialog box's Set Page Title text box, enter a new title.**

   Choose a title that describes the content and purpose of the page (something like *My First Web Site: Home Page*). In Chapter 2, I go into more detail about how to choose a good page title.

7. **Click OK to close the Set Page Title dialog box.**

   The Save As dialog box becomes visible again.

8. **Click Save.**

   The Save As dialog box closes, and FrontPage saves the page. If it's not already visible, the Folder List appears and displays a list of the folders and files that make up your first Web site (see Figure 1-3).

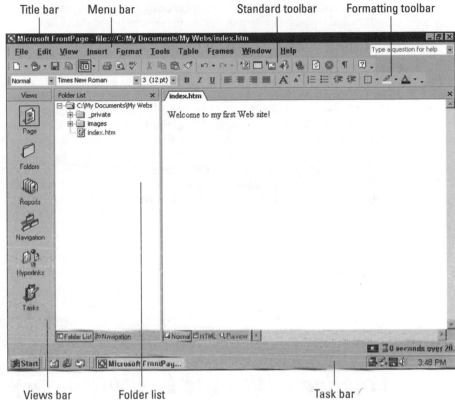

Title bar Menu bar Standard toolbar Formatting toolbar

Figure 1-3:
Your first
Web site.

Views bar Folder list Task bar

Congratulations — you've just laid the groundwork for your first FrontPage Web site! From here, you can do one of three things:

✔ Add more content — text, pictures, and anything else you want to display in your Web site — to the page you just started. The chapters in Part II show you how.

✔ Fill out your Web site with more new Web pages. I explain how to create new pages in Chapter 2.

✔ Set your first Web site aside and create a completely new Web site (read the next section of this chapter for details).

Creating a New Web Site

When you're ready to go beyond the initial site that you created when you first launched FrontPage, you're at the point where the program confuses many folks. After all, the notion of creating a new Web site *before* creating individual Web pages seems backwards. Surely one must first create the pages, then "bind" those pages together to form a site, right?

Not exactly. FrontPage prompts you *first* to create a Web site, and *then* to fill the site with the pages and other files that make up the site's content. This sequence of events makes sense when you know what the program is doing behind the scenes. For FrontPage, the first step in creating a new Web site is creating a folder and earmarking it as the future storage location for all the pages and files that will make up the site. After FrontPage creates that folder, it knows where to save the site's pages and files. FrontPage is now ready for you to begin work building your Web site, whether that's by creating new Web pages, importing existing pages from another location, or whatever. (I discuss the nitty-gritty of site-building in future chapters; I say this only to familiarize you with the general workings of FrontPage.)

When you're ready to create a new Web site, FrontPage provides you with a comfortable balance of direction and flexibility. If you want help getting started, use a Web site template to crank out a boilerplate Web site, complete with linked pages, to which you simply add your own text and graphics. If you need hand-holding, call on a FrontPage wizard to guide you through setting up a site. If you bristle at the prospect of an off-the-rack Web site, you can easily build your own site from scratch.

Creating a Web site by using a template

Templates lay the groundwork for "canned" Web sites you can customize to suit your own needs. Admittedly, sites created with FrontPage templates lack the flair of custom-designed Web sites, but if you're not sure where to begin, they give you a good place to start.

FrontPage comes with six templates:

- **Customer Support Web:** The Customer Support Web enables companies to provide product help and information over the Internet. Customers access the Web site to read product news, have questions answered, brainstorm with other users, and more.

- **Personal Web:** Use this template as the basis for a personal home page. The Personal Web template contains space for a photograph collection, personal information, and a list of favorite sites.

- **Project Web:** The Project Web tracks the status of a project and includes space for project team members, status reports, schedules, an archive, a search form, and a discussion forum.

- **SharePoint Team Web Site:** I briefly discuss this special type of site in Chapter 15.

✔ **One Page Web:** This template forms the basis of a built-from-scratch Web site, which I discuss in more detail later in this chapter.

✔ **Empty Web:** *Template* is really the wrong name for this, um, template, because it creates a FrontPage Web that contains no pages. You'll rarely, if ever, use this template, so don't spend too much time thinking about why anyone would ever want to create an empty Web site.

To create a new Web site by using a template, follow these steps:

1. **With FrontPage running, choose File⟹New⟹Page or Web (if you don't see this option in the File menu, move the pointer over the down-pointing arrow at the bottom of the File menu to view the menu in its entirety).**

   The Task Pane appears at the right of the FrontPage window, as shown in Figure 1-4.

Figure 1-4:
The Task
Pane.

2. **In the Task Pane's New from Template section, click Web Site Templates.**

   The Web Site Templates dialog box appears.

3. **In the dialog box's Web Sites area, click the template you want to use.**

4. **In the Specify the Location of the New Web list box, enter the location of the new Web site, or, click Browse to choose a location from a folder list.**

   By default, FrontPage saves new Web sites inside a subfolder of the My Webs folder (which is located inside the My Documents folder, generally on the C drive). To save the Web site in a different or new folder on your hard drive or local network, enter the folder's file path. If you're not sure how file paths work, refer to the sidebar "File path 101," later in this chapter.

If you click Browse in this step, the New Web Location dialog box appears. In this dialog box, navigate to the location in which you want FrontPage to create the new site, and then click Open. The dialog box closes, and the Web Site Templates dialog box becomes visible again. The path to the location you chose appears in the Specify the Location of the New Web list box.

If you save your new Web site inside a folder that already contains files, the files themselves are not affected, but FrontPage treats the files as part of the new Web site. If, however, you specify a folder that already contains a FrontPage Web site, FrontPage prompts you to choose a different location.

To keep your Web site distinct (and your hard drive well organized), I recommend saving the site in its own unique folder.

5. **In the Web Site Templates dialog box, click OK.**

The dialog box closes, and FrontPage creates the new Web site in the location you specified.

After FrontPage creates the new Web site, the site's files and folders appear in the Folder List. If another Web site is already open in FrontPage when you create a new Web site, the new Web site appears in a separate FrontPage window.

Web pages that come courtesy of a FrontPage template already contain text, hyperlinks, and graphics, which you can change or rearrange to suit your own needs. Chapter 2 shows you how to open pages, and the chapters in Part II tell you everything you need to know about working with Web page content.

File path 101

When you create a Web site in FrontPage, the program prompts you to save the site's pages in a folder on your hard drive. You specify the location of the folder using a notation called a *file path*. The file path describes the location of a file or folder by listing the name of the drive on which the file is stored, followed by the name of the folder (or, in the case of a single file, the filename).

If the folder or file is stored inside another folder, that folder name is preceded by a backslash (\). So, for example, instead of describing the location of a file by saying "the file named `index.htm` that's stored inside the My Webs folder inside the My Documents folder on the C drive," you can just say `C:\My Documents\My Webs\index.htm`.

Note: In this section, I assume you want to *create* your new Web site on your computer or local network, and later *publish* the finished site on a Web server. If you want to create a FrontPage site directly on a server, I explain how in the sidebar "Working with Web sites that are stored on different computers," later in this chapter.

Creating a Web site by using a wizard

A wizard takes you through the site-creation process by presenting you with a series of dialog boxes that prompt you to select different options. FrontPage comes with wizards for its most elaborate Web site templates: the Corporate Presence Web site and the Discussion Web site.

- ✔ **Corporate Presence Wizard:** The Corporate Presence Wizard sets up a corporate Web site complete with graphics. Depending on the options you choose, the site may contain anything from a product catalog to a discussion forum to company contact information.

- ✔ **Discussion Web Wizard:** The Discussion Web Wizard creates an interactive site where visitors post comments and read others' replies about a given topic. Visitors are also able to search for specific information in the text of the Discussion Web replies. Refer to the bonus chapter "Can We Talk" on the CD included with this book to see how to create a discussion group.

FrontPage comes with two additional wizards: the Import Web Wizard and the Database Interface Wizard. I introduce you to the Import Web Wizard later in this chapter.

The Database Interface Wizard helps you hitch your site to a Microsoft Access, Excel, or other ODBC-compliant database. The implications are powerful: Visitors can search the database and display the results in a Web page, add to or change database records using their Web browsers, and much more.

Creating database-driven Web sites with FrontPage is an intermediate-to-advanced task, and goes beyond the scope this book. Fortunately, the FrontPage Help system contains detailed instructions about working with databases, including the system requirements for the host server. To access Help, choose Help⇨Microsoft FrontPage Help.

To create a Web site by using a wizard, follow these steps:

1. **With FrontPage running, choose File⇨New⇨Page or Web.**

   The Task Pane appears.

2. **In the New from Template section of the Task Pane, click Web Site Templates.**

The Web Site Templates dialog box appears.

3. **In the Web Sites area of the dialog box, click the wizard you want to use.**

4. **In the Specify the Location of the New Web list box, enter the location of the new Web site, or click Browse to choose a location from a folder list.**

5. **After you've chosen the Web site's location, click OK in the Web Site Templates dialog box.**

   The dialog box closes, and FrontPage summons the wizard. In a moment, the introductory wizard dialog box appears.

6. **Answer the wizard's questions and then click Next to move on.**

   Proceed through each dialog box in this manner. If you change your mind about a decision you made earlier in the process, click Back as many times as you need to and change your settings.

   When you reach the final wizard dialog box, the Next button appears dimmed.

7. **Click Finish to complete the Web site.**

   Based on your choices, the wizard creates a new Web site. This process may take a moment or two. Relax. Get a snack. Pretty soon, the wizard disappears, and the Web site appears in FrontPage. If another Web site is already open in FrontPage when you create a new Web site, the new Web site appears in a new FrontPage window.

Another piece of the puzzle: FrontPage Server Extensions

Certain FrontPage templates and wizards make use of unique FrontPage features such as keyword site searches and interactive discussion groups. For these and other fancy FrontPage features to function properly, the host Web server on which you eventually publish your Web site must have *FrontPage Server Extensions* installed. FrontPage Server Extensions is a set of programs that works together with the host Web server. Although you can just as easily publish FrontPage Web sites on servers that don't have FrontPage Server Extensions installed, you can't take advantage of certain extra-cool FrontPage goodies. Throughout the book, I point out features that require the assistance of FrontPage Server Extensions (not all do), and I talk in more detail about FrontPage Server Extensions in Chapter 16.

Creating a Web site from scratch

You may already have a vague notion about how you want your Web site to look. A glimmer of an idea is all you need. Templates and wizards can be helpful, but you may not need them — you may prefer to build your site from the ground up.

A from-scratch site is unlike a Web site template, in which FrontPage provides you with a ready-made site framework, or a wizard, in which FrontPage provides you with a ready-made site framework plus a little content. In a from-scratch Web site, you supply the design and content yourself. Here's how to begin:

1. **With FrontPage running, choose File⇨New⇨Page or Web.**

   The Task Pane appears.

2. **In the New from Template section of the Task Pane, click Web Site Templates.**

   The Web Site Templates dialog box appears.

3. **In the dialog box's Web Sites area, click One Page Web.**

   This option creates a new Web site containing a single page: the home page. If you prefer to start *absolutely* from scratch, select Empty Web.

4. **In the Specify the Location of the New Web list box, enter the location of the new Web site, or click Browse to choose a location from a folder list.**

5. **After you've chosen the Web site's location, in the Web Site Templates dialog box, click OK.**

   The dialog box closes, and FrontPage creates a new Web site. If another Web site is already open in FrontPage when you create a new Web site, the new Web site appears in a new FrontPage window.

The stage is now set for you to begin construction on your masterpiece.

Importing an Existing Web Site into FrontPage

If you want to use FrontPage to maintain and update a Web site that was originally assembled using a different program or coded by hand, you must first import that site into FrontPage. The easiest way to accomplish this task is by using the Import Web Wizard, a handy tool that does most of the work for you.

To import a Web site into FrontPage, follow these steps:

1. **With FrontPage running, choose File⇨New⇨Page or Web.**

   The Task Pane appears.

2. **In the New from Template section of the Task Pane, click Web Site Templates.**

   The Web Site Templates dialog box appears.

3. **In the dialog box's Web Sites area, click Import Web Wizard.**

4. **In the Specify the Location of the New Web list box, enter the location of the new Web site, or click Browse to choose a location from a folder list.**

5. **After you've chosen the Web site's location, in the Web Site Templates dialog box, click OK.**

   The dialog box closes. After a brief pause, the Import Web Wizard — Choose Source dialog box appears. Here, you specify the location of the Web site that you want to import. The site's files may be stored in a folder on your computer or local network, or the site may already be published on the World Wide Web.

6. **In the dialog box, specify the current location of the Web site you want to import.**

   • If the Web site is stored on your computer or local network, click the radio button marked From a Source Directory of Files on a Local Computer or Network, and then type the folder's path in the Location text box.

   • If you don't know the folder's location offhand, click Browse to choose from a list of folders on your computer or network. If you want the Import Web Wizard to import the files stored in folders *inside* the folder you specified, select the Include Subfolders check box.

   • If the site is already live on the World Wide Web, click the From a World Wide Web Site radio button and then, in the Location text box, enter the site's Web address (which looks something like www.mysite.com).

   • If you're about to import a site from the World Wide Web, you must activate your Internet connection.

7. **Click Next.**

   The next dialog box that appears depends on the location of the Web site you're importing.

   • If the site's files are stored on your computer or local network, the Import Web Wizard — Edit File List dialog box appears, listing all the files contained in the source folder you specified. This dialog box enables you to exclude files you don't want to import along with the rest of your Web site. To do so, click the names of the files you don't want to import and then click Exclude. To start over with a fresh file list, click Refresh.

- If the site is located on the World Wide Web, the Import Web Wizard — Choose Download Amount dialog box appears. This dialog box enables you to control how much of the Web site you want FrontPage to download and import. To limit the levels of sub-folders FrontPage imports, select the Limit to This Page Plus check box and, in the accompanying text box, enter the number of levels. To limit the amount of total file space taken up by the downloaded files, select the Limit To check box and, in the accompanying text box, enter a number of kilobytes. To tell FrontPage to import only the site's Web pages and image files, select the Limit to Text and Image Files check box.

8. **Click Next.**

   The Import Web Wizard — Finish dialog box appears, congratulating you on a job well done. If you want to double-check your choices, click the Back button; otherwise. . .

9. **Click Finish.**

   The Import Web Wizard performs its magic and, in a moment, your Web site — now a full-fledged FrontPage Web site — appears in FrontPage. (I dare you to say "full-fledged FrontPage Web site" five times fast.) If another Web site is already open in FrontPage when you import a new Web site, the new Web site appears in a new FrontPage window.

Your Web site is now poised for a FrontPage makeover.

Different makes and models of Web servers recognize different filenames as the site's home page. Most Web servers recognize the names `index.htm` or `index.html`, but others recognize `default.htm`, `welcome.htm`, and `home.htm`.

If you import a Web site into FrontPage, and the site's home page filename is something other than `index.htm`. FrontPage changes the filename when it imports the site (and updates all the page's associated hyperlinks to reflect the new name) in order for FrontPage to display the Web site properly.

I only mention this quirk now in case you're wondering why the name change takes place. The home page filename becomes important only when it's time to publish your Web site, so I return to this subject in Chapter 16.

Creating a Subweb

Small, straightforward Web sites are easy to maintain in FrontPage. As the Web site grows, or the number of people involved in the site's creation and maintenance increases, however, keeping track of the Web site's exploding number of pages can turn into a major pain.

If your Web site is starting to resemble an ever-expanding amoeba, consider breaking the Web site into a core *parent* Web site with second-level tiers of information called *subwebs*. A subweb is a complete Web site that lives in a folder inside the parent Web site.

The parent Web site/subweb setup works well when you are creating a large network of interrelated Web sites — for example, a main company site with subwebs for each of the company's different products. The Microsoft Web site offers a good example; check out the Microsoft parent Web site at `www.microsoft.com`, and the FrontPage subweb at `www.microsoft.com/frontpage`.

Another example would be a company-wide intranet site, to which members of different departments contribute material. The entire operation exists inside a single parent Web site, but each department works on its own subweb. In this situation, you can take advantage of FrontPage *permissions* so that site authors from different departments must enter a user name and a password to access their respective subwebs. I talk in detail about how permissions work in Chapter 15.

The parent Web site/subweb arrangement simplifies managing a large site because, although subwebs live inside the parent Web site, FrontPage sees subwebs as distinct Web sites in their own right. You can create hyperlinks between the parent Web site and its subwebs, creating a large network of interrelated Web sites, or you can keep each site separate. The choice is yours.

 If you intend to create a Web site that contains subwebs, you can publish your site on any type of server. If, however, you intend to create *nested* subwebs (subwebs within subwebs), you must publish your Web site on a host Web server that has FrontPage Server Extensions installed. I go into detail about FrontPage Server Extensions in Chapter 16.

You have two choices for creating a subweb: You can either create a new subweb by using a FrontPage template, wizard, or from scratch (the steps that follow show you how), or you can convert a folder inside an existing FrontPage Web site into a subweb (I explain how in Chapter 14).

To create a subweb, do this:

1. **With FrontPage running, choose File⇨New⇨Page or Web.**

   The Task Pane appears.

2. **In the New from Template section of the Task Pane, click Web Site Templates.**

   The Web Site Templates dialog box appears.

3. **In the dialog box's Web Sites area, click the template or wizard you want to use.**

   To create a Web site from scratch, click One Page Web.

4. **In the Specify the Location of the New Web list box, enter the location of the new subweb, or click Browse to choose a location from a folder list.**

   Enter a file path that contains the location of the parent Web site followed by a backslash (\) and then the name of the new subweb's folder. For example, a new subweb named *joe* of the existing Web site *My Webs* stored in the My Documents folder on the C drive would have the following file path: `C:\My Documents\My Webs\joe`. If you're not sure how file paths work, refer to the sidebar "File path 101," earlier in this chapter.

   The subweb folder name you choose should include all lowercase letters and should contain only one word. This makes the site's address easier for your visitors to type after you publish the site on the Web.

5. **After you've chosen the Web site's location, in the Web Site Templates dialog box, click OK.**

   The dialog box closes, and FrontPage creates the new subweb. If another Web site is already open in FrontPage when you create the subweb, the subweb appears in a new FrontPage window. In the parent Web site, the subweb's folder appears in the Folder List with a globe icon on top (see Figure 1-5).

Figure 1-5:
A parent Web site with a single subweb named *myweb*.

You can now update and work with the subweb just like you would any other FrontPage Web site.

Open, Sesame!

You don't need a special incantation to open a FrontPage Web site. Each time you launch FrontPage, the program automatically opens the last Web site you were working on. To open a different Web site, follow these easy steps:

1. **With FrontPage running, choose File⇨Open Web.**

   The Open Web dialog box appears. This standard Microsoft Office dialog box displays the folders on your computer or local network. The left side of the dialog box contains shortcuts to popular storage locations on your hard drive.

2. **In the dialog box, navigate your hard drive or network to the location of the folder that contains the Web site you want to open.**

   Folders containing FrontPage Web sites appear with little globes on top.

3. **Click Open.**

   The Open Web dialog box closes, and the selected Web site opens in FrontPage.

If you open more than one Web site at the same time, FrontPage opens the second Web site in a new window, enabling you to jump back and forth between the two Web sites by clicking their respective buttons in the Windows taskbar, or by pressing Alt+Tab.

 Opening a subweb of the current site is a snap: In the Folder List, double-click the subweb's folder. (If the Folder List isn't visible, on the Standard toolbar, click the Toggle Pane button or choose View⇨Folder List.) You can tell if a folder inside a FrontPage Web site contains a subweb because the subweb's folder is marked with a little globe icon.

Working with Web sites that are stored on other computers

Throughout this book, I assume you do your Web-building on your own computer and then publish your finished Web site on a different computer (most likely a host Web server belonging to your company or your ISP). I recommend this approach because you create Web sites in the privacy of your own hard drive and make only the perfect stuff visible to the world.

In a few instances, however, you may need to create or open a Web site located on another Web server, such as when you're working as part of a site-building team or if you want to adjust your Web site's password protection. (I discuss password protection in Chapter 15.) In FrontPage, you can create and open Web sites directly from remote Web servers as long as: a) you're connected to the Internet or local network, and b) the Web server has FrontPage Server Extensions installed. (For more information about FrontPage Server Extensions, see Chapter 16.)

To create or open a Web site on a remote Web server, follow the steps listed in this chapter with the following change: When you specify the Web site's location, instead of specifying a folder on your own hard drive, enter the remote server's address (it looks something like `http://www.mysite.com`). FrontPage establishes a connection to the remote server. In a moment, the Name and Password Required dialog box appears. In the dialog box, enter the user name and password required for that server, and then click OK. The dialog box closes, and the Web site opens in FrontPage. You can now update and change the site just as if it were stored on your own computer. Just remember, after you save your pages, any changes you make are immediately visible to the world, so proceed with care.

Each time you create or open a Web site on a remote Web server, FrontPage saves a shortcut to that server in the My Network Places folder on your hard drive.

To quickly open a Web site you worked with recently, choose File➪Recent Webs, and then choose the location of the Web site you want to open.

Closing a Web Site

FrontPage enables you to open more than one Web site at a time by displaying each site in a separate window. To close a Web site, simply close the window in which the site is displayed (click the little X-shaped button in the upper-right corner of the window). If you haven't yet saved changes to the site's pages, the Microsoft FrontPage dialog box appears, prompting you to save each open page; click Yes. The dialog box closes, FrontPage saves the changes, and the window closes.

If you have only one Web site open and want to close the site but leave FrontPage running, choose File➪Close Web.

Deleting a Web Site

Remove those dusty old Web sites lurking in the corners of your computer. You're rewarded with a tidy hard drive and lots of extra disk space.

To delete a Web site that's currently open in FrontPage, follow these steps:

1. **In the Folder List, click the Web site's top-level folder and then press the Delete key.**

    The Confirm Delete dialog box appears and warns you that deleting a Web site is a permanent action (in other words, you can't decide after you delete your Web site that you want it back — it's kaput).

2. **In the dialog box, click the Delete This Web Entirely option button and then click OK.**

    The dialog box closes, and FrontPage deletes the Web site.

When you delete a Web site, you delete its subwebs as well.

To delete a subweb, first open the parent Web site in FrontPage. In the Folder List, click the subweb's folder icon and then press Delete. In the Confirm Delete dialog box that appears, click Yes.

You can also delete FrontPage Webs by deleting their folders using Windows Explorer. The benefit here is that deleted Webs go into the Recycle Bin, so you can restore them if you later change your mind.

Exiting FrontPage

When you're done with Web-building for the day, closing up shop takes only a second or two. To exit FrontPage, choose File➪Exit. If any of the site's pages are currently open and unsaved, FrontPage prompts you to save the pages, and then the program closes.

The next time you launch FrontPage, the program opens in whichever view you were using when you last exited (you find out about the different FrontPage views in Chapter 14).

Screaming . . . er, I mean, calling for help

By now, I'm sure you've developed an inkling of the power and complexity of FrontPage. (No doubt that inkling motivated you to buy this book!) Never fear: Help is as close as your mouse. Choose Help➪Microsoft FrontPage Help (or press F1) to access a nicely organized set of FrontPage crib notes. Or, type a question into the list box sitting in the upper-right corner of the FrontPage window, and the Office Assistant will do its best to find an answer.

If you're wondering what a button or menu item does, choose Help➪What's This?, or press Shift+F1. Then click the button or choose the menu item you don't understand. FrontPage flips to the appropriate Help screen. For a reminder about the purpose of a particular button, pass your pointer over the button; in a moment, a yellow Tool Tip appears.

If you still can't find answers to your question, refer to the Cheat Sheet at the front of the book for more places to go for help.

Chapter 2

Working with Web Pages

*M*y artistic period took place between the ages of six and ten, when my teachers set aside part of each school day for creative time. I drew pictures, wrote poems, and perfected my finger-painting technique.

As I got older, my artistic ability dwindled to scribbling on cocktail napkins. Then I discovered Web publishing and entered my renaissance. I no longer work with construction paper or tempera paints; I now use FrontPage to create stacks of colorful Web pages.

In this chapter, you become familiar with basic Web page operations: creating, opening, previewing, and saving pages. If you already feel comfy working with pages and are ready to tinker with page content and design tools, turn to the chapters in Part II.

Creating a New Web Page

FrontPage can whip out a Web page in milliseconds. One click of a button, and FrontPage presents you with a new, empty Web page ready for filling. If the prospect of an empty page intimidates you, lean on FrontPage page templates for a push in the right direction.

Using a template to create pages

Templates are to a page what a jump start is to an engine. If your Web publishing inspiration is tapped out, templates jolt you back into action.

Templates are skeleton pages to which you add your own content and design effects. FrontPage comes with templates for different page layouts, as well as pages that commonly appear in Web sites.

Unlike with Microsoft Word document templates, you cannot attach a FrontPage Web page template to an already existing page. You must use the template as the starting point for a new Web page.

To create a new page with the help of a template, follow these steps:

1. **If you intend to add the new page to an existing FrontPage Web site, open the Web site. If not, or if you're not sure, skip ahead to Step 2.**

   I explain how to open a FrontPage Web site in Chapter 1.

2. **If the Page View isn't already visible, on the Views bar on the left side of the FrontPage window, click Page.**

   The Page View becomes visible. I talk about the different FrontPage views in Chapter 14.

3. **Choose File⇨New⇨Page or Web.**

   If it's not already visible, the Task Pane appears on the right side of the FrontPage window.

4. **In the New from Template section of the Task Pane, click Page Templates.**

   The Page Templates dialog box appears, displaying a smorgasbord of templates (see Figure 2-1).

5. **On the General tab, click the name of the template that you want to use from the list on the left side of the Page Templates dialog box.**

6. **Click OK.**

   The Page Templates dialog box closes, and a new page based on the template appears in Page View. FrontPage also saves a shortcut to the template in the New from Template section of the Task Pane, so the next time you want to create a new page based on that template, you need only click the shortcut.

If the built-in templates don't meet your needs, you can always create your own. I explain how later in this chapter. You can also check out the collection of page templates on the Microsoft Web site; to do so, in Step 4 of the previous list, click Templates on Microsoft.com.

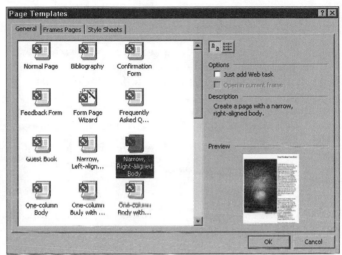

Figure 2-1:
The Page
Templates
dialog box.

Some pages based on FrontPage templates appear with text sitting at the top of the page preceded by the word *comment*. Comments are visible when you edit the page in Page View but not when you view the page with a Web browser. FrontPage uses comments to give you hints about how to customize the template. You can leave the comments there for reference, or you can delete them after you understand how the template works. To delete a comment, click anywhere on the comment and then press the Delete key. I show you how to add your own comments to a page in Chapter 4.

Creating blank pages

You may already have a good idea about what you want to include in the new page. If so, forgo the templates and start from scratch.

 To create a blank page, from the Page, Folders, or Navigation View, click the Create a New Normal Page button on the Standard toolbar. If a Web site is currently open in FrontPage, the new page is added to the site. If no Web site is currently open, FrontPage prompts you for a location when you save the page.

If a new page with a colorful background and/or graphic buttons or hyperlinks in the page margins appears instead of a blank, white page, then the current Web site sports a *theme* or *shared borders*. For more information about themes, turn to Chapter 11. If you're curious about shared borders, flip to Chapter 5.

Creating a page based on an existing page

FrontPage can grab the content from an existing page to use as the starting point for a new page. If your site will contain lots of similarly laid out pages, this feature will save you lots of time. Just follow these steps:

1. **If you intend to add the new page to an existing FrontPage Web site, open the Web site. If not, or if you're not sure, skip ahead to Step 2.**

 2. **If the Page View isn't already visible, click Page on the Views bar.**

3. **Choose File⇨New⇨Page or Web.**

   The Task Pane appears.

4. **In the New from Existing Page section of the Task Pane, click Choose Page.**

   The New from Existing Page dialog box appears.

5. **In the dialog box, navigate to the location of the file you want to use as the starting point for the new page.**

6. **When you find the file, double-click it.**

   The New from Existing Page dialog box closes, and a new page based on the file you selected appears in Page View.

 To save the "skeleton" page for future use, consider saving it as a template. I explain how later in this chapter.

Opening an Existing Web Page

If you already have Web pages hanging around on your hard drive, you can easily open them in FrontPage. It doesn't matter whether the pages are part of a FrontPage Web site; FrontPage willingly opens any Web page. In fact, FrontPage can open pages that aren't even stored on your computer; the pages may live somewhere on your local network or in the wilds of the World Wide Web. FrontPage can even open non-Web page files that are part of your Web site (such as graphic files or Microsoft Office documents) by launching the appropriate program for that type of file.

Opening a page that's part of the current Web site

FrontPage gives you several ways to open pages and files that make up your FrontPage Web site. I list the easiest method here.

First, open the Web site that contains the page you want to open (if you're not sure how to open a Web site, see Chapter 1). Next, double-click a page or file icon in the Folder List, the blue area of the Navigation View, or the Hyperlinks area of the Hyperlinks View. You can also double-click a listing in any of the reports in the Reports View.

To open a page that's part of a subweb inside the currently open Web site, double-click the subweb's folder in the Folder List. The contents of the subweb pop open in a new window. From there, you can proceed as usual to open one of the subweb's files. (What's a subweb, you ask? Check out Chapter 1.)

You can open one page at a time, or you can open several pages and move between them by clicking their tabs at the top of the Page View.

Opening a page stored on your computer or network

You may want to open a page that's part of a FrontPage Web site, but not the Web site that's currently open in FrontPage. No problem. You can even open a Web page that isn't part of a FrontPage Web site — FrontPage isn't particular.

To do so, follow these steps:

1. **In Page View, on the Standard toolbar, click the Open button.**

   The Open File dialog box appears, displaying a list of files and folders contained in the Web site currently open in FrontPage (see Figure 2-2). If no Web site is currently open, the dialog box displays the contents of the last folder you viewed.

Figure 2-2:
The Open File dialog box.

2. **In the dialog box, navigate to the location of the file you want to open.**

   The page may be stored anywhere on your computer or network. The left side of the dialog box contains shortcuts to common file locations including your desktop, your My Documents folder, or your Favorites folder.

3. **In the dialog box's file list, click the file and then click Open.**

   The Open File dialog box closes, and the page opens in Page View.

   If the page is part of a FrontPage Web site, FrontPage opens the Web site as well, and the Web site's files and folders appear in the Folder List.

Opening a page from the World Wide Web

FrontPage enables you to open any Web page stored on just about any Web server in the world. This feature is extremely useful if you want to open a Web page directly from the World Wide Web or from your company *intranet* (an internal company network based on Internet technology, but accessible only to company insiders).

To open a page stored on another Web server, follow these steps:

1. **Activate your Internet or network connection.**

2. **Click the Open button on the Standard toolbar.**

   The Open File dialog box appears.

3. **In the dialog box's File Name text box, type the file's Web address.**

   A Web address (also known as a *URL* or *Uniform Resource Locator*) looks similar to the following address:

   ```
   http://www.server.com/file.html
   ```

4. **Click Open.**

   The Open File dialog box closes. If the file is part of a Web site stored on a Web server that supports FrontPage Server Extensions, the Enter Network Password dialog box appears. In the dialog box, type your user name and password and then click OK. The dialog box closes, and FrontPage opens both the page and the Web site.

   If the host Web server doesn't support FrontPage Server Extensions, FrontPage opens a copy of the page for you to edit (not the live page itself). When you later save the page, FrontPage prompts you to choose a saving location on your own computer or network.

When you open a Web site stored on a server to which you have password access, you are working on the *live version* of the Web site. Your changes are visible to the world as soon as you save the page.

A note about Web site security

Opening Web pages stored on other Web servers brings up the topic of security. After all, if people can use FrontPage to open any page anywhere, what's to keep them from fooling around with someone else's Web site files (aside from their consciences)?

Web servers keep files safe by using an identification system of user names and passwords. If you want to make changes to files stored on a particular server, the server's administrator must give you a unique user name and password that you must enter before you can proceed. This means that, although anyone with FrontPage can open just about any Web page, only those folks with password access can actually make changes to the pages sitting on the server and have those changes be visible on the World Wide Web.

(You can set up password protection for your own FrontPage Web sites; I discuss the topic in Chapter 15.)

For FrontPage to be able to work with the server's password system, the server must be running a set of programs called FrontPage Server Extensions. Without FrontPage Server Extensions, FrontPage doesn't know how to access the server's list of authorized user names and passwords.

Therefore, you may use FrontPage to edit only live pages that are stored on servers to which you have password access and those servers must be running FrontPage Server Extensions. I discuss FrontPage Server Extensions in much more detail in Chapter 16.

Converting Other Documents into Web Pages

Document conversion is one of the most lovable FrontPage features, because much of your Web site's content may already exist in other formats. FrontPage can convert the following popular document formats into Web pages in the blink of an eye:

- Microsoft Word documents (for Windows, Versions 2.*x*, 6.0/95, 97-2000; for Macintosh, Versions 4.0-5.1, 6.0/95) (with the filename extension DOC)
- Microsoft Works 4.0 documents (WPS)
- WordPerfect 5.*x* and 6.*x* documents (DOC, WPD)
- Microsoft Excel and Lotus 1-2-3 worksheets (XLS, XLW, WK1, WK3, WK4)
- Windows write files (WRI)
- RTF documents (RTF)
- Text documents (TXT)

If you have information stored in a file format other than those listed here, FrontPage attempts to recover text from any file format.

When you use FrontPage to convert a word-processing or RTF file into a Web page, FrontPage maintains much of the document's text and paragraph formatting by converting the formats to the closest HTML style. Incidentally, RTF stands for *Rich Text Format*, a format all kinds of word-processing programs can read. Folks often use RTF when they want to share formatted documents with others who are using different types of software or computer systems.

FrontPage can also convert spreadsheet worksheets into Web pages. If you've never worked with a *spreadsheet,* it's a type of program that simplifies numerical calculations. Lotus 1-2-3 and Microsoft Excel are spreadsheet programs loved by number crunchers everywhere. Spreadsheet *worksheets* (what the program calls its documents) are arranged in rows and columns of information.

Unless you use Office Web components, when you use FrontPage to convert a worksheet, the resulting Web page contains static numbers, and you lose the ability to use functions and equations. Office Web components come with specific system requirements; I discuss them in Chapter 13.

Text documents contain no formatting whatsoever. No bold or italics, no tables or curly quotes (" ") — just regular old characters and spaces. FrontPage can convert a text document to a Web page in one of the following ways:

- ✔ **One formatted paragraph:** Page View stuffs all the document's paragraphs into a single paragraph, to which the program applies the Formatted style. In a Web page, the Formatted style appears as a mono-spaced font — in most Web browsers, the font appears as Courier. If your text document contains rows and columns of information separated by spaces or tabs, this style is a good choice.

- ✔ **Formatted paragraphs:** FrontPage maintains the separation between individual paragraphs and applies the Formatted style to each one.

- ✔ **Normal paragraphs:** You use this option most often. FrontPage applies the Normal style to each paragraph in the document. The Normal style is the default style for Web page text. The Normal style appears as a proportional font — most browsers display Times.

- ✔ **Normal paragraphs with line breaks:** FrontPage applies the Normal style to the document's paragraphs and retains line breaks. Use this style if you want your document's line breaks to remain intact.

- ✔ **Treat as HTML:** If the text file contains HTML tags, this option tells FrontPage to treat the tags as valid HTML and not to place the tags into the body of the Web page.

Conversion considerations

To convert or not to convert? It's a worthwhile question, because you have a few options when deciding how to include non-Web page files in your Web site. Here's a quick rundown:

✓ **Using FrontPage to convert the file into a Web page works well for text files, simply formatted word-processing files, or files in which all you need is static data.** If you just want to grab content from a file to dump into a Web page, this is the way to go.

✓ **Importing the file into your Web site in its native format makes more sense for long or complex documents, such as reports or publications, or if you want users to have access to dynamic information in a document (such as equations and functions in a spreadsheet worksheet).** The upside is that visitors can open the documents on their own computers as long as they have programs that know how to read the documents. The downside is that non-Web page files can be quite large and therefore take a long time to download. For details on how to import files into a FrontPage Web site, see Chapter 14.

✓ **Many Web sites make formatted documents available as PDF files.** PDF files look just like snapshots of the original files, but download quickly because the files are compact. Visitors can install a free PDF viewing program to view and print the file (I include this viewing program, called Acrobat Reader, on this book's CD-ROM; for more information, see Appendix B.) This is a good way to make a complex document such as a brochure easy for your visitors to download. However, you must buy a separate program called Adobe Acrobat to be able to create PDF files.

Office (2000 and later) users have some additional options. Word, Excel, and PowerPoint can each save documents as Web pages. The Office Web page conversion features are more sophisticated than FrontPage's, and often work better for complex or highly formatted documents (see each Office program's Help system for details). Office 2000 and later also contains a feature called *Web components*. Web components enable Office users to embed in Web pages some of the Office functionality many know and love, including spreadsheets, PivotTables, and charts. For more information about Web components, see Chapter 13.

If you don't want to convert an entire document, you can cut or copy data from other programs and then paste the data into an open page in FrontPage.

Now that you know your options, here's how to proceed:

1. **In FrontPage, create a new page.**

   I discuss how earlier in this chapter.

   If you want to place converted content inside an existing Web page, open that page and place the cursor where you want the content to appear.

2. **Choose Insert⇨File.**

   The Select File dialog box appears.

3. **In the dialog box's Files of Type list box, choose the type of file you want to convert, and then navigate your computer or network to the location of the file.**

4. **In the dialog box, double-click the file.**

   The Select File dialog box closes, and one of the following three things happens:

   - If FrontPage knows how to proceed, it converts the document's content and places the content into the Web page. (You can skip the rest of the steps in this section.)

   - If the document is a text file, the Convert Text dialog box appears. This dialog box offers you five ways to convert text, which I describe earlier in this section.

   - If FrontPage needs guidance, the Open File As dialog box appears. This dialog box prompts you to select the format in which you want FrontPage to convert the file's content. Your choices are HTML, RTF, or Text (FrontPage automatically highlights the option it thinks is best).

5. **In the Convert Text or Open File As dialog box, select the option you want to use, and then click OK.**

   The dialog box closes, and FrontPage proceeds to convert the document's content according to your preference.

FrontPage's conversion features can't reliably handle certain word-processing special effects such as annotations, footnotes, and embedded objects. In the case of embedded clip art, charts, and spreadsheets, FrontPage can convert the objects into Web-ready graphics. Other effects don't weather the conversion so well.

If in doubt, try the conversion. If you don't like the way FrontPage converts your document, close the page without saving it. Because your original document remains safely unchanged on your hard drive, you can choose a different conversion method later.

Previewing a Page

As you create pages in FrontPage, the pages look similar to how they appear as viewed with a Web browser. In techno-speak, this similarity is called *WYSI-WYG* (pronounced *wizzy-wig*), which stands for *What You See Is What You Get*.

Even so, previewing your pages is a good idea. Previewing gives you a more accurate representation of how your pages will appear to your visitors after the site has been published. FrontPage enables you to quickly preview your pages by using two methods: by using FrontPage's built-in Preview, or by opening the pages in a separate Web browser such as Microsoft Internet Explorer or Netscape Navigator.

Previewing pages using FrontPage's built-in Preview

The built-in Preview shows you how your page would look and act in a Web browser — specifically, the version of Microsoft Internet Explorer you have installed on your computer. Unlike previewing your page with a separate browser, you don't need to first save the page to preview it, which is handy for on-the-fly previewing. The built-in Preview also has the advantage of living inside FrontPage, so you don't need to launch a separate program or switch between windows to preview your pages.

The built-in Preview works only if you have Microsoft Internet Explorer 3.0 or later installed on your computer. FrontPage doesn't have a browser built into its midst; it uses Internet Explorer to display what's visible in the built-in Preview. Therefore, if you don't have the program installed, FrontPage has no way of rendering a page preview.

Furthermore, the built-in Preview can't accurately display working versions of certain FrontPage Web site effects.

Previewing pages using a Web browser

For the extra few seconds of lag time while the program launches, I recommend previewing your pages in an honest-to-goodness Web browser. By using a Web browser to preview your pages as you work, you get the most accurate representation of what your visitors will see when they check out your Web site.

Even better, if you have more than one Web browser installed on your computer, you can choose which browser you'd like FrontPage to launch. You can also select different window sizes so that you can see how your page looks to visitors who have monitors of lower resolution than yours.

Because FrontPage makes previewing your pages in several browsers so easy, consider downloading and installing more than one browser program (preferably ones that can display different features) if you have the room on your hard drive. The insight you gain about how different pages may look in different browsers is worth the extra bit of effort that installing the extra browsers requires.

For more general information about browser-specific Web publishing effects, see Chapter 3. For tips on how to account for browser-specific differences in your site's design, refer to Chapter 4.

 For an overview of the display capabilities of different Web browsers, visit Webmonkey's Browser Chart at hotwired.lycos.com/webmonkey/ reference/browser_chart/. You can download different Web browsers from Download.com at www.download.com.

 To preview your page in your default Web browser, in Page View, click the Preview in Browser button on the Standard toolbar.

To choose the browser in which you want to open the page or to control the window size, follow these steps:

1. **Choose File⇨Preview in Browser.**

   The Preview in Browser dialog box appears (see Figure 2-3).

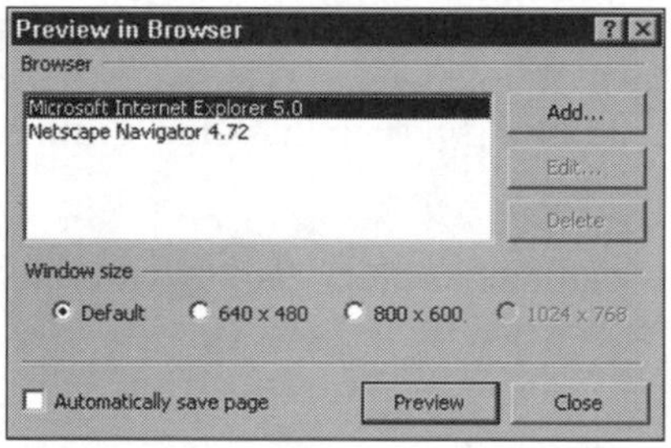

Figure 2-3:
The Preview
in Browser
dialog box.

2. **In the dialog box's Browser list, click the name of the browser you want to use.**

3. **Click the option button for the window size that you want to view.**

   A monitor's *resolution* refers to the number of pixels the monitor can display on-screen. The numbers listed next to each radio button represent standard resolution values. The larger the number, the higher the resolution of the picture and the more "real estate" a monitor can display.

4. **Click the Automatically Save Page check box to prompt FrontPage to save the page each time you use the Preview in Browser command.**

5. **Click the Preview button.**

   The dialog box closes, and FrontPage opens your page in the browser of your choice.

To edit the page, return to FrontPage by clicking the Microsoft FrontPage button in the Windows taskbar (or press Alt+Tab to switch between open windows). Make any changes you want and then save the page. To view changes, click the Preview in Browser button again or switch back to your browser and click the browser's Reload or Refresh button.

Printing a Page

Web pages don't make the best transition to print because the concept of "a page" on the World Wide Web is tied to a chunk of information rather than to a physical piece of paper. Even so, you may, from time to time, need to print your Web pages if, say, your Net-challenged boss wants to check on your work.

Before you commit to paper, choose File⇨Print Preview to see how the Web page will look on the printed page.

To print a page, do the following:

1. **Choose File⇨Print or click the Print button on the Standard toolbar.**

   The Print dialog box appears.

2. **If not already visible in the dialog box's Name list box, choose the name of the printer you want to use.**

3. **In the Print Range area, click the All radio button to print all pages, or click the Pages radio button to specify a range of pages.**

   "Pages" in this case refers to the number of pieces of paper it takes to print all the information in your Web page. If you click Pages, type the number of the first page in the range in the From text box and the number of the last page in the range in the To text box.

   Unfortunately, in FrontPage, you can only print one Web page at a time. If you want to print all the pages inside your Web site, you must open each page separately and follow this set of steps.

4. **In the Number of Copies text box, type the number of copies you want to print.**

5. **If you are printing more than one copy of the page and want to collate the copies, click the Collate check box.**

6. **Click OK to spur your printer into action.**

Keep in mind that FrontPage print settings affect how FrontPage prints your pages, not how your pages print after you publish them on the World Wide Web. If your visitors want to print your Web site, their Web browsers' print settings determine how the finished product looks.

Saving a Page

Your Web publishing masterpiece is only as grand as the last time you saved your pages. So save your work often. My fingers instinctively press Ctrl+S every time I write a particularly brilliant sentence.

You can save a page as part of the Web site currently open in FrontPage, else-where on your hard drive or network, directly on the World Wide Web, or as a FrontPage template.

 If you've made lots of changes to your page but haven't yet saved the changes, you can erase all the changes and revert to the previously saved version of the page. To do so, click the Refresh button on the Standard tool-bar. After FrontPage asks if you want to revert to the previously saved ver-sion of the page, click Yes.

 If you can't remember which open pages you've saved recently, glance at the pages' tabs in Page View. On a tab, a filename followed by an asterisk (*) indi-cates that you haven't saved changes to a page yet. To quickly save all your open pages, choose File⇨Save All.

Saving a page on your computer or network

Follow these steps when you want to save a page anywhere on your com-puter or local network. Most often, you will save new pages inside FrontPage Web sites, but you can just as easily choose another location. To save a page on your computer or local network, follow these steps:

 1. **Click the Save button on the Standard toolbar.**

   The Save As dialog box appears (see Figure 2-4).

 If you're saving an existing page, no dialog box appears — the command just saves your changes. If you want to save the page in a different loca-tion, choose File⇨Save As to display the Save As dialog box.

   By default, FrontPage saves pages as follows:

   • If a Web site is currently open in FrontPage and you create a new page, FrontPage prompts you to save the new page as part of that FrontPage Web site.

   • If no Web site is currently open in FrontPage and you create a new page, FrontPage prompts you to save the page in the My Documents folder.

• When you make changes to an existing page, FrontPage saves the changes in the same location, *except* if you originally opened the page from a site on a different Web server on which you don't have authoring access. In that case, FrontPage prompts you to save the page in a location on your computer or network.

Figure 2-4: The Save As dialog box.

2. **If you want to save the page in a different location, in the Save in list box, navigate to the location on your computer or network.**

3. **To change the page title, click the Change Title button in the dialog box.**

   The Set Page Title dialog box appears.

   When you view a Web page in a Web browser, the title appears in the browser's *title bar* — the colorful strip at the top of the browser window. Page titles also appear in search indexes (such as Yahoo! and Excite) and in visitors' lists of browser bookmarks. The title should sum up the page's content in a way that's meaningful to visitors. For example, whereas the title *My Home Page* could apply to millions of different pages all over the World Wide Web, *Asha Dornfest's Home Page* tells the visitor exactly what to expect.

4. **In the dialog box's Page Title text box, type a new title, and then click OK.**

   The dialog box closes and the Save As dialog box becomes visible again.

5. **If you want to change the page's filename, enter a new name in the File Name list box.**

   If you don't specify a filename extension, FrontPage adds HTM to the name you enter here when you save the page.

Tips and tricks for naming files

Here are a few tips to keep in mind as you consider what to name your Web pages:

✔ **Filename.** Keep your filenames short and sweet. I recommend sticking to one-word names that use only lowercase letters. This saves your visitors from having to type a long, involved filename when they want to view the page in a Web browser.

✔ **Home page filename.** The host Web server, on which you will eventually publish your finished Web site, determines your home page filename. Most Web servers recognize the filename index.htm or index.html as the Web site's home page (this is the default

home page name FrontPage uses), but other servers recognize different names. Before you publish your Web site, ask your system administrator or a helpful person at your ISP which home page filename you should use.

✔ **Filename extension.** Should you use the HTM or HTML filename extension? It's up to you — they're interchangeable. FrontPage automatically appends the HTM extension to whatever filename you choose, but if you prefer to use HTML, when you save the file, add .html to the filename you specify. You can also change the filenames of existing pages; I explain how in Chapter 14.

6. **Click Save.**

    The dialog box closes, and FrontPage saves the page.

    If the page you're saving contains pictures, the Save Embedded Files dialog box appears. I explain how to use this dialog box later in the chapter.

If you open a page from one location and then save the page to a different location, FrontPage saves a copy of the edited page. The original, unchanged page remains in its original spot.

Saving a page as part of a "live" Web site

You can save a page as part of a Web site that's stored on another Web server to which you're connected via your company intranet or the Internet. By doing so, you are, in effect, publishing the single page. (For the complete story about publishing your Web site, see Chapter 16.)

To save a page as part of a Web site stored on a remote Web server, you must have authoring access to that Web site, and the host Web server must support FrontPage Server Extensions. For more information about publishing your Web site (including the importance of FrontPage Server Extensions), flip to Chapter 16.

If the host Web server doesn't support FrontPage Server Extensions, you must publish your page using the steps listed in Chapter 16. Don't worry — it's just as easy.

To save your page in a Web site stored on a different Web server, follow these steps:

1. **Activate your Internet connection.**

2. **Follow Steps 1 through 4 in the previous section, "Saving a page on your computer or network."**

3. **In the File Name list box, enter the Web address to which you want to publish the page, and then click Save.**

   The Web address you specify must include the address of the server (it looks something like `http://www.server.com`) followed by a forward slash and the filename. If the file is to be stored in a folder or subweb on the server, the folder reference must precede the filename, like this:

   ```
   http://www.server.com/foldername/filename
   ```

   Note: File paths on Web servers work just like file paths on your own computer, except that file paths on Web servers contain forward slashes, not backslashes. For a crash course in file path notation, see Chapter 1.

   After you click Save, the Enter Network Password dialog box appears.

4. **In the dialog box, type your user name and password, and then click OK.**

   The dialog box closes, and FrontPage saves the page as part of the Web site.

Saving pages containing pictures

If you save a page that was originally opened from a location outside the current FrontPage Web site and that page contains graphics, FrontPage is smart enough to ask if you want to save the associated graphic files as well. If FrontPage didn't take this extra step, the pictures in the page wouldn't show up, because no associated graphic files would be available to display. (You discover the mechanics of Web graphics in Chapter 6.)

When you save a page containing pictures, in addition to saving the page, FrontPage pops open the Save Embedded Files dialog box. This dialog box enables you to save the graphic files as well as change the graphics' filenames and specify the folder in which the graphics are stored. You can also click the Picture Options button in the dialog box to specify details about the graphic file's format details. After you specify your preferences, click OK to save the graphics.

Saving a page as a FrontPage template

You can save any page as a FrontPage page template. This feature saves countless hours if you create lots of pages with standard layouts. Even better, if you are working with a Web design team, you can create *shared templates* that everyone on the team can access.

1. **With the page you want to save as a template open in Page View, choose File⇨Save As.**

   The Save As dialog box appears.

2. **In the Save as Type list box, choose FrontPage Template and then click OK.**

   (Because you're creating a template, you don't have to fill in a page title or filename.) The Save As dialog box closes, and the Save As Template dialog box appears.

3. **Type a descriptive title in the Title text box.**

4. **In the Name text box, type a filename.**

   Just type a short word — FrontPage automatically applies the appropriate filename extension (TEM) to the filename you choose.

5. **In the Description text box, type a short description of the template's function.**

6. **To create a shared template that other site authors can use when they're working on the Web site, mark the Save Template in Current Web check box.**

7. **Click OK.**

   FrontPage saves the page as a template.

   If the page that you're saving contains pictures, the Save Embedded Files dialog box appears. Earlier in the chapter, I explain how to use this dialog box.

The next time you create a Web page based on a template, you'll see your template sitting with all its friends on the General tab of the Page Templates dialog box.

Part II
Creating Envy-Inducing Web Pages

The 5th Wave   By Rich Tennant

"I couldn't say anything. They were in here
with that FrontPage program we bought them
that encourages artistic expression."

In this part . . .

Mastering FrontPage is one thing. Understanding how to construct a great-looking, easy-to-navigate Web site is another. Part II helps you do both.

In this part, you discover how to build Web pages from the ground up. You delve into the inner workings of the Page View, your tool for everything from creating hyperlinks to adding interactive forms to your Web site.

Chapter 3

Web Design Fundamentals

. . . .

. . . .

*T*he desktop-publishing revolution taught wannabe designers a lesson: Buying a big, fat desktop-publishing program doesn't guarantee professional looking newsletters and reports. The crucial ingredient — design sense, or a "good eye" — isn't built into the software.

In the same way, creating great-looking Web sites requires a thorough understanding of FrontPage's capabilities *and* an eye for what makes a Web site work. This chapter gets you thinking about design so you can build a site that's easy to navigate, loads quickly, and looks fantastic.

Clients and Servers 101

To understand Web design, you first need to understand the basic relationship between clients and servers on the Web. The client-server relationship is the yin and yang that makes the Internet work.

A *server* is any computer that contains and distributes information. A *client* is the program that retrieves and processes or displays that information. Web servers store and serve Web pages, and web clients (better known as *Web browsers*) display the pages on your screen. Clients and servers are useless without each other, much like separate halves of a piece of Velcro.

If you're unclear about the client-server relationship, think of your television. After you turn on your TV, the device hunts for signals from a broadcast station, assembles the signals into *Ally McBeal,* and displays the show on your TV screen. In this example, the broadcast station is the server, and your TV set is the client. Without the signals sent by the broadcast station, your TV is an empty box. By the same token, without TVs to pick up and display these signals, broadcast stations have no purpose. Figure 3-1 illustrates the client-server relationship.

When you publish a site on the Web, you place all the site's linked files on a Web server. The server waits patiently, listening for client requests from the Internet or company intranet. As soon as the server receives a request (for instance, a visitor types the file's address into his or her browser and hits Enter), the server springs into action and delivers the requested file. How the file looks after appearing on your visitor's screen depends in large part on the particular features of the visitor's computer and Internet setup, such as the choice of browser software, operating system, and size and resolution of the monitor.

Return to the TV analogy for a moment. The broadcast station (the server) spits signals into the ether, which your TV (the client) picks up and translates into *Ally McBeal* (the file). You're watching the same show as everyone else. What you see on your color, 27-inch screen, however, looks different from what your neighbor sees on the old black-and-white set in her kitchen (see Figure 3-2).

In a fit of mischief, you adjust the contrast setting on your TV, and Ally McBeal's face turns green. She doesn't turn green all over America — just on your set — and the broadcast station can't do a thing about it.

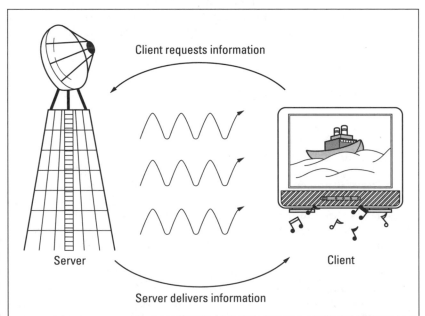

Client requests information

Server delivers information

Figure 3-1:
The client-server relationship.

Server

Client

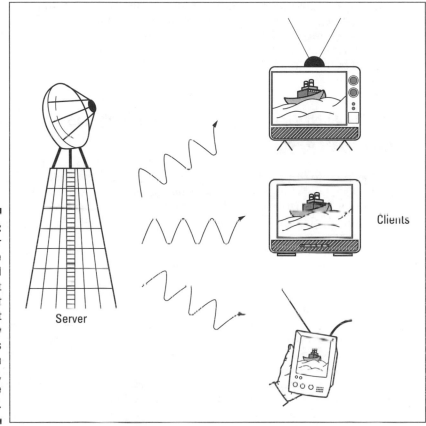

Figure 3-2:
The server
serves the
original
content, but
how that
content
ultimately
looks
depends, in
large part,
on the
client.

The moral of this story is that you have only so much control over how your Web site looks after it ends up on your visitors' screens. Read on if you want to discover more about the specific differences between clients and how to accommodate those differences in your site's design.

Cross-Platform Mania

Designing for the Web is often compared to taming a large, hairy beast. Whereas print design enables you to control how the finished product looks down to the finest detail, Web design can be, at times, a crapshoot. Why? Because the Web is a *cross-platform medium,* which means that people browse the Web by using any number of hardware devices, software programs, and operating systems. Each piece of the platform affects how Web sites ultimately look after the sites show up on the visitor's screen.

The challenge (or, as those less tactful may say, pain-in-the-butt) is to design sites that account for platform variations and still manage to look good. Doing so is not difficult after you accept a few truisms about the Web as a publishing medium. You soon realize that the Web design beast, although still big and hairy, is really just a teddy bear after you come to know it.

Web truism #1: Your visitors use different computers

Just as people drive to work in buses, Bugs, and BMWs, folks cruise the Net with all sorts of computers. Some drive old clunkers with tiny black-and-white monitors. Others speed along with turbo-charged processors and a big, full-color display. The beauty of the Web is that the vehicle doesn't matter — whether you use a Mac, a PC, a UNIX workstation, or even a television, all you need is a Web browser, and you're ready to roll. The problem, however, is that Web sites look different depending on the visitor's hardware setup.

A particular Web site viewed on different computers doesn't necessarily look so different that you wouldn't recognize the site, but elements such as color, text alignment, and font size are all affected (in varying degrees) by your visitor's monitor size or resolution and choice of operating system. I created my personal site on a PC running Windows, for example, and I gave my page a lovely lemon-yellow background color. To my chagrin, my designer friend — a Mac user — looked at my page with his Web browser and told me that my page was a sickly green. (Fortunately, this problem was easy to fix — I share the secret in Chapter 6.)

Web truism #2: Your visitors use different browsers

Not only do your visitors use different computers, they also use different programs to browse the Web. As with platform differences, Web pages appear slightly different in each Web browser — and even in older versions of the same browser.

The vast majority of the Web-surfing population uses some version of Netscape Navigator or Microsoft Internet Explorer, the big guns in the browser field. The rest use other browsers, such as Lynx (a text-only browser), browsers designed to accommodate disabilities, proprietary browsers belonging to online services, or foreign-language browsers (to name a few).

Browser-specific design effects further complicate the situation. In an effort to encourage folks to use their products, Netscape and Microsoft each use technology that produces impressive design effects — but only if viewed by the companies' own browsers and, even then, only by the most recent version. If you're one of the unfortunate few using another browser, or you use an older version of Internet Explorer or Navigator, too bad.

Fortunately, FrontPage gives you some level of control over browser-specific effects as you design your Web site. I show you how to use this feature in Chapter 4.

Web truism #3: Your visitors connect to the Internet at different speeds

Speed is an obsession on the Internet. A few seconds spent waiting for a Web site to appear on-screen feels like an eternity. Seconds stretch into agonizing minutes for those of your visitors using slow Internet connections.

What causes a Web site to load at tortoise speed? Some factors are beyond your control, such as the speed of the Web server that hosts the Web site or the amount of traffic clogging the network at that particular moment.

Other factors directly relate to the design of the Web site itself. Graphics are the most common culprit. Big pictures with lots of colors take a long time to load and are not always worth the time that visitors spend waiting.

The length of a Web page also affects its speed. Pages containing several screens full of text load more slowly than shorter pages.

Other sloths include multimedia goodies, such as sounds, videos, and embedded miniprograms called Java applets or ActiveX components. These extras, so loved by designers with lightning-fast Internet connections, are the bane of regular folks surfing with a 28.8 Kbps modem.

Web truism #4: Your visitors come from diverse cultures

Consider your visitors' cultural backgrounds to be as central to your design as platform differences. Differences in language and outlook affect how your visitors experience your Web site just as much as their choices of computer or browser. Beyond its appearance, your site must speak to people of different cultures, nationalities, and value systems. Keep a diverse audience in mind as you build your site. By making sure that each page is easy to navigate and is clearly written, you make your site accessible to the largest audience possible.

FrontPage also has sophisticated foreign language capabilities, both in the program's interface, and in the program's ability to create Web pages that contain different languages. For details, refer to the Help system coverage by choosing Help⇨Microsoft FrontPage Help.

Five Steps to a Brilliant Web Site

If you read the preceding section, you're now aware of the Web-design truisms, and you can account for these factors as you design your site. The following sections describe how to do so in five easy steps.

Give your site a purpose

As I write this book, my purpose isn't to document the Internet or even to explain every nook and cranny of FrontPage. My purpose is to show you how to use FrontPage to quickly create a beautiful Web site — and have fun at the same time.

Your site needs a similar clarity of purpose to be effective. Focus on what you want your site to accomplish: Do you want to educate your visitors? Do you want to sell them a product? Do you just want to share your warped vision of the world? After you decide what you want your site to do, make the purpose clear to your visitors right away so they know what to expect if they decide to stay for a while.

You can state your site's purpose directly. Or you can use a more subtle approach by listing your site's different parts, thereby enabling your visitors to know, at a glance, what kind of information they can find there.

Remember your visitors

Establishing a purpose can be daunting unless you concentrate on your most important visitors: your *target audience*. Just as *Seventeen* targets teenyboppers and *Wired* targets technology addicts, your site must target a specific group of people.

Visualize your target audience. No, don't try to divine your visitors' hair color or astrological signs. Ask yourself the following questions: "Are they technically savvy? How old are they? What kind of information do they want?" The more answers you come up with, the better you can communicate your message to your visitors.

Cultivate an image

Elvis, Nike, and Howard Stern all have something your Web site needs: an image. Your site's image is everything it says without words — in advertising and design lingo, its *look and feel*. So think about how you'd want your target audience to describe your site — "friendly," "cutting edge," "useful," "bizarre" — and choose your site's tone, graphics and layout accordingly.

Make your site easy to navigate

If you've ever driven a car in San Francisco, you know it's not what one would call a user-friendly city. One way streets, nosebleed hills, and elusive parking make driving in San Francisco a daunting experience for the first-time visitor. (Of course, you can always double-park while you hop out for a cappuccino, which more than makes up for the hassles.)

Your Web site should be just the opposite. Your site must be easy to navigate the very first time around. Guide your visitors with clearly categorized information and thoughtfully placed links. (Link bars help your visitors, too; check out Chapter 5 for details.) Break information into manageable bits, keeping pages short and easy to read. If your visitors get lost, give them a map containing links to all the pages in your site or, even better, set up the site so that visitors can search your site for keywords. (You can perform this task by using the FrontPage Web Search component, which I describe in Chapter 13.)

Plan for the future

Web sites, like little babies, grow. It's inevitable. As time goes on, you're bound to add new pages and even new sections to your site. Build some growing room into your site's organization. Minimize repetitive tasks by creating page templates. Use shared borders and the Include Content Web components to automate the inclusion of standard elements in your pages. (You can read about shared borders in Chapter 5 and Web components in Chapter 13.) Most important, keep the growth of your Web site in perspective by refining your site's purpose and by remaining focused on your target audience.

The Web loves to talk about itself, hence the enormous number of Web sites devoted to the topic of Web design. Here are a few I like:

✔ Webmonkey at `hotwired.lycos.com/webmonkey/`

✔ Builder.com at `www.builder.com`

✔ Web Review at `www.webreview.com`

Or, if you're looking for some good books on the topic of Web design, check out *Web Design & Desktop Publishing For Dummies,* 2nd Edition, by Roger C. Parker (IDG Books Worldwide, Inc.), or *The Non-Designer's Web Book,* 2nd Edition, by Robin Williams and John Tollett (Peachpit Press).

Proof That HTML Is Easy

And you thought you'd sneak out of here without hearing anything about HTML, the language used to create Web pages. You don't need to know HTML to publish fully functional, great-looking Web sites with FrontPage. If you want to get serious about Web publishing, however, HTML fluency has no substitute. HTML evolves faster than Microsoft can crank out new versions of FrontPage, so knowing HTML enables you to integrate the latest, hottest Web-design effects into your site right away.

You don't need programming experience to learn HTML because HTML isn't a programming language. HTML is a *markup language,* which means that it's just a series of codes that signal your Web browser to display certain formatting and layout effects. These codes, called *tags,* are easy to pick up. Don't believe me? Keep reading: I prove my point in the following paragraphs.

Figure 3-3 shows a line of text in a Web page as it looks when viewed with a Web browser.

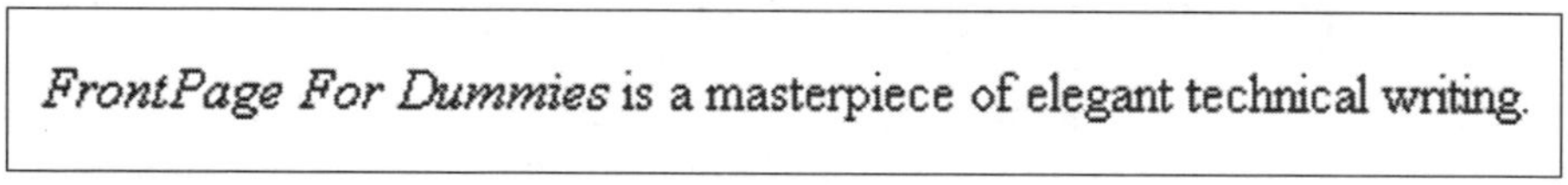

Figure 3-3:
Regular and italic text, as seen in a Web browser.

FrontPage For Dummies is a masterpiece of elegant technical writing.

Figure 3-4 shows the HTML tags behind that same line of text. The HTML tags that define italic text (<i> and </i>) surround the words *FrontPage For Dummies.* The opening tag, <i>, tells the Web browser where the italic text begins, and the closing tag, </i>, indicates where the italics end.

That's the basic premise behind HTML. Not as difficult as you thought, eh? So consider taking a crack at HTML. If you're serious about becoming a Web designer, it's the thing to do.

Figure 3-4:
The HTML
source
behind the
text pictured
in Figure
3-3.

```
<i>FrontPage For Dummies</i> is a masterpiece of elegant technical writing.
```

FrontPage contains several features that simplify working with your page's underlying HTML. To access a page's HTML tags, with the page open in Page View, click the HTML button (it's located next to the Preview button in the lower portion of the Page View window). The Help system contains detailed information about working with FrontPage's HTML features. To access Help, choose Help➪Microsoft FrontPage Help (or press F1).

No doubt my HTML teaser has captivated your imagination. Find out more by visiting one or several of the wonderful HTML tutorials on the Web. Visit www.ashaland.com/webpub/about.html for an overview. Or add *HTML For Dummies,* 3rd Edition (IDG Books Worldwide, Inc.), by Ed Tittel and Steve James, to your computer book library.

Chapter 4

Tweaking Your Text

● ●

In This Chapter

▶ Adding text

▶ Designing with browser and server compatibility in mind

▶ Creating stylish fonts and paragraphs

▶ Building lists

▶ Adjusting paragraph alignment, indenting, and spacing

▶ Adding borders and shading

▶ Inserting a timestamp

▶ Inserting symbols, invisible comments, and horizontal lines

● ●

*Y*ou didn't buy this book just to find out how to use FrontPage. Figuring out FrontPage is a means to an end; your ultimate goal is to create a spectacular Web site. In this and the following chapters, I show you how to build beautiful pages using the FrontPage Page View.

The Page View contains a gazillion tools and commands that control various aspects of a Web page. In this chapter, I concentrate on the tools that affect the main ingredient of a page: text.

What Does the Page View Do?

You use the Page View to open and add stuff to the individual pages that make up your Web site.

Before programs like FrontPage hit the scene, you had to create and work with Web pages by fiddling with HTML. HTML stands for *HyperText Markup Language,* a set of codes that defines the layout and structure of a Web page. These codes (called *tags*) control how the page looks and acts. (Figure 4-1 illustrates a bare-naked Web page with its HTML tags in full view.) As you surf the Web, your Web browser translates HTML tags into the nice, neat Web page you see on-screen (see Figure 4-2).

Figure 4-1:
Please avert
your eyes:
This page's
HTML tags
are
showing.

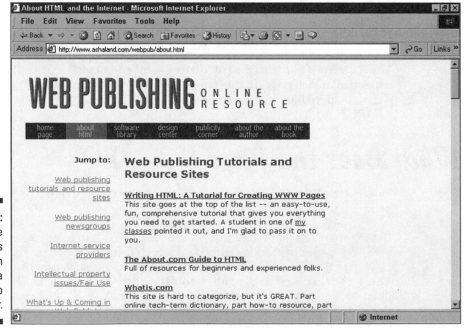

Figure 4-2:
The same
page as
seen
through a
Web
browser.

TECHNICAL STUFF

HTML isn't just for geeks

Although you don't need to learn HTML to create Web pages with FrontPage, a bit of HTML knowledge certainly doesn't hurt. In fact, learning HTML is well worth your time. HTML is constantly evolving, with new tags and design effects making impressive debuts. Future versions of FrontPage are sure to support these features, but you don't want to wait for (or, heaven forbid, pay for) an upgrade so that you can use hot, new effects in your site, do you? So consider learning a bit of HTML. You gain a greater understanding of Web publishing, and you can take advantage of HTML's latest features. At the very least, you can impress your colleagues at the next staff party.

In Chapter 3, I introduce you to some elementary HTML, just to prove how easy the stuff is.

Until recently, you had to know HTML to create a Web page. Although memorizing tags is not difficult, doing so does take time. Because most of us would rather frolic on the beach than spend weekends in front of the computer, the process of learning HTML (along with programming the VCR) stayed tucked away in the techie zone.

That is, until programs like FrontPage came along. The Page View does the HTML grunt work for you, freeing your brain cells for creative tasks. You get to choose menu items and click buttons, and the Page View generates all the HTML behind the scenes — which means that you can create sophisticated Web pages without sacrificing precious beach time.

Getting Started

Words, letters, numbers, characters. Text. It seems rather prosaic alongside the World Wide Web's flashy graphics and interactive effects. Yet text is the most important part of each page that you create, because the text makes up the majority of the content. You may dazzle your visitors with cutting-edge visuals and multimedia tricks, but the content — fresh, interesting, useful information — keeps people coming back for more.

Adding text to a page

Enough with the lecture. I promised to get you started on a Web page, didn't I? Okay, so launch FrontPage and open your Web site, jump to the Page View, create a new blank page, and start typing. Or, open and type on an existing page. (If you're not sure how to launch or get around in FrontPage, flip through the chapters in Part I.)

If you want more room to type, you can increase your screen real estate by hiding the Views bar and the Folder List. To toggle the current setting, choose View➪Views Bar and View➪Folder List.

Sanity-saving shortcuts

FrontPage shares many attractive features with its Microsoft Office siblings. Page View contains the following timesaving features that may tempt you to give your computer a big, affectionate squeeze:

- ✔ **Undo:** If you type (or, worse, delete) something that you didn't want typed (or deleted), the Undo button on the Standard toolbar enables you to take back what you've done, up to the last 30 actions.

- ✔ **Redo:** You can redo anything you've undone by clicking the Redo button.

- ✔ **Cut, Copy, and Paste:** You can cut, copy, and paste stuff (text, images — just about anything that you can select with your pointer) between open pages in FrontPage and between documents in different programs. Just click the Cut, Copy, or Paste button. If you want more control over how FrontPage formats the text you are about to paste into your document, choose Edit➪Paste Special.

- ✔ **The Office Clipboard:** All Office XP/2002 programs include the Office Clipboard, which enables you to cut, copy, and paste multiple items across Office programs. To turn on the Office Clipboard (which lives in FrontPage's Task Pane), choose Edit➪Office Clipboard.

- ✔ **Drag and drop:** You can drag and drop text, graphics, and other elements to different locations on pages.

- ✔ **Find and Replace:** The Edit➪Find command enables you to jump directly to the location of a character, word, or phrase. You can even replace all instances of that character/word/phrase with another character/word/ phrase by using the Edit➪Replace command. Both the Find and the Replace functions work inside a single page or across the entire Web site. These functions can even sift through the pages' HTML tags (a useful feature if you're HTML-literate). To search for a document across Webs or other Office applications, choose File➪Search.

- ✔ **Thesaurus:** The built-in Thesaurus (accessible by choosing Tools➪Thesaurus) instantly boosts your vocabulary by thousands of words.

- ✔ **Spell checking:** Click the Spelling button to take care of last-minute typo cleanups. If you activate the spell checker while in Page View, FrontPage spell checks the open page. If you are in any other view, FrontPage gives you the option to spell check the entire Web site in one go. FrontPage also knows how to check spelling as you type. Red squiggly lines appear inside the page beneath words that are either misspelled or unrecognizable to FrontPage. To correct a mistake, right-click the word and then choose the correct spelling from the pop-up menu that appears. If the word is spelled correctly but is unfamiliar to FrontPage, add the word to the FrontPage dictionary by right-clicking the word and then choosing Add to Dictionary. (To turn on and off automatic spell checking, choose Tools⇔Page Options. On the General tab of the Options dialog box that appears, select the Check Spelling as You Type check box. Click OK to close the dialog box.)

✔ **Customizable toolbars:** You can show, hide, rearrange, and customize any of the FrontPage toolbars. To show or hide toolbars, choose View⇔Toolbars and then choose the name of the toolbar you want to show or hide (in the Toolbars list, check marks indicate toolbars that are currently visible). To customize your toolbars, click the down arrow on the right side of the toolbar, and then choose Add or Remove Buttons⇔Standard. From the pop-up menu that appears, choose the buttons you want to show or hide. You can also *float* toolbars; pass the pointer over the left edge of the toolbar until the pointer turns into a crossed arrow. Click and drag the toolbar anywhere inside the FrontPage window, and then drop it. To dock the toolbar back in its original position, double-click the title bar on the top of the toolbar.

✔ **Right-click pop-up menus:** FrontPage contains shortcuts to commonly used commands in pop-up menus that appear after you pass the pointer over an element (a piece of text, a hyperlink, a graphic, anything) and click the right mouse button. The pop-up menu that appears contains commands pertaining to the element you just clicked.

✔ **Tool Tips:** If you can't remember a toolbar item's function, pass your pointer over the item; in a moment, a yellow Tool Tip appears telling you the item's name.

✔ **Personalized desktop setup:** The Tools⇔Customize command gives you access to all sorts of options for setting menu commands, toolbars, and other desktop settings just the way you like them.

Keeping Web Browser and Server Compatibility in Mind

Using FrontPage, you can choose a Web browser platform for which you want to optimize your site, and you can also pick and choose among browser-specific design effects. You need to think about this now — *before* you embark on site-building — because, based on your choices, FrontPage makes decisions about how it carries out text formatting and other design tasks. Furthermore, FrontPage makes available in its menus and toolbars only those effects that will work in your chosen platform.

(If you're not sure what browser-specific design effects are, read Chapter 3 for an introduction to the Web's client-server nature and how it affects Web design.)

You'll find a handy table that summarizes browser support for different Web design effects at `hotwired.lycos.com/webmonkey/reference/browser_chart`.

You can also specify the type of host Web server on which you'll eventually publish your site. This feature is most helpful if you intend to publish your site on a Web server that doesn't support FrontPage Server Extensions, because it automatically disables effects that require FrontPage Server Extensions to work. (I talk in detail about what FrontPage Server Extensions are and do in Chapter 16.)

To control how FrontPage uses platform-specific effects, follow these steps:

1. **Choose Tools⇨Page Options.**

   The Page Options dialog box appears. (Even though the command is called Page Options, the compatibility settings apply to the entire Web site, including the site's subwebs.)

2. **Click the Compatibility tab to make that group of options visible.**

3. **From the Browsers list box, choose the name of the Web browser group for which you want to design.**

   FrontPage only lists two traditional Web browsers — Internet Explorer and Netscape Navigator — because these browsers account for the vast majority of the Web browsing population.

4. **From the Browser Versions list box, choose the browser version number for which you want to design.**

   Later versions of both browsers support more design features than earlier versions.

5. **From the Servers list box, choose the name of the Web server program used by your ISP or company Web server.**

   If your host Web server program isn't listed, or if you don't know which Web server program to choose, select Custom.

6. **If the host Web server has FrontPage Server Extensions installed, make sure that the Enabled With Microsoft FrontPage Server Extensions check box is selected.**

7. **If you want to enable or disable a particular type of design effect, in the Available Technologies section, select or deselect the check box corresponding to that effect.**

8. **Click OK.**

    The Page Options dialog box closes, and FrontPage saves your compatibility settings.

From now on, FrontPage makes available only those effects that will work with the platform you've chosen. All other effects appear dimmed in FrontPage menus and dialog boxes.

In my experience, not all browsers display certain effects the same way even though FrontPage says otherwise. For example, even though both Internet Explorer and Netscape Navigator (Versions 4.0 and later) support JavaScript and Dynamic HTML, each browser displays the effects slightly differently. Therefore, if you use browser-specific effects in your Web site, be sure to thoroughly preview your page by using more than one Web browser. If you're not sure how to preview a page, see Chapter 2.

Foolin' with Fonts

In FrontPage lingo, *font* refers to how text looks on your Web page. Characteristics such as bold or italics, size, color, and typeface all make up a character's font. Characters — the thingies that appear on-screen after you press keyboard buttons — can be an unruly bunch. FrontPage comes with an arsenal of font style tools that can rein in those rowdy . . . er, characters.

Using font tools

Font tools are stored in the Font dialog box and on the Formatting toolbar. The Font dialog box (shown in Figure 4-3) contains every tool you need to control your characters. The options in this dialog box enable you to change the font, style, color, size, and effect of text in your page. To access the Font dialog box, choose Format⇨Font.

The Formatting toolbar (shown in Figure 4-4) contains buttons for the text tools you use most often. If the toolbar isn't already visible, choose View⇨ Toolbars⇨Formatting.

Figure 4-3:
The Font
dialog box.

Figure 4-4:
The
Formatting
toolbar.

You can use font tools in either of the following two ways:

- ✔ Type a bunch of text, select the text that you want to format, and then turn on the appropriate tool, either by choosing an option in the Font dialog box or by clicking a button on the Formatting toolbar.
- ✔ Turn on the tool first, type the formatted text, and then turn off the tool when you're done.

You can apply more than one font format to a piece of text. You can, for example, make a word both bold and italic at the same time.

 The Format Painter button on the Standard toolbar enables you to copy formatting from one piece of text and then apply that formatting elsewhere. To do so, select the text that contains the formatting you want to copy, click the Format Painter button, and then select the text to which you want to apply

The thrill of themes

One of the most alluring features in FrontPage 2002 is its extensive collection of graphical *themes*. Themes are coordinated sets of fonts, colors, graphics, and backgrounds that you can apply to your Web site. Chapter 11 goes into detail about themes, but I mention them here because they affect each of the text-tweaking tricks covered in this chapter. For example, if you create a new Web page that is formatted using a theme, it will already have a set font. If you insert a horizontal line, a custom-designed graphic line appears in place of the standard gray stripe. Keep these variations in mind as you progress through this chapter.

the formatting. To apply the formatting to more than one clump of text, select the text that contains the formatting you want to copy, double-click the Format Painter button, select the text to which you want to apply the formatting, and then click the Format Painter button when you're finished.

To turn off all font styles as you type, press Ctrl+spacebar. To remove all font styles from a selected chunk of text, choose Format➪Remove Formatting.

Changing text font

Usually, when folks talk about a document's font, they're referring to its *typeface*, or the style and shape of the characters. The right choice of font sets the tone for your document and makes the text easy to read.

 If you use custom fonts in your Web pages, your visitors' computers must also have these fonts installed in order for your text to appear correctly on their screens. If your visitors don't have a particular font on their machines, any text you format in that font appears to them in their browsers' default font. For example, if you use the Garamond font in your pages and a visitor who doesn't have Garamond installed on her machine browses your page, she sees your page's text in Times (the default font for most browsers).

To change text font, on the Formatting toolbar, choose a new font from the Font list box.

To set the default font for FrontPage, choose Tools➪Page Options. In the Options dialog box that appears, click the Default Font tab, and then select the desired fonts from the Default Proportional Font and Default Fixed-Width Font list boxes. Click OK to close the dialog box.

Being bold (or italic or underlined or...)

Bold and italic text make up the foundation of the font-formatting team. You pull these formats out like a trusty hammer every time you build a page. Apply these attributes for emphasis or to add variety to your text.

In addition to bold and italic, you have a bunch of other text effects at your disposal, such as subscript, superscript, strikethrough, and small caps. One effect deserves special mention: the *Blink* effect. Blink, a Netscape-specific effect, causes text to flash on and off like a faulty neon sign outside a cheap motel. Trust me — the instances are very few where the Blink effect is anything but tacky.

To apply a font effect, do one of the following things:

- ✔ Click the appropriate button on the Formatting toolbar.
- ✔ Choose Format➪Font to open the Font dialog box. Choose a style from the Font Style list, or select the check box next to the effect you want (if any). If you're not sure how a particular effect looks, select the check box to see a preview of the effect in the Preview area of the dialog box. When you're done, click OK.

The Overline, Capitalize, Small Caps, and All Caps font effects come courtesy of *cascading style sheet* commands (CSS). Browsers that are unable to display style sheets can't display these effects. Additionally, older browsers are unable to display the Strikethrough effect, because it's a relatively new addition to HTML. I talk more about style sheets in Chapter 12.

Changing text size

Text size in print documents is measured in absolute units called *points* or *picas*. Because of the way HTML works, text size in Web pages is based on a relative system of *increments*.

HTML text sizes range in increments from 1 (the smallest size) to 7 (the biggest). In FrontPage, the point-size equivalents for each increment range from 8 points (for size 1) to 36 points (for size 7). The catch: The number of points each increment value turns out to be when viewed with a Web browser is determined by *each visitor's individual browser settings,* not by FrontPage.

Here's where you run into some cross-platform prickles, because you can't assume that all of your visitors' browsers are set to display text sizes the same way. For example, by default, FrontPage creates Web pages with size 3 text, which the Page View displays as 12-point type. A nearsighted visitor browsing your site, however, may have set her Web browser to display size 3 text as 18-point type. (This scenario is a good illustration of the client-server relationship at work. Refer to Chapter 3 for more information.)

Cascading style sheet wizardry

Cascading style sheets (or CSS) enable you to sidestep many of the limitations inherent in Web design. A style sheet is a collection of formatting and style instructions that tell the Web browser how to display the page.

FrontPage contains built-in support for style sheets so you can create virtually any font or paragraph style you like (with caveats, of course). See Chapter 12 for details.

The moral of this story: Although you can control the increment size of the text on your page, you can't control each increment's point-size equivalent as it appears in visitors' Web browsers. (The visitor controls his or her own browser settings.)

To change text size, on the Formatting toolbar, choose a size from the Font Size list box.

Another way to change text size is to use the Heading paragraph style. I show you how to use paragraph styles in the section "Creating Stylish Paragraphs," later in this chapter.

Changing text color

You can dress up your text in any color of the rainbow (plus a few fluorescent shades that don't appear in nature). Color gives your text panache, calls attention to important words, and, if coordinated with the colors of the page's graphics, unifies design.

To change the color of selected text, click the down arrow attached to the Font Color button to display a list box of standard colors, as shown in Figure 4-5. Click the desired color swatch to apply that color to your text.

Figure 4-5: Using the Font Color button.

If you don't see a standard color you like, you can choose from a palette of 135 browser-safe colors. (I explain what I mean by *browser-safe* in Chapter 6.)

You can even grab colors from any object on your screen, such as a graphic or an icon. To do so, follow these steps:

1. **Click the down arrow next to the Font Color button and then choose More Colors.**

   The More Colors dialog box appears, as shown in Figure 4-6.

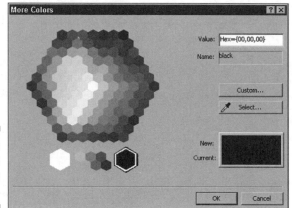

Figure 4-6:
The More
Colors
dialog box.

2. **In the dialog box's color palette, click the color you like.**

   Or, if you would rather grab a color from an existing object, click the Select button. The pointer turns into a little eyedropper. Move the eyedropper over an object on your screen that contains the color you want to use (the active color appears in the New box), and then click to select the color.

3. **Click OK.**

   The More Colors dialog box closes, and FrontPage applies the selected color to your text.

Each time you apply a color to your page, FrontPage adds that color to the Document's Colors section in all color-related list boxes (I introduce you to the list boxes later in the book). This thoughtful extra makes applying colors elsewhere in your page easy, and it helps you keep an eye on your page's overall color scheme.

You can turn the Font Color drop-down menu into a *floating menu* so that it's visible on your screen all the time (handy if you're applying color to several items, or if you want to keep track of your page's color scheme). To do so, click the Font Color button and then move your pointer over the border at the top of the menu that drops down. After the line changes color, click and drag the menu anywhere on your screen, and then release the mouse button.

To change the body text color for the entire page, choose Format⇨Background to display the Background tab of the Page Properties dialog box. From the Text list box, select the color swatch you like and then click OK. You can also base your page's body text color on that of another page. You discover how in Chapter 5.

Changing character spacing

FrontPage makes it easy to increase or reduce the amount of blank space separating selected characters. To do so, follow these steps:

1. **Choose Format⇨Font to display the Font dialog box.**

2. **In the dialog box, click the Character Spacing tab to make the options visible.**

3. **From the Spacing list box, choose Expanded or Condensed.**

4. **In the accompanying By box, enter the number of pixels by which FrontPage will expand or contract the selected text.**

   Note: The Position options in this dialog box enable you to control the amount of space between regular text and superscript or subscript text.

5. **Click Apply to see how the spacing change looks before closing the dialog box, or click OK to close the dialog box and apply the character spacing.**

The character spacing options come courtesy of cascading style sheet commands (CSS). Browsers that are unable to display style sheets won't display these effects.

Creating Stylish Paragraphs

Unlike font effects, which you can apply to individual letters and words, paragraph styles operate on entire paragraphs. Use paragraph styles if you want to make widespread changes throughout your page.

A FrontPage paragraph differs from the paragraph as defined by your composition teacher. To FrontPage, every time you press the Enter key, you create a new paragraph. Even if you type only one word and then hit Enter, FrontPage considers the word a paragraph.

Practicing safe styles

I remember the first time I used a word processor. I was seduced by the millions of text styles at my disposal and proceeded to use most of them in my first document. (I think it was a letter to a pen pal.) The finished product looked like a cut-and-paste ransom note you might see in an old private-eye movie. The text was readable, but it was a gaudy mess.

I'm not implying that you lack restraint. I relate the example only to illustrate how moderate use of font and paragraph styles enhances a page's readability and visual appeal, whereas overuse sends your readers screaming to a new Web destination.

FrontPage contains the following paragraph styles:

- ✔ **Normal** is the default style for paragraphs. Nothing fancy — just regular old left-aligned paragraphs with a proportional font. (The Times font appears in most Web browsers.)

- ✔ **Formatted** creates paragraphs with a fixed-width font (Courier for most browsers).

- ✔ **Address** is a holdover from the olden days of Web design (around 1993). Back then, the Address style was used to designate the page creator's e-mail address so visitors could get in touch. Today, folks format their contact information any number of ways, so the Address style has, for the most part, become obsolete. Besides, the style creates italic text just as the italic font style does, so why use the old clunker?

- ✔ **Headings** help identify clumps of information inside a page. Large headings, usually located at the top of the page, identify what the page is all about, and smaller headings, sprinkled throughout, divide the page's information into manageable bits. Headings in Web pages come in six sizes. Strangely enough, Heading 1 is the largest size, and Heading 6 is the smallest.

- ✔ **Lists** group related bits of information together by using bullets, numbers, or special text formatting. I discuss lists in detail in the next section of this chapter.

To change the style of a paragraph, follow these steps:

1. **Place the cursor inside the paragraph you want to format, or select more than one paragraph.**

2. **On the Formatting toolbar, choose the style you want from the Style list box.**

The List of Lists

Lists. I love 'em and hate 'em. I love 'em because lists promote the illusion that I'm in control. I hate 'em because lists show me just how much work I still need to do.

Lists in Web pages, on the other hand, do nothing but make life easier by organizing your page's information so that your text is easy to read and understand.

Bulleted and numbered lists

Bulleted lists are not lists that were attacked with an assault weapon. Such lists are groups of items, each of which is preceded by a solid dot, called a *bullet*. A *numbered list* looks like a bulleted list, except that numbers stand in for the bullets. Numbered lists are great if you need to present a series of ordered steps.

To create a bulleted or numbered list, follow these steps:

1. **Place the cursor in the page where you want the list to begin.**

2. **Click the Bullets button or the Numbering button.**

   A bullet or number appears at the beginning of the first line.

3. **Type the first list item and then press Enter.**

   A bullet or number appears on the next line.

4. **Type your second list item (and so on).**

5. **After you're done adding items to your list, press Enter twice to end the list.**

You can convert existing paragraphs into bulleted or numbered lists by selecting the paragraphs that you want included in the list and then clicking the Bullets button or the Numbering button.

To split a long list into two separate lists, click at the end of a list item and press Enter twice. The list splits into two lists and, in the case of numbered lists, renumbers itself automatically.

If the plain dots or numbers sitting in your lists don't appeal to your aesthetic senses, dress 'em up. The List Properties dialog box enables you to change the shape of your bullets or replace the dreary black spots with pictures. If you want to give a numbered list a makeover, you can use the List Properties dialog box to apply Roman numerals or change the list's starting number.

To access the List Properties dialog box, click within the list you want to format, and then choose Format⇨Bullets and Numbering.

Here's another idea: Apply a theme to your Web site. Each theme has its own set of graphic bullets. I show you how to use themes in Chapter 11.

Definition lists

A *definition list* enables you to present information in dictionary format — with the term you want to define listed first and its definition listed on the following line, slightly indented. Definition lists turn up infrequently but can come in handy every now and then, such as for a long list of names and addresses.

Although you can create definition lists several ways (as you can the other types of lists), the easiest way is to follow these steps:

1. **Place the cursor in the location where you want the list to begin.**

2. **From the Style list box on the Formatting toolbar, choose Defined Term.**

3. **Type your first term and then press Enter.**

   FrontPage creates a new line, slightly indented.

4. **Type the term's definition and then press Enter.**

   FrontPage creates a new line, flush left.

5. **Type your second term — and so on.**

   Repeat Steps 3 and 4 for each new term and its definition.

6. **To end the definition list, press Enter twice.**

List-in-a-list

Sometimes a simple list doesn't cut it. Say you need something more sophisticated, such as a multilevel outline or a numbered list with bullets following certain items (similar to the one shown in Figure 4-7). No problem!

Figure 4-7:
A number-
bullet
combo list.

```
1.  Top level list item 1
2.  Top level list item 2
       o  Second level list item 1
       o  Second level list item 2
3.  Top level list item 3
4.  Top level list item 4
```

To create such a fancy-shmancy combo list, follow these steps:

1. **Create a bulleted or numbered list.**

   The list should contain every item, regardless of level.

2. **Highlight the item or items you want to move down (or up) a level, and then click the Increase Indent (or Decrease Indent) button twice.**

   The list items move down (or up) a level.

3. **To change the items' numbering or bullet style, with the items still highlighted, click the Bullets or Numbering button.**

   For more bullet and number style options, instead of clicking Bullets or Numbering, right-click the selection and choose List Properties from the pop-up menu. Choose the numbering or bullet style you want from the List Properties dialog box, and then click OK to close the dialog box.

Collapsible outlines

You can transform multilevel lists into *collapsible outlines*. When viewed with a Web browser, the levels in a collapsible outline expand and contract when clicked.

To create a collapsible outline, follow these steps:

1. **Create a multilevel list.**

   To do so, follow the steps in the preceding section, "List-in-a-list."

2. **Highlight the list and then choose Format➪Bullets and Numbering.**

   The List Properties dialog box appears.

3. **In the dialog box, select the Enable Collapsible Outlines check box.**

   If you want the outline to appear initially collapsed, select the Initially Collapsed check box.

4. **Click OK.**

   The dialog box closes. The list looks no different than before. To see how the collapsible outline works, preview the page by using Internet Explorer 4.0 or later.

Collapsible outlines work only when the page is viewed with Internet Explorer 4.0 or later. Visitors using other browsers see a regular multilevel list.

Adjusting Paragraph Alignment, Indenting, and Spacing

By default, FrontPage paragraphs (with the exceptions of headings and lists) are single-spaced, line up with the page's left margin, and contain no indentation (that is, no extra space exists between the margin and the paragraph). Also, a little bit of space precedes and follows each paragraph. You can change these default paragraph settings one of two ways: the easy-but-basic way, and the slightly-more-involved-but-with-greater-control way.

✔ **Easy-but-basic way to change paragraph alignment:** Click inside the paragraph (or select multiple paragraphs) and then click the Align Left, Center, Align Right, or Justify button (Justify creates paragraphs with neat-and-tidy text that lines up along both the left and right margins.).

✔ **Easy-but-basic way to indent a paragraph:** Click inside the paragraph (or select multiple paragraphs) and then click the Increase Indent button. You may click the button as many times as you want to achieve the desired effect. To decrease the level of an indented paragraph, click the Decrease Indent button.

✔ **Slightly-more-involved-but-with-greater-control way to change paragraph alignment, indentation, and spacing:** Go through the steps that follow.

    1. **Click inside the paragraph (or select multiple paragraphs).**

    2. **Choose Format⇨Paragraph.**

       The Paragraph dialog box appears.

    3. **From the Alignment list box, choose the alignment option you want.**

    4. **From the list boxes in the Indentation section, specify the amount of indentation (in pixels) you want.**

       The Before Text list box controls indentation along the left margin, and the After Text list box controls indentation along the right margin. The Indent First Line list box enables you to apply a different indentation setting to the first line of the paragraph.

    5. **From the list boxes in the Spacing section, specify the amount of spacing (in pixels) you want.**

       The Before list box controls the amount of space before the paragraph; the After list box controls the amount of space after the paragraph; the Word list box controls the amount of space between words in the paragraph; and the Line Spacing list box controls (you guessed it) the space between the lines in the paragraph.

    6. **Click OK.**

       The Paragraph dialog box closes, and FrontPage applies the formatting to the selected paragraph(s).

New paragraphs versus line breaks

Whenever you press the Enter key, FrontPage thinks you want to create a new paragraph. If you simply want to create a new line without creating a new paragraph, use a line break instead. To create a line break, press Shift+Enter.

To distinguish between line breaks and new paragraphs in your page, click the Show/Hide ¶ button on the Standard toolbar. Line breaks are flagged with left-pointing arrows.

The options in the Paragraph dialog box come courtesy of CSS commands. Browsers that are unable to display style sheets won't display these effects.

If you want more control over the placement of your paragraphs than the Paragraph dialog box can give you, consider using an invisible table (see Chapter 8), or check out the FrontPage positioning features (see Chapter 12).

Adding Borders and Shading

Want to surround the selected paragraph with a box? Or give the paragraph a colorful background so it visually jumps off the page? These effects and more await you in the Borders and Shading dialog box.

Adding a border

To quickly add a border to the selected paragraph, click the down arrow next to the Border button and choose a border style you like. For a little more control, do this:

1. **Click inside the paragraph (or select multiple paragraphs) and then choose Format⇨Borders and Shading.**

   The Borders and Shading dialog box appears, as shown in Figure 4-8.

2. **In the Setting area of the dialog box, click the option that corresponds to the type of border you want.**

3. **In the Style box, click the name of the border style you want.**

4. **Choose a border color from the Color list box.**

   If you choose More Colors, the More Colors dialog box appears. I explain how to use the More Colors dialog box in the previous section, "Changing text color."

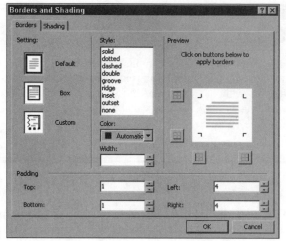

Figure 4-8:
The Borders
and Shading
dialog box.

5. **Enter a border width (in pixels) in the Width box.**

6. **To turn on or off individual borders, in the Preview area, click the button that corresponds to the border you want to change.**

7. **To add empty space between the paragraph text and the surrounding border, enter pixel values in boxes in the Padding area of the dialog box.**

8. **Click OK to close the dialog box and apply the border settings.**

Adding shading

In FrontPage, *shading* refers to the paragraph's foreground and background attributes. The paragraph's foreground attribute is its text color, and its background attributes are the color or picture that sits behind the selected paragraph's text.

 To quickly apply a background color to selected text, click the Highlight Color button. To add more complex shading, do this:

1. **Click inside the paragraph (or select multiple paragraphs) and then choose Format⇨Borders and Shading.**

   The Borders and Shading dialog box appears.

2. **In the dialog box, click the Shading tab to make those options visible.**

3. **To change the paragraph's background color, choose an option from the Background Color list box.**

4. **To change the paragraph's foreground (text) color, choose an option from the Foreground Color list box.**

5. **To place a picture in the paragraph's background, in the Background Picture text box, type the graphic file's path, or click Browse to select the file from a folder location.**

   If you click Browse, the Select Background Picture dialog box appears. If you're not sure how to use this dialog box, I provide directions in Chapter 6.

6. **To control how the picture repeats in the paragraph background, select an option from the Repeat list box.**

   By default, the picture repeats itself over and over until it fills the selected paragraph's background area. Repeat-X causes the picture to repeat horizontally, and Repeat-Y causes the picture to repeat vertically. No-Repeat causes the picture to appear only once.

7. **To change the position of the picture relative to the paragraph, choose options from the Vertical Position and Horizontal Position list boxes.**

   For example, if you choose a vertical position of top and a horizontal position of left, the image appears in the top-left corner of the paragraph's background.

   Note: The Attachment list box controls whether the background image moves when the visitor scrolls down the page (by default, the image appears fixed in place with the text scrolling on top). Because the effect is only visible in Microsoft Internet Explorer, I recommend leaving the default setting as it is.

8. **Click OK to close the dialog box and apply the shading settings.**

The options in the Borders and Shading dialog box and the Highlight Color effect come courtesy of CSS commands. Browsers that are unable to display style sheets won't display these effects. Furthermore, browsers that do support CSS don't display borders and shading consistently. If you decide to use these effects, be sure to preview your Web site in more than one browser make and version.

Inserting Symbols

Symbols are the odd little characters that occasionally make an appearance in Web pages. Some symbols turn up in scientific writing, and others, such as the copyright symbol, are more commonplace.

To include a symbol in your page, follow these steps:

1. **Place the cursor in the page where you want the symbol to appear.**

2. **Choose Insert⇨Symbol.**

   The Symbol dialog box appears.

3. **In the dialog box, click the character you want to insert.**

4. **If this character is the one you want, click Insert; if not, keep hunting and clicking until you find the right character and then click Insert.**

   The symbol appears on your page at the location of the cursor.

5. **Click Close to close the Symbol dialog box.**

A few (very few) browsers are unable to display certain symbols in Web pages. Keep this point in mind if your Web site is symbol-heavy, and preview, preview, preview.

Inserting Comments

You can insert explanatory text and reminders to yourself (or to other members of your Web-building team) in the form of *comments*. Comments are notes that appear only in FrontPage, not as a visitor views the page with a Web browser. To insert a comment, follow these steps:

1. **Place the cursor in the page where you want the comment to appear.**

2. **Choose Insert⇨Comment.**

   The Comment dialog box appears.

3. **In the Comment text box, type your comment and then click OK.**

   The dialog box closes, and the comment appears in your page as colorful text.

To edit a comment, double-click the comment. To delete a comment, click the comment and then press the Delete key.

Keep in mind that comments aren't *completely* invisible; your visitors can see the comments if they look at your page's underlying HTML tags.

Inserting a Time Stamp

Some folks like their Web pages to display the date and time the page was last edited, so visitors know they are looking at timely information. FrontPage can automate this task for you, as follows:

1. **Place the cursor in the page where you want the time stamp to appear.**

2. **Choose Insert⇨Date and Time.**

   The Date and Time dialog box appears.

3. **In the dialog box, choose a display option.**

   If you want the time stamp to reflect when you (or another author) last edited the page, choose Date This Page Was Last Edited. If you want the time stamp to reflect edits *and* automatic updates (such as if a Web component automatically inserts information into the page), choose Date This Page Was Last Automatically Updated.

4. **In the Date Format list box, choose the date format you prefer.**

5. **In the Time Format list box, choose the time format you prefer.**

6. **Click OK to close the dialog box and insert the time stamp into your page.**

Inserting Horizontal Lines

Horizontal lines are thin gray stripes that run the width of your Web page. How do they fit into a chapter about tweaking text, you ask? Because, as is true of font and paragraph styles, horizontal lines help group together bunches of related information. (Work with me here.) You can use a horizontal line if you need a quick way to divide your Web page into different sections. You can even change the line's width and height for a little variety.

Keep in mind that overusing horizontal lines can wreak design havoc. A line or two can provide a much-needed visual break. Too many lines make your page look as though it's trapped behind bars.

To insert a horizontal line, place the cursor in the page where you want the line to appear and choose Insert➪Horizontal Line. To customize how the line looks, follow these steps:

1. **In the page, double-click the horizontal line.**

   The Horizontal Line Properties dialog box appears.

2. **In the Width area of the dialog box, type a value into the text box and then click the Percent of Window or Pixels radio button.**

   You can indicate the width as a percentage of the width of the browser window, or you can specify an absolute number of pixels.

3. **In the Height text box, type the line's height (its thickness) in pixels.**

4. **In the Alignment area, click the Left, Center, or Right radio button.**

5. **Choose a color from the Color list box.**

6. **If you want the line to appear solid instead of engraved, select the Solid Line (No Shading) check box.**

7. **Click OK to close the dialog box and insert the line into the page.**

To delete a horizontal line, click the line and then press the Delete key.

Chapter 5

Hyperlinks: Your Web Site's Ticket to Ride

. . . .

In This Chapter

▶ Creating hyperlinks

▶ Linking to downloadable files and e-mail addresses

▶ Editing hyperlinks

▶ Fixing broken hyperlinks

▶ Removing hyperlinks

▶ Using bookmarks to jump to a specific spot in a page

▶ Working with link bars

▶ Using shared borders

. . . .

Hyperlinks are the gems that make surfing the Web so addictive. Click a link, and you find yourself somewhere else — maybe on another page in your Web site or, just as easily, on a page stored on a server in Sri Lanka or Cheyenne. Too bad Web surfing doesn't earn frequent flyer miles.

The heady nature of Web travel may lead you to believe that hyperlinks are difficult to create. Relax and discover how easily you can hitch your Web site to the global conga line known as the Internet.

The Hyperlink Two-Step

Hyperlinks are bits of text or pictures that act as springboards to other locations. Hyperlinks between pages and files in a Web site *(internal hyperlinks)* transform the site from a jumble of separate files into a cohesive unit. Hyperlinks to locations outside the Web site *(external hyperlinks)* connect the site to the rest of the Internet.

After you launch FrontPage and open the Web site and/or the page you want to edit, creating a hyperlink is a two-step process. Here are the basic steps (the rest of this chapter fills in the details):

1. **In the page, select the thing you want to transform into a hyperlink.**

   I call this "thing" the *hyperlink source.* The hyperlink source is the object people click. A hyperlink source can be a character, a word, a phrase, or a picture. (Chapter 6 explains how to insert a picture into your page.)

2. **Connect the hyperlink source to the place you want visitors to end up after they click the hyperlink.**

   From now on, I call this location the *hyperlink destination.* A hyperlink destination can be a spot in the same page, in another page or file inside the same Web site, or in a different site on the Internet. A hyperlink destination can also point to an e-mail address or initiate a file download.

Keep practicing these steps, and you can soon do the hyperlink two-step with the best of 'em.

Linking to an existing file or Web page

Most often, when you create a hyperlink, you already have the link's destination in mind. As long as you know that destination's location — whether it's a page inside the same Web site or a different Web site altogether — you're ready to roll.

To link to an existing page or file, follow these steps:

1. **In the page, select the object you want to turn into a hyperlink (the hyperlink source).**

   Highlight a bit of text, click a picture, double-click a word — whatever.

 2. **On the Standard toolbar, click the Insert Hyperlink button.**

   The Insert Hyperlink dialog box appears, as shown in Figure 5-1.

3. **Click the Existing File or Web Page icon in the dialog box's Link To section (if it's not already selected) to make those options visible.**

4. **Depending on location of the page or file to which you want the hyperlink to lead, specify the hyperlink destination.**

   • If the destination file is part of the currently open FrontPage Web site, in the dialog box's file list, click the file. If the file is stored inside a folder or a subweb, double-click the folder or subweb to open it and then click the file.

    When a page is currently open in Page View, *two* instances of that page appear in the dialog box's file list. You can click either icon in this step.

- If the destination file is located on the World Wide Web, type its address (also known as its *URL*) in the Address box. A World Wide Web URL looks similar to the following addresses:

```
www.server.com
www.server.com/filename.htm
www.server.com/foldername/filename.htm
```

If you can't remember the URL, in the dialog box, click the Browse the Web button (it looks like a globe with a magnifying glass on top) to launch your Web browser. Surf to your destination, switch back to FrontPage by clicking FrontPage's button in the Windows taskbar, and — huzzah! — the URL appears in the Address box.

- If the page or file is elsewhere on your hard drive or network, read the sidebar "Linking to a file stored on your computer or local network" for a heads up about potential problems with this type of hyperlink. If you're sure you want to create the link, in the dialog box, navigate to the location of the file and then click it.

5. **Click OK.**

   The dialog box closes, and a hyperlink is born.

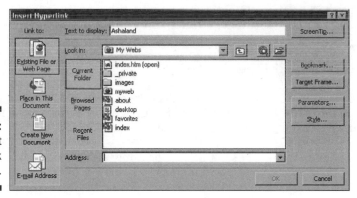

Figure 5-1:
The Insert Hyperlink dialog box.

If the hyperlink source is text, that text now displays the proud markings of a link: underlining and color.

You can still apply font and paragraph styles — bold, italic, and so on — to text hyperlinks as you can to regular text. You can also get rid of the default underlining that appears when you transform regular text into a hyperlink. To do so, click inside the link, and click the Underline button on the Formatting toolbar.

If the hyperlink source is a picture, the image itself looks no different than before its transformation. Trust me — the image is now a *graphic hyperlink.* If you want proof, pass your pointer over any text or graphic hyperlink, and the

---

Choosing hyperlink words wisely

Hyperlinks immediately attract attention, especially if your visitors quickly scan the page for information. Choose the clearest, most meaningful text for promotion to linkhood. Avoid the temptation to create links that say things such as "<u>Click here</u> to see a picture of Harold, my pet ferret." (The underlined words are the hyperlink in the previous sentence.) Instead, choose a word that clues the visitor in on what's sitting at the other end of the hyperlink. If you want to immortalize Harold in your home page, you're better off using the following link text: "See a picture of <u>Harold, my pet ferret</u>."

---

link destination appears in the status bar at the bottom of the FrontPage window.

To differentiate graphic hyperlinks from regular pictures in your Web pages, you can give graphic hyperlinks a border. The borders of graphic hyperlinks are the same color as text links, giving visitors a visual cue to click the picture to jump elsewhere. I show you how to add borders to pictures in Chapter 6.

Instant hyperlink shortcut! Drag an icon from the Folder List and drop it into the page currently open in Page View. (If the Folder List isn't visible, click the Folder List button on the Standard toolbar or choose View➪Folder List.) FrontPage creates a link to the selected destination page, using the destination page's title as the hyperlink text.

If you type an Internet URL or an e-mail address inside the body of your page and then press the spacebar or Enter, FrontPage automatically turns the URL/address text into a hyperlink to that location.

Keep in mind that the steps in this section apply to links leading to *any* type of file, not just Web pages. For example, say you want to create a hyperlink that, when clicked, enables visitors to download a file. No problem. Simply import the item into your Web site (see Chapter 14 for details), and then create a hyperlink leading to that item. When a visitor clicks that link, if the visitor's Web browser doesn't know how to open that file type, the browser automatically prompts the visitor to download the file (try it and see).

Linking to a new page

As you build your Web site, the inspiration for a new page could strike at any time. That's okay — FrontPage doesn't require you to create pages first and links later. If you decide you want to link to a new page that does not yet exist, follow these steps.

1. **In the page, select the hyperlink source.**

2. **On the Standard toolbar, click the Insert Hyperlink button to open the Insert Hyperlink dialog box.**

3. **In the dialog box's Link To section, click Create New Document to make those options visible.**

4. **In the Name of New Document text box, type the new page's filename.**

    Unless you specify the extension HTM or HTML as part of the filename, FrontPage automatically appends HTM to whatever you enter here.

    The Full Path notation under the text box tells you where FrontPage saves the new page. If a Web site is currently open, FrontPage adds the new document to that Web. If no Web site is open in FrontPage, the new page is saved in your computer's root directory (most likely C:\). If you're happy with the saving location, skip on to Step 7. To change the saving location, proceed to Step 5.

5. **To save the new page in a location other than the one described in the Full Path notation, click the Change button.**

    The Create New Document dialog box appears.

6. **In the dialog box, navigate to the location where you want FrontPage to save the new page, type a filename in the File Name list box, and then click OK.**

    The Create New Page dialog box closes, and the Insert Hyperlink dialog box becomes visible again.

7. **In the dialog box's When To Edit section, click the appropriate option button.**

    If you're ready to set aside the current page to work on the new page right now, leave Edit the New Document Now selected. Otherwise, click Edit the New Document Later.

8. **Click OK to close the dialog box and create the hyperlink.**

    If you told FrontPage that you want to edit the new page now, then the new, blank page opens in Page View (the current page remains open as well). If you told FrontPage you want to edit the new page later, the current page becomes visible, and FrontPage creates the new page, but doesn't open it.

Linking to an e-mail address

The quickest way to help your visitors get in touch is to include a link to your e-mail address (also known as a *mailto link*) inside each page in your site. That way, if visitors have comments (or, dare I say it, complaints), they can click the mailto link that pops open an e-mail window in the Web browser. From there, they can fire off messages in seconds.

For mailto links to work, the visitor's browser must either have a built-in e-mail component or be able to hook up with a separate e-mail program.

The no-brainer approach to creating a link to your e-mail address is to type your e-mail address in the page followed by a tap on the spacebar or Enter key. FrontPage automatically transforms the address text into a link.

Otherwise, do this:

1. **In the page, select the hyperlink source.**

2. **Click the Insert Hyperlink button to open the Insert Hyperlink dialog box.**

3. **In the dialog box's Link To section, click E-mail Address.**

   The contents of the Insert Hyperlink dialog box change accordingly.

4. **In the E-mail Address text box, type an e-mail address.**

   The address should look something like this: `name@address.com`. When you start typing your address, FrontPage automatically tacks `mailto:` to the beginning. That's okay.

5. **Optionally, in the Subject text box, type a subject line for the e-mail message generated by this link.**

6. **Click OK.**

Another way to encourage visitor feedback is to provide an interactive form. I show you how in Chapter 9.

(By the way, to instantly place a link to your e-mail address at the bottom of every page in your site, place the mailto link inside a *shared border*. I show you how to use shared borders later in this chapter.)

Linking to a file stored on your computer or local network

FrontPage enables you to create a link from your Web page to a file stored elsewhere on your computer's hard drive. The problem is, when you publish your finished Web site on a host Web server, the link no longer works because the location of the hyperlink destination file is specific to your computer's file system, not the Web server's.

Sometimes this feature comes in handy, such as if you're creating a local Web presentation to be displayed only on your computer or local network (not on the World Wide Web). If you decide to use this option, proceed with care, and double-check the link after you've published your site to be sure the link works properly.

Editing Hyperlinks

Just as you can change your hair color, you can easily change your hyperlinks. You can change the text that makes up the link, the destination to which the link leads, its appearance, and even how it behaves.

Changing a hyperlink's text or destination, and adding a ScreenTip

A visit to the Edit Hyperlink dialog box enables you change the text that makes up a hyperlink, change its destination, or add a *ScreenTip*. A ScreenTip is a caption-like label that pops up when the visitor passes the cursor over the link (similar to the ToolTip that appears when you hover your cursor over a toolbar button in FrontPage).

ScreenTips appear only to those of your visitors using Microsoft Internet Explorer 4.0 and later.

1. **In the page, click the hyperlink you want to change.**

2. **Click the Insert Hyperlink button to open the Edit Hyperlink dialog box.**

3. **To change the hyperlink text visible in the page, type new text in the Text to Display text box.**

4. **To change the link's destination, click a different file in the file list or type a different URL in the Address list box.**

   Refer to the section "Linking to an existing file or Web page" earlier in the chapter for detailed instructions on how to specify a link's destination.

5. **To add a ScreenTip, click the ScreenTip button to display the Set Hyperlink ScreenTip dialog box. Type the ScreenTip text into the appropriate text box, and then click OK.**

   The Edit Hyperlink dialog box becomes visible again.

6. **Click OK to close the dialog box.**

Note: The steps outlined in this section work only on hyperlinks that are *not* part of a FrontPage link bar. I talk more about link bars later in this chapter.

Displaying a hyperlink's destination in a new browser window

You may have experienced this trick during your own Web wanderings: You click a link inside a Web page, and, instead of replacing the contents of the current browser window, the hyperlink destination shows up in a second browser window.

This effect, called *changing the hyperlink's target*, comes in handy for several situations. Some Web sites program all their external links (links that point to locations outside the Web site) to pop open new windows when clicked, so visitors get a clear visual cue when they "leave" the site. Other sites use this effect to display supplementary information without replacing the contents of the original window (a good example would be a product catalog with a link leading to a size chart that appears in its own window).

To change a hyperlink's target, do the following:

1. **In the page, click the hyperlink you want to change.**

2. **Click the Insert Hyperlink button to open the Edit Hyperlink dialog box.**

3. **In the dialog box, click the Target Frame button.**

   The Target Frame dialog box appears. (You'll use this dialog box often if you decide to use *frames* in your site — hence the name "Target Frame." I tell you all about frames in Chapter 10.)

4. **In the dialog box's Common Targets list box, click New Window, and then click OK.**

   The Target Frame dialog box closes, and the Edit Hyperlink dialog box becomes visible again.

5. **Click OK to close the dialog box.**

Note: The steps outlined in this section work only on hyperlinks that are *not* part of a FrontPage link bar. I talk more about link bars later in this chapter.

Changing hyperlink color

Hyperlinks stand out from regular text because hyperlinks appear in a different color from their ordinary text siblings. The default hyperlink color is blue, but you can change the link's color so that the hyperlink coordinates nicely with the color scheme of your page.

Hyperlinks actually have three distinct colors: the default color, the active color, and the visited color. These colors appear when a visitor views the page in a Web browser.

- **The default color** is the link's color before the visitor follows the hyperlink trail. When a visitor arrives at your page for the first time, all the page's links appear in the default color, because the visitor hasn't yet followed a link.

- **The active color** is the color the link becomes "mid-click." The active color lets visitors know they are indeed activating that particular link.

- **The visited color** is the color the link changes to after visitors follow a link and then return to your page. The visited color lets visitors know which links they've already followed and which ones they haven't yet explored.

You can select unique hyperlink colors for each page you create. Or you can set up a consistent color scheme by basing the hyperlink color on the colors in another page in your site. You also can apply a theme to your Web site; each theme contains a nicely coordinated set of hyperlink colors. (I cover themes in Chapter 11.)

Selecting unique colors

To select unique link colors for a page, follow these steps:

1. **With the page open in Page View, choose Format➪Background.**

   Note: If the current Web site page is formatted with a theme, this menu option appears dimmed because themes contain a preset group of text and hyperlink colors.

   The Page Properties dialog box appears with the Background tab visible. The current link color settings appear in the list boxes labeled Hyperlink, Visited Hyperlink, and Active Hyperlink, as shown in Figure 5-2.

2. **Choose a new color from one or all the list boxes corresponding to each hyperlink state.**

   If you choose More Colors, the More Colors dialog box appears. I explain how to use the More Colors dialog box in Chapter 4.

3. **Click OK.**

   The dialog box closes, and the page's links change color.

To see how the active and visited colors look, preview the page in a Web browser.

The steps in this section change the hyperlink colors for all the hyperlinks in the page. You can use the Font Color button to change the colors of individual hyperlinks, but color changes made this way show up only in recent versions of advanced browsers. Older browsers only know how to display page-wide color changes.

Creating a table of contents

A table of contents displays the titles of all your site's pages in a hierarchical list, with links to each page. The table of contents also lists any external links that you add to your site's navigation structure (see Chapter 14 for information about the purpose of a navigation structure). Visitors love tables of contents for the bird's-eye view they provide, but even the best-intentioned Web designer dreads creating a table of contents for a big Web site, especially if he or she is constantly adding and changing pages.

Here's where the Table of Contents Web component swoops in to the rescue. FrontPage can crank out a fully linked table of contents and updates it if pages change.

To create a table of contents, do the following:

1. **In your page, place the cursor where you want the table of contents to appear.**

2. **Choose Insert⇨Web Component.**

   The Insert Web Page Component dialog box appears.

3. **In the dialog box's Component Type list box, click Table of Contents.**

4. **In the dialog box's Choose a Table of Contents list box, click For This Web Site, and then click the Finish button.**

   The Table of Contents Properties dialog box appears.

5. **In the Page URL for Starting Point of Table text box, type the filename of the page that you want to appear at the top of the table of contents.**

   Or click Browse to select a page from a list of files in your Web site. By default, FrontPage specifies the site's home page as its starting point.

6. **From the Heading Font Size list box, choose the heading size for the first item in the table of contents.**

Choosing a relatively bold heading (such as Heading 1 or Heading 2) sets the first item apart from the rest so that the item acts as a title for the table of contents.

7. **If you want each page in your site to appear in the table of contents only once, click the Show Each Page Only Once check box.**

   If you don't select this option, pages that link to more than one page in your site appear more than once.

8. **If you want the table of contents to display pages in your site that don't link to other pages, click the Show Pages with No Incoming Hyperlinks check box.**

   If you mark this check box, the only access point to the page is through the table of contents, because the page isn't linked to the rest of your Web site.

9. **If you want FrontPage to automatically update the table of contents as you edit pages and add new pages to your Web site, click the Recompute Table of Contents When Any Other Page Is Edited check box.**

   If you don't select this option and still want to update the table of contents, you need to recalculate your site's hyperlinks each time a page changes or you add a new page. (To recalculate hyperlinks, choose Tools⇨Recalculate Hyperlinks.)

10. **Click OK.**

   The dialog box closes, and a placeholder for the table of contents appears in the page.

To see how the actual table of contents looks, preview the page by choosing File⇨Preview in Browser (the built-in FrontPage Preview displays only the placeholder).

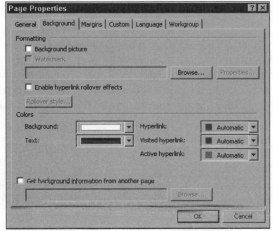

Basing colors on another page

You can base hyperlink color (as well as the two other background attributes — the default text color and the page background color or picture) on another page in your Web site. If you choose this option, you can make background color changes to a single page and have those changes automatically appear in every page that uses those background settings.

To base background colors on those of another page, follow these steps:

1. **With the page open in Page View, choose F<u>o</u>rmat⇨Background.**

   Note: If the current Web site or page is formatted with a theme, this menu option appears dimmed, because themes contain a preset group of text and hyperlink colors.

   The Page Properties dialog box appears with the Background tab visible.

2. **Click the Get Background Information from Another Page check box.**

3. **Next to the corresponding text box, click the Browse button.**

   The Current Web dialog box appears.

4. **In the dialog box, select the page and then click OK.**

   The Current Web dialog box closes, and the file's path appears in the text box.

5. **Click OK.**

   The Page Properties dialog box closes, and the page's background and hyperlink colors change accordingly.

Adding a rollover effect

Here's an eye-catching little trick: Add a *rollover effect* to your text hyperlinks so that when visitors pass their pointers (or *roll*) over the hyperlink, something special happens to the hyperlink text. Perhaps the text turns a different color or grows a couple of sizes. Whatever you choose, the effect is surprising and fun. To add a rollover effect to your page's hyperlinks, do the following:

1. **Select Format⇨Background to display the Background tab of the Page Properties dialog box.**

2. **In the Formatting area, check the Enable Hyperlink Rollover Effects check box, and then click the Rollover Style button.**

   The Font dialog box appears.

3. **Choose the text effect that you want the page's hyperlinks to display when a visitor rolls over the hyperlink.**

   Chapter 4 contains instructions on using the Font dialog box. (The default rollover setting turns hyperlinks bold and red.)

4. **Click OK to close the Font dialog box.**

5. **Click OK again to close the Page Properties dialog box and apply the rollover effect.**

When you preview your page, you'll see the rollover effect in action.

 Hyperlink rollover effects come courtesy of Dynamic HTML, and are visible only in Microsoft Internet Explorer and Netscape Navigator, Version 4.0 or later. Furthermore, this particular effect works inconsistently when viewed with Netscape. In browsers that don't support the effect, such hyperlinks look like any other text hyperlink.

Verifying and Fixing Hyperlinks throughout Your Web Site

Broken hyperlinks are like ants at a picnic. One or two ants are mildly annoying, but if enough ants show up, they ruin the entire afternoon.

A hyperlink breaks if the destination page that the link points to becomes unreachable. A link may break because the Web server on which the destination page is stored goes down or because the page's author renames the page. After a visitor clicks a broken hyperlink, instead of delivering the requested page, the destination Web server delivers an error message stating that it can't find the page. Major Web-surfing bummer.

The most common cause of broken hyperlinks — renaming a page in your Web site and then forgetting to update the hyperlinks elsewhere in the Web site that lead to the page — is a moot point in FrontPage, because the program automatically updates hyperlinks if you rename or move a page. (I describe this feat of wonder in Chapter 14.)

Certain situations are beyond FrontPage's control, however, and cause hyperlinks in your Web site to break:

- You delete a file that another page in the Web site is linked to.
- You import an existing Web site into FrontPage and leave out some files.
- You mistype a URL while creating a hyperlink to a site on the Internet.
- You create a link to a site on the Internet, and that site changes location or otherwise becomes unreachable.

Fortunately, FrontPage comes with a little marvel called the Verify Hyperlinks command. The Verify Hyperlinks command performs the following miracles:

- It finds all the broken or unchecked links in your Web site and lists them in the Broken Hyperlinks report.
- It checks links to external Internet sites to make sure they work properly.
- It enables you to fix individual broken links.
- It updates the corrected links in selected pages or throughout the entire Web site.

Verifying hyperlinks

You need to find broken hyperlinks before you can fix them. Happily, FrontPage roots out broken hyperlinks for you.

Verifying hyperlinks involves locating broken internal links (links between pages and files that reside inside the Web site), and double-checking external links to make sure they work.

To verify the hyperlinks in your Web site, follow these steps:

1. **Activate your Internet connection.**

2. **Save all open pages, if you haven't already (choose File⇨Save All).**

3. **Choose View➪Reports–>Problems➪Broken Hyperlinks.**

FrontPage switches from Page View to the Broken Hyperlinks report in the Reports View. The report displays a list of broken internal hyperlinks and as-yet-unverified external hyperlinks (see Figure 5-3). Broken internal links (if any exist) are flagged with the status label Broken and a broken chain link icon, and unverified external links are flagged with the label Unknown and a question mark icon.

Also, the Reporting toolbar becomes visible.

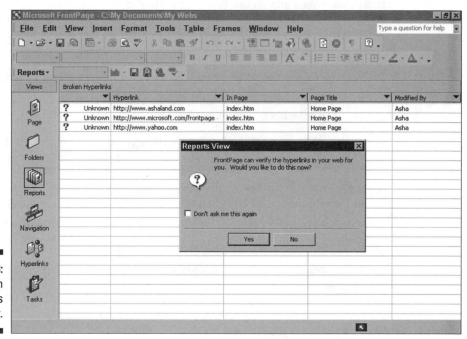

Figure 5-3: The Broken Hyperlinks report.

4. **On the Reporting toolbar, click the Verifies Hyperlinks in the Current Web button.**

The Verify Hyperlinks dialog box appears.

5. **In the dialog box, click Start.**

If your Web site contains lots of external links, the verification process takes quite a while. Be sure that you have a few minutes to spare.

After you click Start, FrontPage verifies each external link by contacting the destination Web server and then making sure that it can reach the page. As the verification process is going on, a progress message appears in the FrontPage status bar letting you know what's happening. As FrontPage checks each link, its status label in the report changes from a question mark to either a green check mark followed by OK (indicating valid links) or a broken chain link followed by Broken (indicating broken links). When the verification process is complete, FrontPage lists a summary of its findings in the status bar.

 To stop the verification process, press the Esc key. To resume verifying hyperlinks, click the Verify Hyperlinks button on the Reporting toolbar.

Fixing broken hyperlinks

After FrontPage has unearthed the broken links, you need to fix them. To do so, follow these steps:

1. **If you haven't already, follow the steps in the preceding section, "Verifying hyperlinks."**

2. **From the Broken Hyperlinks report, double-click the broken hyperlink that you want to fix.**

   The Edit Hyperlink dialog box appears, as shown in Figure 5-4.

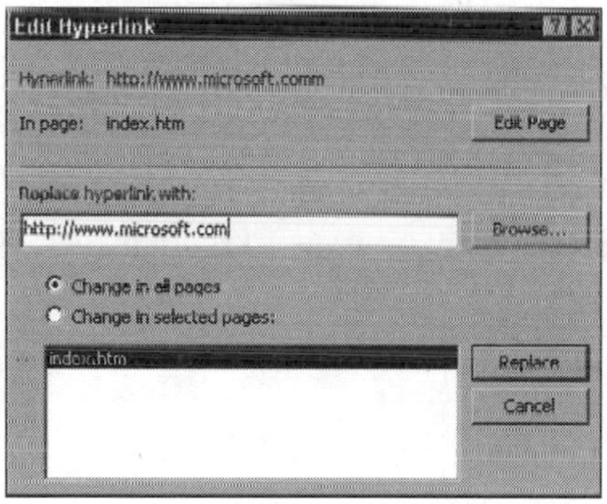

Figure 5-4:
The Edit
Hyperlink
dialog box.

3. **Decide whether you want to edit the page containing the hyperlink or update the hyperlink destination itself; then take the appropriate action.**

   To edit the page containing the link, click the Edit Page button. The page opens in Page View so that you can fix the ailing link. When you switch back to the Reports View, repaired internal links disappear from the list, and the status of repaired external links change from Broken to Unknown (FrontPage must verify the newly-edited link in order to give it a passing mark.).

   To edit the link itself, in the Edit Hyperlink dialog box, type a new URL in the Replace Hyperlink With text box. If you can't recall the URL, click Browse to launch your Web browser. Browse to the destination, and when you switch back to FrontPage, the destination URL is visible in the text box. To change the link in selected pages (rather than throughout the entire Web site), click the Change in Selected Pages option button and then click the names of the pages you want to update in the box underneath. Click Replace to fix the hyperlink and close the dialog box.

4. **Continue repairing broken hyperlinks by repeating Steps 2 and 3.**

I recommend verifying your site's hyperlinks at least every couple of weeks. Web pages move and change all the time, breaking hyperlinks in your Web site. FrontPage makes checking your links so easy — why not make it a regular habit?

Unlinking Hyperlinks

Suppose you became so intoxicated with the power of hyperlink creation that, looking at your page now, you see more links than regular text. Perhaps you overindulged. Perhaps removing a few links so that the others may shine would be wise. To obtain forgiveness for your excesses, follow these steps:

1. **Click the link you want to unlink.**

2. **Click the Insert Hyperlink button to open the Edit Hyperlink dialog box.**

3. **In the dialog box, click Remove Link.**

   The dialog box closes, and your link returns to regular text (or, if the link's a picture, returns to its original state).

Using Bookmarks

A *bookmark* is an invisible spot inside a Web page that can be used as the destination of a link. Bookmarks enable you to control more closely where visitors end up after they click a hyperlink. A link without the benefit of a bookmark drops visitors off at the top of the destination page. When a visitor clicks a hyperlink that leads to a bookmark inside a page, the visitor jumps straight to the bookmark location.

To link to a bookmark in your page, you must first create the bookmark and then create the hyperlink that leads to the bookmark.

Creating bookmarks

A bookmark can be the current location of the cursor or any selected bit of text: a word, a phrase, or even a letter. Text defined as a bookmark looks (and acts) no different from regular text; the text is simply flagged with an invisible marker to which you can point a hyperlink.

To create a bookmark, follow these steps:

1. **In the page, select the clump of text you want to turn into a bookmark.**

   Or place the cursor in the location where you want the bookmark to sit without selecting any text.

   The bookmark eventually becomes the hyperlink destination.

2. **Choose Insert➪Bookmark.**

   The Bookmark dialog box appears. If you selected text in Step 1, the text is visible in the Bookmark Name text box. (FrontPage wisely assumes that you want to give the bookmark the same name as the text it's made of.) Otherwise, the text box is empty.

3. **If the text box is empty (or if you want to choose a different name), in the Bookmark Name text box, type a brief name.**

   A good name describes the bookmark's function or location.

4. **Click OK.**

   The dialog box closes. If the bookmark is made of text, a dotted line appears underneath the selected text. If the bookmark is a single point, a flag icon appears at the location of the bookmark. (In real life, bookmarks are invisible. Visitors viewing your page with a browser can't distinguish bookmarks from regular text.)

5. **Click Save to save the new bookmark information.**

Linking to a bookmark

Bookmarks are like ballroom dancers: They need a partner to do their thing. Without a hyperlink, a bookmark is as lonely as a wallflower.

Linking to bookmarks inside a page helps visitors find their way around long pages that otherwise require lots of scrolling and searching to navigate.

You can create a link at the top of the page to bookmarks in the interior of the same page so that visitors can jump around with swift clicks of the mouse. Likewise, you can create a link at the bottom of the page to a bookmark at the top of the page so that visitors don't have to scroll to return to the beginning of the page.

Any bookmark on any page in your Web site is an eligible candidate for a link. To forge this link, follow these steps:

1. **In the page, select the hyperlink source.**

   This step is the same as that for creating a regular link: Select the word, phrase, or picture you want to turn into a hyperlink.

 2. **Click the Insert Hyperlink button to open the Insert Hyperlink dialog box.**

3. **In the dialog box's file list, click the page that contains the bookmark to which you want to link, and then click the Bookmark button.**

   Or, if the bookmark is in the same page as the hyperlink, in the dialog box's Link To area, click Place in This Document.

   Depending on which item you click, either the Select Place in Document dialog box appears, or the Insert Hyperlink dialog box changes its options to display essentially the same information — the bookmarks inside the selected page.

4. **From the list of bookmarks, click the bookmark to which you want to link.**

5. **Click OK (and if the Insert Hyperlink dialog box is still open, click OK again to close it).**

   The dialog box closes, and the bookmark and hyperlink live happily ever after. (Trumpets sound.)

Dismantling bookmarks

Get rid of any bookmarks that outlive their usefulness. The procedure is quick and painless (for both you and the bookmark). If the bookmark is made up of text, right-click inside the bookmark you want to dismantle, and from the pop-up menu that appears, choose Bookmark Properties. In the Bookmark dialog box that appears, click Clear. If the bookmark is marked with a flag icon, place the cursor in front of the flag icon and then press the Delete key.

Helping Visitors Find Their Way with Link Bars

As I was thinking of a way to explain link bars, a scene from a Saturday morning cartoon popped into my head. Bugs Bunny is lost in the desert, and while searching for an oasis, he comes upon a signpost stuck into sand. The signpost contains markers pointing every which way: "This way to Cairo," "This way to New York," "This way to Mars."

Link bars give your visitors a similar array of choices. Link bars are a collection of hyperlinks leading to the other pages inside your Web site. By placing a link bar inside each page of your site, you help your visitors find their way around. Think of link bars as signposts: "This way to the home page," "This way to the feedback form." With a single click, visitors are whisked off to the destination of their choice.

FrontPage gives you two methods for creating link bars. You can let FrontPage generate link bars based on a navigation structure you build, or you can create custom link bars containing links of your choosing. Each method has its advantages and disadvantages. Read on to find out more.

 If you want your link bar to appear in the same position inside more than one page in your Web site (a good Web design decision, in my opinion), place the link bar inside a *shared border*. I show you how to create and use shared borders later in this chapter.

Letting FrontPage generate a link bar

Wouldn't it be nice if you could map out your site — draw a flow chart illustrating how each of the site's pages relate to each other, and how a user would navigate the site — and let FrontPage create all the links between the pages based on that map? Well, you can. FrontPage can generate a link bar based on the layout of a map you create called a *navigation structure*. (The navigation structure lives in the FrontPage Navigation View, which you get to know in detail in Chapter 14.)

After you've created a navigation structure, you can tell FrontPage to generate link bars based on the structure's different "levels" relative to the current page (that is, the placement in the structure of the page into which you're inserting the link bar).

Inserting a navigation structure-based link bar

FrontPage generates link bars based on the settings in the Link Bar Properties dialog box, shown in Figure 5-5. (I show you how to access this dialog box in a moment.) The Hyperlinks to Add to Page section of the dialog box enables you to select the level of hyperlinks that appear in the link bar. Here's where the layout of the navigation structure makes a difference, because the layout determines which pages appear in each level.

Your choices are as follows:

- **Parent Level.** This option lists hyperlinks leading to the pages in the level above the current page.
- **Same Level.** This option lists hyperlinks leading to the pages in the same level as the current page.

✔ **Back and Next.** In Web sites that rely on a linear, slideshow-like flow of information, this option lists hyperlinks to the previous page and the next page, both of which are on the same level as the current page.

✔ **Child Level.** This option lists hyperlinks leading to the pages in the level below the current page.

✔ **Global Level.** This option lists hyperlinks leading to pages that sit at the topmost level of the site.

✔ **Child Pages under Home.** This option lists hyperlinks leading to pages in the level beneath the site's entry page, regardless of the level of the current page.

You also can include links to two additional pages:

✔ **Home Page.** The home page is the site's entry page.

✔ **Parent Page.** The parent page sits in the level above the current page and contains a link to that page.

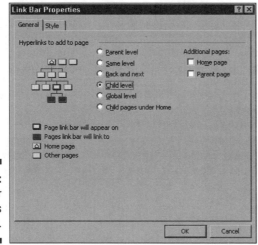

Figure 5-5:
The Link Bar
Properties
dialog box.

To insert a link bar based on the site's navigation structure, do the following:

1. **Using the Navigation View, create a navigation structure for your site.**

   The chart doesn't need to be complete (you can add pages as you go along) but should at least reflect the site's core structure. I explain how to create a navigation structure in Chapter 14.

2. **Switch back to Page View, and place the cursor where you want the link bar to appear on the page.**

   The following steps are easier if you make the Page View's Navigation Pane visible (do so by clicking the Navigation button at the bottom of the Folder List). The Navigation Pane displays the navigation structure you created in the Navigation View. You'll want to refer to it when, in Step 7, you specify the link bar's contents.

3. **Choose Insert⇨Navigation.**

   The Insert Web Component dialog box appears, with the Link Bars component type selected.

4. **In the dialog box's Choose a Bar Type list box, click Bar Based On Navigation Structure, and then click Next.**

   New options that enable you to choose how the link bar looks appear in the dialog box.

5. **In the Choose a Bar Style list box, click the illustration that reflects how you'd like the link bar to look, and then click Next.**

   Be sure to scroll down the Choose a Bar Style list box; FrontPage includes some elegant graphical possibilities. If you create a text-based link bar, you can change the text formatting using any of the FrontPage font tools (see Chapter 4 for details).

   After you click Next, new options that enable you to choose whether you want a horizontal or vertical link bar appear in the dialog box.

6. **In the Choose an Orientation box, click either the horizontal or vertical orientation illustration, and then click Finish.**

   That Finish button is a bit of a tease, as you're not actually finished. The Insert Web Component dialog box is replaced by the Link Bar Properties dialog box, which requires just a few more mouse clicks.

7. **In the Hyperlinks to Add to Page section of the dialog box, choose the option(s) you want.**

   If you decide you want to change how the link bar looks, click the dialog box's Style tab, and choose new options. Otherwise. . . .

8. **Click OK.**

   The dialog box closes, and the link bar appears in the page. Figure 5-6 illustrates one example of a navigation structure-based link bar.

Figure 5-6:
Link bars
help visitors
find their
way around
your Web
site.

If an italicized message appears in the page where the link bar buttons should be, some sort of problem exists. Chances are that you chose a link bar setting that conflicts with the page's placement in the navigation structure. For example, the page sits at the bottom level of the chart, and you specified that the link bar should contain Child level links — none of which exist. Or you may have attempted to insert a link bar into a page that hasn't yet been added to the navigation structure, and therefore FrontPage has no way to construct the link bar. The message appears only in FrontPage to alert you to a link bar problem; when you preview the page using a Web browser, you don't see a thing.

To change the link bar's settings, double-click the message to display the Link Bar Properties dialog box, choose new options, and then click OK. You may also switch to Navigation View to reshuffle the navigation structure or to add or remove link bar links (I show you how to do so in the following section).

Adding links to a navigation structure-based link bar

As you add new pages to your Web site, you can easily add them to the navigation structure. When you do, links to those pages automatically appear in the site's link bars (see Chapter 14 for instructions on how to add pages to your navigation structure).

Although the main purpose of navigation bars is to help visitors get around inside your Web site, FrontPage gives you the option to add link bar links that point to external Web sites as well. To do so, follow these steps:

1. **On the Views bar, click the Navigation button to switch to Navigation View.**

2. **Click anywhere inside the navigation structure, and then click the Add Existing Page button on the Navigation toolbar.**

   Don't confuse the Add Existing Page button on the Navigation toolbar with the Insert Hyperlink button on the Standard toolbar. They look the same, but they do different things.

   After you click the Add Existing Page button, the Insert Hyperlink dialog box appears.

3. **In the dialog box, specify the page or file to which you want to link.**

   The options in this dialog box enable you to select any page or file inside the current Web site or its subwebs, or to specify a URL pointing to an external site. For details on how to use this dialog box, see the previous section in this chapter, "The Hyperlink Two-Step."

4. **Click OK.**

   The dialog box closes, and an icon corresponding to the new link appears in the navigation structure. To change the icon's placement, drag it to a new location inside the structure.

Removing links from a navigation structure-based link bar

You may eventually want to add a page to the navigation structure, but not have a link to the page appear inside the site's link bars. Here's how to exclude pages from link bars:

1. **In Navigation View, click the icon in the navigation structure that corresponds to the page that you want to exclude from link bars.**

 2. **On the Navigation toolbar, click the Included in Navigation Bars button to toggle the link bar setting.**

   The icon turns from yellow to gray indicating that a link to the page no longer appears in the site's link bars.

When you exclude a page from link bars, FrontPage automatically excludes that page's Child pages as well. If you want to restore those pages' positions in link bars, click their respective icons and then click the Included in Navigation Bars button. Note also that pages excluded from link bars can't contain FrontPage page banners (I tell you about page banners in Chapter 13).

Changing the button labels on a navigation structure-based link bar

If your link bar is made up of graphic buttons, you might find that some of the text labels are too long to fit on top of the button. To change the label text, do this:

1. **In the Navigation View or the Page View's Navigation Pane, click the icon that corresponds to the label you want to change.**

   The icon turns blue.

2. **In the icon, click the text label.**

   The text label becomes highlighted.

3. **Type a new text label and then press Enter.**

 4. **Switch back to Page View (or, if you're already in Page View, click inside the open page) and, if necessary, click the Refresh button on the Standard toolbar to display the label change.**

When you change a text label in the navigation structure, FrontPage uses the label as the page title (if you're not sure why this matters, flip to Chapter 2 and read the section about saving a page on your computer or network). To change the page title while leaving the navigation structure label unchanged, in the Page View's Folder List or Navigation Pane, right-click the page's icon, and choose Properties from the pop-up menu that appears. In the Properties dialog box that appears, type a new title in the Title text box, and then click OK.

Creating a custom link bar

If your site's structure isn't straightforward enough to fit within the limitations of the FrontPage navigation structure setup, you can still take advantage of link bars. You can create custom link bars that are independent of the site's navigation structure. Custom link bars require a little more initial work than navigation structure-based link bars, but are more flexible and will save you lots of time as your site grows. You can also create several custom link bars that you can insert in different pages or sections of your Web site.

Custom link bars work only if you publish your site on a host server that has the 2002 version of FrontPage Server Extensions installed. I talk about FrontPage Server Extensions in more detail in Chapter 16.

Inserting a custom link bar

1. **In the page, place the cursor where you want the link bar to appear.**

2. **Choose Insert⇨Navigation.**

   The Insert Web Component dialog box appears, with the Link Bars component type selected.

3. **In the dialog box's Choose a Bar Type list box, click Bar with Custom Links, and then click Next.**

   New options appear in the dialog box. These options enable you to choose how the link bar looks.

4. **In the Choose a Bar Style list box, click the illustration that reflects how you'd like the link bar to look, and then click Next.**

   After you click Next, new options that enable you to choose whether you want a horizontal or vertical link bar appear in the dialog box.

5. **In the Choose an Orientation box, click either the horizontal or vertical orientation illustration, and then click Finish.**

   Nope, you're not really finished. The Create New Link Bar dialog box appears prompting you to name your link bar.

6. **In the dialog box's Name text box, type a brief name.**

   Depending on the setup of your Web site, you can create more than one custom link bar (say, one link bar for the site's top-level pages, and another for the site's individual sections). So, choose a name that reminds you of the link bar's placement or purpose in the site.

7. **Click OK.**

   The dialog box closes, and the Link Bar Properties dialog box appears (see Figure 5-7). Note that, despite the same name, this dialog box is different than the dialog box that appears when you create a link bar based on your site's navigation structure.

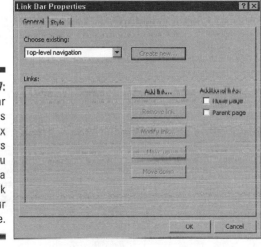

Figure 5-7: The Link Bar Properties dialog box appears when you insert a custom link bar into your page.

8. **In the dialog box, click Add Link.**

   The Add to Link Bar dialog box appears. This dialog box looks and acts very much like the Insert Hyperlink dialog box. For instructions on how to use this dialog box, refer to the section "The Hyperlink Two-Step" earlier in this chapter.

9. **In the dialog box, specify the details for the first hyperlink in the custom link bar, and then click OK.**

   The Add to Link Bar dialog box closes, and the Link Bar Properties dialog box comes back into view.

10. **To add another link, click Add Link, and repeat Step 9 as many times as is necessary to complete the link bar.**

    If you want the link bar to contain links to the home page or the current page's parent page, in the Add to Link Bar dialog box, click the corresponding check boxes.

11. **When the link bar is complete, click OK in the Link Bar Properties dialog box.**

    The dialog box closes, and the link bar appears in the page.

FrontPage can also generate link bars containing a linear set of back and next links. These link bars lead the visitor through links you specify sequentially (similar to a slide show). You can either create a new custom link bar with back and next links, or you can convert a link bar you created earlier.

To insert back and next links into a page, do the following:

1. **In the page, place the cursor where you want the link bar to appear.**

2. **Choose Insert⇨Navigation.**

    The Insert Web Component dialog box appears, with the Link Bars component type selected.

3. **In the dialog box's Choose a Bar Type list box, click Bar with Back and Next Links, and then click Next.**

4. **In the Choose a Bar Style list box, click the illustration that reflects how you'd like the link bar to look, and then click Next.**

5. **In the Choose an Orientation box, click either the horizontal or vertical orientation illustration, and then click Finish.**

    If this is the first custom link bar you're creating, the Create New Link Bar dialog box appears, prompting you to choose a name for the new link bar. Type a brief name in the dialog box's Name text box and then click OK. The dialog box closes, and the Link Bar Properties dialog box becomes visible.

    If you've created other custom link bars, the Link Bar Properties dialog box appears.

6. **If you're converting an *existing* custom link bar into a back-and-next link bar (as opposed to creating a new link bar), choose the link bar's name from the Choose Existing list box.**

7. **Add links to the new link bar, or modify the existing link bar you selected in Step 6.**

    Follow the previous set of steps in this section for detailed instructions.

8. **When the link bar is complete, click OK in the Link Bar Properties dialog box.**

    The dialog box closes, and a hyperlink with the text *Next* appears on the page. If you open each successive page represented in the link bar and add a back-and-next link bar to those pages (or, if you place the link bar inside a shared border, a task that's explained later in this chapter), FrontPage keeps track of the pages' sequence and inserts the appropriate links. Pretty neat.

If you don't like the words *Back* and *Next*, you can change them. To do so, choose Tools⇨Web Settings to display the Web Settings dialog box. In the dialog box, click the Navigation tab, type different labels into the appropriate text boxes, and then click OK to close the dialog box.

Editing a custom link bar

Custom link bars are easy to change. To do so, double-click the link bar on the page to display the Link Bar Properties dialog box. In the dialog box, make any changes you like:

- ✔ Change the order of the links by clicking the link names in the Links list box and then clicking Move Up or Move Down.
- ✔ Change link text or destinations by clicking the link name and then clicking Modify.
- ✔ Add new links by clicking Add Link.
- ✔ Remove links by clicking Remove Link.

When you're done making changes, click OK to close the dialog box.

Deleting a link bar

If FrontPage link bars don't do the trick for your site, you can delete any link bar and create hyperlinks the old-fashioned way. In the Page View Folder List, click the Navigation button to display the Navigation Pane. The Navigation Pane contains an icon for each custom link bar you've created. To delete a link bar, click its icon and then press the Delete key. The Delete Link Bar dialog box appears, explaining that, by deleting the link bar, you also remove the link bar from any pages in which it's currently sitting. Click OK to proceed.

If you simply want to remove a link bar from a page, but you don't want to delete the link bar altogether, click the link bar on the page to select it, and then press the Delete key.

Using shared borders

Well-designed Web sites are easy to get around. Link bars help in this regard, but to be truly effective, link bars must appear in every page in the Web site — ideally in the same spot in each page. Consistently designed pages help visitors familiarize themselves with your site's layout. The more they explore, the easier finding their way becomes for them.

To help you maintain a consistent layout in your Web pages, FrontPage provides a feature called *shared borders*. Shared borders enable you to place items — link bars, page banners, copyright notices, logos, or anything else — in the margins of your pages, and to have those items automatically appear in the same position in every page in your Web site.

You can use shared borders anytime you want to include something on every page, but I find that shared borders really show their stuff when paired with link bars and page banners (you find out about page banners in Chapter 13). By placing a link bar inside a shared border, you avoid having to manually add a link bar to each page. Not only that, FrontPage automatically updates the link bar throughout the site as you change and add to the link bar or the site's navigation structure.

To add shared borders to your Web site, follow these steps:

1. **In any view, choose Format⇨Shared Borders.**

   The Shared Borders dialog box appears, as shown in Figure 5-8.

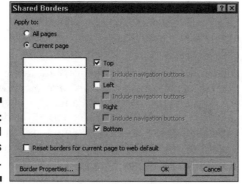

Figure 5-8:
The Shared
Borders
dialog box.

2. **In the dialog box's Apply To section, click the All Pages option button, and then click the check boxes that correspond to the areas in your page where you want to place shared items.**

   For example, if you want a link bar to appear on the left side of every page in your Web site, click the Left check box.

   If you want FrontPage to include standard link bars in the top, left, or right border, mark the corresponding Include Navigation Buttons check boxes. I find that adding link bars by hand is easier, but if you'd rather let FrontPage pick up some of the work, by all means, try this feature out. You can always change the link bar settings later.

3. **To give the shared border a background color or background picture, click Border Properties in the Shared Borders dialog box, choose options from the Border Properties dialog box, and then click OK to close the Border Properties dialog box.**

Shared border formatting is visible only on Web sites published on host Web servers that support the latest version of FrontPage Server Extensions. If you publish your site on a server that doesn't support FrontPage Server Extensions (or that has an older version installed), the shared border *content* will appear, but the *background formatting* will not.

4. **Click OK to close the Shared Borders dialog box.**

The dialog box closes, and FrontPage applies the selected borders to each page in your site.

When you next open the pages in Page View, you see dotted lines demarcating the shared borders at the margins of the page. The space inside the shared border boundary acts no differently from the rest of the page, except that when you add anything to a shared border, that item appears in the same position in every page in the Web site.

When you look at the page using a Web browser, the dotted lines disappear, and only the shared border content is visible. You can change or turn off shared border settings for individual pages. For example, you may want link bars to appear in every page of your site except the home page. In that case, you can turn off the shared borders for the home page, but maintain shared borders in the rest of your site.

To change the shared border settings for an individual page, do the following:

1. **To change shared border settings in the page currently open in Page View, click the cursor anywhere inside the page. To change shared border settings in more than one page in this site, select the pages you want to edit in the Folder List while pressing the Ctrl key.**

2. **Choose Format⇨Shared Borders.**

The Shared Borders dialog box appears.

3. **In the dialog box's Apply To section, click the Current Page option button (if you've selected more than one page, the Selected Page(s) option button appears there instead), and make whatever changes you like.**

To return to the Web site's original shared border settings, click the Reset Borders for Current Page to Web Default check box.

4. **Click OK.**

The dialog box closes, and FrontPage changes the border settings accordingly.

Chapter 6

You Oughta Be in Pictures

. . . .

. . . .

*T*ext is important. Text is, in fact, the foundation of your Web site, the basic building block of a page, blah, blah, blah. Although that statement is essentially true, let's be honest — the Web hasn't achieved global fame because it contains a bunch of words. The pairing of information and pictures is what transforms the Web from a heap of data into a colorful adventure.

Web graphics, when used properly, create a mood and help visitors navigate your site. High-quality, well-chosen images lend style and legitimacy to your site, but, as with all Web design effects, too much of a good thing can be toxic. Cheesy clip art detracts from the site's overall image and, worse, slows its load time.

In this chapter, I let you in on tricks to keep your graphics looking good and loading fast. And, of course, I show you how to use the graphics capabilities of FrontPage.

Bitmaps and Drawn Graphics . . . They're Two Different Animals

FrontPage enables you to add two fundamentally different types of graphics to your Web pages: *bitmaps* and *drawn graphics*. I won't spend a lot of time explaining the technical differences between the two, but having a general sense of their capabilities helps you better understand your options.

Most often, when working with graphics in Web pages, you're working with bitmaps. Bitmaps are made up of bunches of colored dots (or *bits*). As such, these graphics can't be resized without losing quality and falling prey to *the jaggies* (the unsightly ragged edges that appear when you change a bitmap's size).

Drawn graphics (also known as *vector graphics*) consist of lines and curves. Because these graphics are essentially the result of a mathematical calculation by the computer, they can be stretched, reshaped, grouped together, colored, and generally messed with any which way. Using FrontPage's drawing tools, you can create and manipulate shapes, lines, fancy text known as WordArt, and plenty more.

Because bitmaps and drawn graphics have such different qualities and capabilities, I talk about them separately in this chapter. Most of the chapter is devoted to bitmaps, as you'll use this type of graphic most often. I discuss drawn graphics at the end of the chapter.

Understanding the Quirks of Web Graphics

Web graphics can bewilder the novice Web publisher. No need to worry. As long as you stick to the guidelines in this chapter, you should have a graphic-filled, stress-free Web publishing experience.

Getting to know the Web-friendly bitmap formats

The alphabet soup of bitmap graphic file formats is enough to send anyone into fits of intimidation. Good news: Web-friendly graphics come in only three formats: GIF, JPEG, and PNG. The GIF format is the most commonly used format on the Web. The JPEG format (pronounced *jay-peg*) can stuff a wide

Is it pronounced GIF or JIF?

A dispute rages in the Web publishing community over the pronunciation of the acronym GIF. Is GIF pronounced with a hard *g,* as in *graphic,* or is the term pronounced *jif,* like the peanut butter brand? I say GIF with a hard *g* (after all, GIF stands for *Graphic Interchange Format*), but know-it-alls live in both camps (including the creator of the GIF format, who says *jif*). No matter how you say GIF, prepare to be corrected.

range of color into a small file size. The PNG format (say *ping*) is the new kid on the block and surpasses both GIF and JPEG in many ways.

Which format do you choose? The definitive answer is . . . it depends. GIF displays a maximum of 256 colors and is therefore best suited to high-contrast, flat color pictures, such as logos and cartoons. JPEG can display thousands of colors, so that format is your best choice for pictures containing subtle color changes or a wide range of color, such as photographs and complex digital art.

To learn more about Web graphics, read the excellent *Web Graphics 101* at builder.com/Graphics/Graphics101/index.html.

The GIF format has a few extra cards up its sleeve: transparency and interlacing, both of which I discuss later in the chapter.

What about PNG? This relatively new graphic format, developed specifically for Web use, is the wave of the future. PNG is able to display more colors than GIF, and it contains more transparency options than both GIF and JPEG, to name only two of its virtues.

PNG is destined to replace GIF and JPEG as the standard image format on the Web. Unfortunately, browser support for PNG files is still taking hold. Only recent versions of advanced browsers, such as Netscape Navigator (Version 4.0 or later) and Microsoft Internet Explorer (Version 4.0 or later), display the format. Older or less sophisticated browsers are left in the dust. Therefore, until most Web surfers use a PNG-compatible browser, you're wise to stick with GIF and JPEG for now.

Want to know more about PNG? Check out "A Basic Introduction to PNG Features" by Greg Roelofs at www.libpng.org/pub/png/pngintro.html.

FrontPage takes the guesswork out of file formats, because it automatically converts most Web-challenged formats into GIF or JPEG. I talk more about the conversion process later in this chapter.

Picky palettes

In Chapter 3, I relate a harrowing episode from early in my Web publishing career: I colored my Web site with what I thought was a soothing lemon-yellow background, but when my friend looked at the page on his computer, the same color appeared pallid green. I made the mistake of ignoring an important Web graphic rule: *Stick to the browser-safe palette of colors.*

GIFs can display a range, or *palette,* of 256 colors. The tricky thing about color palettes, however, is that the colors are operating system specific. In other words, colors look different when you view them on a PC running Windows than when you view them on a Mac. Bright colors look about the same, but unusual or pastel colors may appear surprisingly different on different platforms.

If your graphic contains a color that isn't present in your visitor's system palette, your visitor's Web browser attempts to display the color by *dithering* — that is, by mixing other colors together to approximate the color in the graphic. Dithered graphics, while better than nothing, lack clarity and definition.

You can reduce dithering by sticking to the *browser-safe* palette for your Web graphics. This palette gives you a range of 216 colors available to most of your visitors whatever their platform. If you create graphics by using these colors or apply this palette to the graphics that you convert to GIF, the dithering problem shrinks considerably. And you don't have your friends calling and asking why you used such a gross color for the background of your page.

For more information about the browser-safe palette, visit `the-light.com/netcol.html`. Refer to your graphics program's documentation for instructions on how to apply the palette to your graphics.

Keeping graphics zippy

Web truism #3 states, "Your visitors connect to the Internet at different speeds." (I discuss the four Web truisms in Chapter 3.) If your visitors must wait more than a few seconds for the page to appear in their browsers, your site risks falling victim to *clickitis,* the chronic condition that causes surfers to click elsewhere whenever they must wait a moment for something to download to their machines. Keeping load times brief prevents clickitis. Here are some ways to ensure that your graphics don't drag:

 ✔ **Reduce image dimensions.** Wherever possible, keep the picture file's dimensions small.

✔ **Limit colors.** You can shave precious seconds off the download time while maintaining your picture's quality if you use a graphics program to reduce the number of colors in your pictures.

✔ **Keep resolution low.** Save your graphic files at a resolution of 72 ppi (pixels per inch). This resolution, while too low for high-quality print images, works just fine for images that are displayed on a computer monitor. Anything higher and you're adding unnecessary bulk to your graphic's file size.

✔ **Repeat pictures.** As much as possible, use the same pictures throughout your site. Web browsers *cache* graphic files, which means that the browser saves a copy of the picture on the visitor's hard drive. The first time someone visits your site, the browser downloads the graphic files from the host server. After the initial download, the browser displays the cached files instead — which load almost instantly.

If you'd like to find out more about the nuts-and-bolts of Web graphics, pick up a copy of *Designing Web Graphics.3* by Lynda Weinman (New Riders Publishing). This book isn't cheap, but it's the definitive guide to how Web graphics work.

FrontPage displays a rough estimate of the page's download time on the right side of the status bar. If you click the time estimate, you can select a different connection speed and watch the time estimate change. Keep an eye on the download time as you add graphics to your page.

Practicing graphic restraint

Pictures are the road hogs of the Information Superhighway, but pictures also make the Web such a pleasant drive. A conscientious Web publisher balances these opposing forces by using pictures judiciously and firing the bulk of the creative power into the site's content.

The "more is better" trap is easy to fall into when adding pictures to your site. I urge you to practice restraint. Each additional picture increases the overall load time of the page and should only be added if seeing the picture is worth the wait. Use only those pictures that communicate your site's purpose and make getting around the site easier or more pleasant for your target audience.

Finally, make sure your visitors can understand your site without the pictures. Some surfers turn off their browser's image-loading option to speed up browsing sessions. (I show you how to deal with this situation later in the chapter.)

Adding a Picture to Your Page

When you insert a picture in a Web page, FrontPage adds a reference inside the page's HTML tags that points to the location of the graphic file. The reference tells the visitor's browser to display the picture inside the page at the location of the reference. In other words, when you look at a Web page that contains pictures, you're actually looking at more than one file simultaneously: the Web page (the file that contains the text and the references to the pictures) and each individual graphic file.

Inserting a picture is not unlike creating a hyperlink, because you simply link two different files: the Web page and the graphic file. So, similar to a hyperlink, a picture reference can point to a graphic file stored inside the Web site or on a remote Web server.

If the graphic files that you want to display in your Web site aren't already saved in a Web-friendly format, you're in luck: FrontPage automatically converts BMP, TIF, WMF, RAS, EPS, PCX, PCD, and TGA files to GIF or JPEG. (FrontPage converts graphics with 256 or fewer colors into GIF, and it converts graphics with more than 256 colors into JPEG.) FrontPage also knows how to insert PNGs into your pages, but because many browsers don't yet support PNG, I recommend sticking with GIF and JPEG for now.

If you want greater control over the conversion process, you should first open and convert your graphic file in a program specifically geared toward graphic work such as Adobe Photoshop or Jasc Paint Shop Pro. By the way, the CD included with this book contains an evaluation version of Paint Shop Pro 7 — be sure to take this excellent program for a test drive. If you get hooked on this program (as I think you might), turn to *Paint Shop Pro 7 For Dummies,* by Dave Kay (IDG Books Worldwide, Inc.) for help.

Most graphics programs enable you to tweak any aspect of the graphic file and then save the file in the Web-friendly format of your choice.

Inserting a picture

If you have graphics already stored on your computer or network, plugging the pictures into a page is easy. Follow these steps:

1. **In Page View, open the page into which you want to insert the graphic, and then place the cursor where you want the picture to appear.**

   FrontPage only knows how to place the cursor inside a line of text or at the bottom of the page. If the cursor location doesn't exactly correspond to where you want the picture to sit inside your page, just do the best you can. I talk about other ways to position pictures later in this chapter.

2. **On the Standard toolbar, click the Insert Picture from File button.**

   The Picture dialog box appears, as shown in Figure 6-1. The dialog box displays a list of your computer's files and folders.

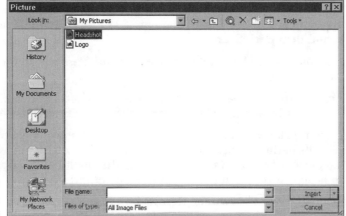

Figure 6-1:
The Picture
dialog box.

3. **In the dialog box's file list, navigate to the location of the picture that you want to insert, and then double-click the file's icon.**

   The dialog box closes, and the picture appears inside the page.

The next time you save the page, the Save Embedded Files dialog box appears and asks whether you want to import the inserted picture into the Web site. Click OK to import the file. See Chapter 2 for more details on how this dialog box works.

You can copy a picture from another application and paste the picture into your page directly from the Clipboard. You can also drag a graphic file from the Folder List, your desktop, or Windows Explorer and drop the file into the page.

Using clip art

When you installed FrontPage, the program quietly slipped a bunch of clip art onto your hard drive. FrontPage gives you access to a bevy of colorful images you can use to adorn your Web site.

To insert FrontPage clip art into a Web page, follow these steps:

1. **In the page, place the cursor where you want the clip art to appear.**

2. **Choose Insert➪Picture➪Clip Art.**

   The Add Clips to Organizer dialog box appears. This dialog box appears only the first time you use clip art. At the same time, options for inserting clip art appear in FrontPage's Task Pane on the right side of the window.

3. **In the dialog box, click Later to skip the time-consuming cataloging process for now.**

   The Add Clips to Organizer dialog box closes.

4. **To find clip art, in the Task Pane, type a key word in the Search Text box, and then click Search.**

   For example, if you type the word **cake**, FrontPage finds all the clips containing images of cake.

   You can narrow the search by choosing a search location from the Search In list box, or by selecting file types from the Results Should Be list box.

   After you click Search, the contents of the Task Pane change to display the results of the clip art search. FrontPage displays thumbnail images of the pieces of clip art (and, if relevant, other multimedia clips such as sounds and videos) that match your search criteria.

5. **If necessary, scroll down the Results box to see all the art FrontPage found for you. When you see an image you like, click the image to insert it into your page.**

   Each piece of clip art is huge. You can adjust the dimensions of an image by using the Picture Properties dialog box. I explain how later in this chapter.

The next time you save your page, the Save Embedded Files dialog box offers to import the clip art file into your Web site. Click OK to import the file. (For more details on how to save pages containing pictures, refer to Chapter 2.)

FrontPage's clip art search-and-retrieval system is actually a separate program called the Microsoft Clip Organizer. The Clip Organizer can do much more than display clip art based on a simple search. The program can catalog all the image and multimedia clips on your computer, organize them into related groups called *collections,* and even grab clips from the Web.

Gobs of graphics

Where do you find ready-made pictures to plop into your Web site? In addition to FrontPage clip art, plenty of excellent Web galleries encourage you to grab their pictures for your own personal use. Start with the Webreference.com graphics collection at www.webreference.com/authoring/graphics/collections.html.

Or decorate your Web site with a FrontPage theme. Themes contain nice-looking banner and button graphics and can easily spice up an entire Web site. I talk about themes in Chapter 11.

To find out more about how the Clip Organizer works, make sure the Insert Clip Art options are visible in the Task Pane and click the Clip Organizer link. The Microsoft Clip Organizer dialog box appears. (If you haven't yet let the Clip Organizer catalog the contents of your computer, the Add Clips to Organizer dialog box appears. If you'd like to run the catalog operation, in the dialog box, click Now. Otherwise, click Later.) In the Microsoft Clip Organizer dialog box, choose Help⇨Clip Organizer Help to access the Clip Organizer help system.

Controlling How a Picture Is Displayed

After you insert a picture into your page, you have some control over how the picture is displayed. For example, you can specify how the picture aligns with surrounding text, change its display dimensions, and more. Read on for details.

Aligning a picture with surrounding text

When you insert a picture in the same line as text, you can control how the picture aligns with that text. Follow these steps:

1. **In the page, double-click the picture.**

   The Picture Properties dialog box appears with the Appearance tab visible, as shown in Figure 6-2.

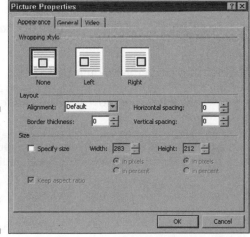

Figure 6-2:
The Appearance tab of the Picture Properties dialog box.

2. **In the dialog box's Layout area, choose an option from the Alignment list box.**

Here are your choices:

- **Left:** Places the picture in the left margin and wraps surrounding text around the right side of the picture.

- **Right:** Places the picture in the right margin and wraps surrounding text around the left side of the picture. (Figure 6-3 illustrates both the Left and Right alignment options.)

   Note: In the dialog box's Wrapping Style area, clicking Left or Right achieves the same thing as selecting Left or Right from the Alignment list box.

- **Top:** Aligns the top of the picture with the text.

- **Texttop:** Aligns the top of the picture with the top of the tallest text in the line.

- **Middle:** Aligns the middle of the picture with the text.

- **Absmiddle:** Aligns the middle of the picture with the middle of the tallest text in the line.

- **Baseline:** Aligns the picture with the text baseline. The *baseline* is the invisible line that the page's text sits on, something like the lines on a piece of binder paper.

- **Bottom:** Aligns the bottom of the picture with the text.

- **Absbottom:** Aligns the picture with the bottom of the text in the line.

- **Center:** Works just like the Middle option.

4. **Click OK.**

The dialog box closes, and the picture alignment changes accordingly.

If you use the Left or Right option to align a picture, adjacent text flows, or *wraps,* around the picture. You can control the amount of text that wraps around the picture by inserting a *line break* where you want the wrapping to stop. A line break creates a new, blank line and moves all the text following the line break beneath the picture.

Pressing Shift+Enter creates a normal line break. (I discuss this type of line break in Chapter 4.) The line breaks described here work specifically with left- and right-aligned pictures.

This picture is aligned using the **Left** alignment option. This picture is aligned using the **Left** alignment option. This picture is aligned using the **Left** alignment option. This picture is aligned using the **Left** alignment option. This picture is aligned using the **Left** alignment option.

This picture is aligned using the **Right** alignment option. This picture is aligned using the **Right** alignment option. This picture is aligned using the **Right** alignment option. This picture is aligned using the **Right** alignment  option. This picture is aligned using the **Right** alignment option. This picture is aligned using the **Right** alignment option.

Figure 6-3:
The results
of the Left
and Right
alignment
options.

To insert a line break, follow these steps:

1. **Position the cursor on the page where you want to insert the line break.**

2. **Choose Insert⇨Break.**

   The Break dialog box appears.

3. **Click the option button next to the type of line break you want.**

   The type of line break you select depends on how the picture is aligned:

   - **Clear Left Margin.** If the picture is left-aligned, choose this option to cause text after the line break to shift to the first empty space in the left margin below the picture.

   - **Clear Right Margin.** If the picture is right-aligned, choose this option to cause text after the line break to shift to the first empty space in the right margin below the picture.

   - **Clear Both Margins.** If the page contains several pictures — some that are left-aligned and others that are right-aligned — choose this option to cause text to shift to the first empty space where both margins are clear.

4. **Click OK to close the dialog box and insert the line break.**

Placing graphics right where you want them

New Web designers (especially those who are used to working with page layout programs such as PageMaker or Quark) are often frustrated by how difficult simply placing a picture where they want on the page can be. In Web pages, graphics sit in line with the page's text flow, which means that you have limited control over the picture's position.

Fortunately, Web design has a loophole: the table. By structuring the layout of your text and graphics inside a table and then turning off the table's borders, you can create beautifully laid-out pages. You find out more about tables in Chapter 8.

Another option is positioning, which enables you to place a picture in any spot on the page, independent of the page's text or other content. Positioning even makes layering text and pictures possible in your pages. Positioning can nudge your Web site toward the cutting edge of design, but only for those visitors using state-of-the-art Web browsers. I explain the ins and outs of positioning in Chapter 12.

Controlling the amount of space surrounding a picture

You can control the amount of breathing room surrounding each picture. By adjusting horizontal and vertical spacing, you set the amount of space that separates a picture from its surroundings. To adjust picture spacing, follow these steps:

1. **In the page, double-click the picture.**

   The Picture Properties dialog box appears with the Appearance tab visible.

2. **In the Horizontal Spacing text box, type the number of pixels of blank space that you want to insert to the left and right of the picture.**

3. **In the Vertical Spacing text box, type the number of pixels of blank space that you want to insert above and below the picture.**

4. **Click OK to close the dialog box and adjust the spacing.**

Adding (or removing) a border around a picture

Borders are useful only if the picture in question is the basis of a hyperlink. Although you can place a black border around a regular picture by using this feature, in my opinion, the border looks darn ugly.

On the other hand, borders around graphic hyperlinks can make your site easier to navigate. Graphic hyperlink borders are the same color as the page's text link colors, cueing neophyte Web surfers to click the picture to activate the link. On the *other* other hand, borders may cause visual clutter and, worse, may clash with the colors in the picture.

You can solve this design dilemma by choosing your hyperlink graphics carefully — use pictures that implicitly whisper, "Click me." For example, graphics that look like raised buttons just beg to be clicked. Even the greenest of visitors knows to click this type of picture to activate its associated hyperlink.

To give your picture a border, or to remove the border surrounding a graphic hyperlink, follow these steps:

1. **In the page, double-click the picture.**

   The Picture Properties dialog box appears with the Appearance tab visible.

2. **In the dialog box's Border Thickness box, type the thickness, in pixels, of the picture border.**

   I recommend nothing thicker than 2 pixels. Anything much thicker tends to look gaudy, but experiment to see what you prefer. To remove borders from graphic hyperlinks, specify a border thickness of 0 pixels.

3. **Click OK to close the dialog box and apply the border setting.**

The best way to add a border to regular (non-hyperlinked) pictures is to open the graphic file in a graphics program and edit the file itself. Later in this chapter, I explain how to launch your graphics program from within FrontPage.

Setting display dimensions

FrontPage enables you to specify the width and height of a picture as it appears when viewed with a Web browser. By doing so, you don't affect the size of the graphic file itself; you affect only the dimensions of the picture as they appear inside a Web page. It's kind of like looking at a small object through a magnifying glass; the glass makes the object look bigger, but the size of the object doesn't change.

You can use FrontPage to adjust the dimensions of your Web graphics, either in pixels or as a percentage of the browser window size.

To resize a graphic quickly, in the page, click the graphic and then drag the size handles that appear around the graphic.

Resampling a picture

Earlier in the chapter, I explain how to set a picture's display dimensions, and I mention that by changing dimension settings, you don't affect the dimensions of the graphic file itself, only the size as it appears inside a Web page. Well, I'm about to go back on my word.

If you decide you prefer the new size of the picture, you can tell FrontPage to *resample* or optimize the picture to match its new size. Resampling doesn't perform magic, but it can smooth out the rough edges that sometimes

appear when you resize a picture. Resampling can also reduce the file size a bit. To resample a picture, click the picture, and then, click the Resample button on the Pictures toolbar that appears.

Keep in mind that when you resample a picture, FrontPage prompts you to save the changed graphic when you next save the page. Later in this chapter, I explain how to save a changed graphic as a separate file so that you can revert back to the original if you change your mind.

For more precise control over dimensions, follow these steps:

1. **In the page, double-click the picture.**

   The Picture Properties dialog box appears with the Appearance tab visible. The Width and Height text boxes already contain the picture's dimensions.

2. **To change the picture's dimensions, click the Specify Size check box, and then type new numbers in the Width and Height text boxes.**

   You can specify a number of pixels, or you can choose a percentage of the browser window. To maintain the correct proportion, click the Keep Aspect Ratio check box.

3. **Click OK to close the dialog box and adjust the picture's dimensions.**

Specifying ALT text

Some Web surfers, desperate to save seconds, turn off their browsers' capability to display pictures. Instead of a graphically exciting Web site, like the example shown in Figure 6-4, the result is a no-nonsense, fast-loading, text-only site, with empty placeholders where the pictures normally sit, as shown in Figure 6-5.

Visitors who want to dispense with pretty pictures to get just the facts love this feature. But what about you? You painstakingly designed your site's graphics only to discover that some of your visitors never even see them!

This is a Web publishing reality you must accept. All you can do is specify *alternative text* (known in Web design circles as *ALT text*) for each of your pictures. ALT text appears inside the placeholder where the original graphic would have appeared if image-loading were turned on. Generally, you use ALT text to describe the graphic, giving visitors an idea of what the graphic contains and enabling visitors to decide whether the graphic is worth the load time.

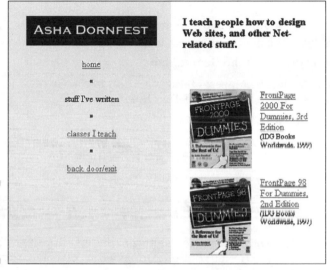

Figure 6-4:
My Web site
in full
regalia.

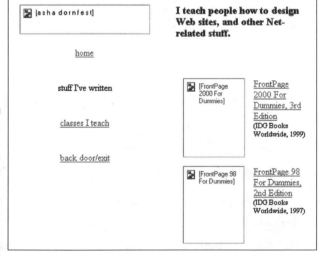

Figure 6-5:
My Web site
with my
browser's
image-
loading
function
turned off.

ALT text comes with a bonus: Some browsers display ALT text as a caption of sorts, popping the text up in a little box when the visitor hovers the pointer over a picture.

Give every picture in your Web site meaningful ALT text. By doing so, you give visitors yet another way to enjoy your Web site (a thoughtful touch that many Web surfers appreciate).

To specify ALT text, follow these steps:

1. **In the page, double-click the picture to display the Picture Properties dialog box.**

2. **In dialog box, click the General tab.**

3. **In the Alternative Representations section of the General tab, type a brief, descriptive blurb in the Text box.**

4. **Click OK to close the dialog box.**

   Although nothing appears to have changed in your page, FrontPage has inserted the ALT text into your page's HTML tags.

Placing a text label on top of a picture

If a picture on your page needs a descriptive caption, or if you want to transform your favorite pictures into buttons or banners, you can easily do so by placing a bit of text on top of the picture.

The tool you use for this effect resides on the Pictures toolbar, shown in Figure 6-6. You can make this toolbar visible by clicking a picture in the page or by choosing View➪Toolbars➪Pictures.

Figure 6-6:
The Pictures
toolbar.

To create a text label, follow these steps:

1. **In the page, click the picture you want to edit.**

2. **On the Pictures toolbar, click the Text button.**

   After you click the Text button, an empty rectangular area with a flashing insertion point appears in the center of the picture.

3. **Type your desired text and then click anywhere outside the picture.**

   The picture is deselected, with the new text label sitting at the center of the picture.

To reposition the text label inside the picture, click the picture. A rectangular box appears around the text label. Click inside the rectangular box and then drag the label to a new position.

You can also format the text by using any of the text tools in the Font dialog box (available by choosing Format⇨Font) and on the Formatting toolbar.

Editing the Picture Itself

FrontPage has limited image-editing capabilities that can save you the hassle of launching a separate program for little touch-ups.

When you use FrontPage to edit a graphic file, the Save Embedded Files dialog box appears the next time you save the page and prompts you to save the new, changed version of the picture. If you click OK to save the picture, you overwrite the original picture. To be safe, consider renaming the changed picture (which prompts FrontPage to save the changed picture as a separate file) so that you can revert to the original picture if you mess up or change your mind. To do so, in the Save Embedded Files dialog box, click the Rename button, type a new filename, and then click OK to close the dialog box and save the file.

Creating a transparent GIF

The concept of a transparent GIF is more easily demonstrated than explained, so I'm going to show you one first and then tell you about the concept in a moment. Figure 6-7 shows the difference between a regular GIF and a transparent GIF. The graphic on the left is a regular GIF. See how the graphic's background color wrestles with the background color of the page? This problem disappears if you make the GIF's background color transparent, like the background of the graphic on the right. The transparent GIF blends nicely with the rest of the page.

A transparent GIF has one of its colors erased (generally the background color) so that the color of the page shows through. The Pictures toolbar contains a "magic eraser" that can make regular GIFs transparent with a couple of clicks.

Figure 6-7:
A regular
GIF is on
the left; a
transparent
GIF is on
the right.

Regular GIF   Transparent GIF

A GIF can have only one transparent color. Whichever color you slate for erasure disappears throughout the graphic. Unless the color you choose is unique, your GIF resembles Swiss cheese, because see-through spots appear throughout the picture. To avoid this problem, make sure that the GIF's background color does not appear anywhere else in the graphic. If you're working with ready-made graphics, you may need to alter them in a graphics program first.

To transform a regular GIF into a transparent GIF, follow these steps:

1. **Insert the GIF of your choice into your page.**

2. **In the page, click the picture.**

3. **Click the Set Transparent Color button on the Pictures toolbar that appears, and then, in the picture, move the pointer over the color you want to erase.**

   As you move the pointer over the picture, the pointer turns into a little pencil eraser with an arrow sticking out of the top.

4. **Click the mouse button.**

   The color disappears!

To change a picture's transparent color, click the Set Transparent Color button and then click a different color inside the picture. The original color reappears, and the newly chosen color becomes transparent.

To turn a transparent GIF back into a regular GIF, click the Set Transparent Color button and then click the transparent area. The old color comes back.

If you try this trick on a JPEG graphic, FrontPage prompts you to convert the picture to GIF format. (GIF and PNG are the only Web graphic formats that can be made transparent.) Proceed with care, however, because the GIF format can't accommodate as many colors as JPEG can, and your picture's quality and file size may suffer as a result.

Cropping a picture

Cropping a picture involves trimming parts of the picture away, leaving only the stuff you like. To crop a picture, do this:

1. **In the page, click the picture you want to crop.**

2. **Click the Crop button on the Pictures toolbar.**

   A set of handles and a cropping border, shown in Figure 6-8, appear inside the selected picture. The handles, which are shaped like little squares, allow you to change the shape of the cropping border (the dotted lines). Just click and drag one of the handles, and keep reshaping the cropping border until it completely surrounds the part of the picture you want to keep intact. You can also click inside the cropping border and drag the border around without reshaping it. After you crop the picture, the stuff inside the cropping border stays, and the stuff outside the border goes.

Figure 6-8:
Cropping a
picture.

3. **After you get the cropping border right where you want it, click the Crop button again.**

   Snip! The unwanted portion of the picture goes away.

If you decide you don't like the newly cropped picture, click the Undo button on the Standard toolbar to start over.

Applying a special effect to a picture

The Pictures toolbar contains a few tools that apply special visual effects to your pictures. To use any of these effects, click the picture you want to change and then click the corresponding button:

✓ **Rotate Left and Rotate Right.** These options rotate the picture 90 degrees to the left or right.

✓ **Flip Horizontal and Flip Vertical.** These options flip the picture horizontally and vertically.

✓ **Increase Contrast and Decrease Contrast.** These options increase or decrease the picture's contrast.

✓ **Increase Brightness and Decrease Brightness.** These options increase or decrease the picture's brightness.

✓ **Line Style.** This button becomes active when you select an AutoShape or a piece of WordArt in your page. If the element that you select has any type of line in it, this button controls the line's style and thickness.

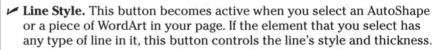

✓ **Format Picture.** This button becomes active when you select an AutoShape or piece of WordArt in your page. Click the button to open the Format dialog box for either type of graphic. This dialog box gives you a bunch of options for customizing the image.

✓ **Color.** Click this button to see four pop-up options: Grayscale, Black & White, Washout (useful when you want inactive graphic hyperlink buttons to look inactive in your page), and Automatic (which returns the graphic to its original or most recently saved self).

✓ **Bevel.** Click this button to transform a regular, flat picture into a raised button of sorts. This effect works best with square and rectangular graphics.

✓ **Restore.** If you're not happy with any of the effects, click the Restore button to return the picture to its original state. (Just be sure *not* to save the changes first; otherwise the Restore button won't work.)

Launching a separate graphics program

Want to add some finishing touches to your graphic? You can launch a separate graphics program right from within FrontPage. To do so, you must first associate your graphics program with FrontPage. (Refer to Chapter 2 for instructions.) After FrontPage knows which graphics program to launch, in the page, right-click any graphic, and choose Edit Picture from the pop-up menu that appears. The associated editing program launches with the selected graphic open and ready for a makeover.

Deleting a picture

Erasing a picture from your page hardly takes a thought. Just click the picture and press the Backspace or Delete key. That's it.

Using Thumbnails to Speed Up Your Page

Adding pictures to a Web page increases the page's overall load time. Because Web surfers' annoyance level rises with every second they must wait for a page to appear on-screen, you're wise to limit the number of pictures to keep the site loading fast.

But what if your site relies on pictures? Say you're building an online catalog or a Web-based art gallery. For these sites, the pictures are the main attraction. Are you (and your visitors) doomed to a slow-moving site?

Thankfully, no. Your salvation is called a *thumbnail*. A thumbnail is a tiny version of the picture that you want to display in your page. Because small pictures load faster than big pictures, thumbnails take only moments to appear on-screen. The thumbnail is hyperlinked to the full-sized picture, so if visitors want to see more detail, they can click the thumbnail. (Presumably they are willing to wait a few moments for the full-sized version to appear.) Figure 6-9 shows you how thumbnails work.

Thumbnails are wonderful because visitors wait only for the pictures they really want to see. Furthermore, you can insert several thumbnails into a page and still keep the load time minimal.

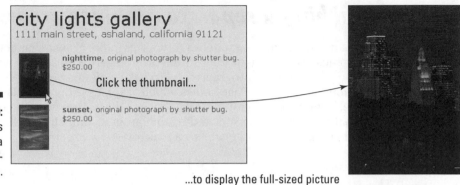

Figure 6-9:
Thumbnails
speed up a
picture-
laden page.

...to display the full-sized picture

Keep in mind that a page with bunches of graphics, no matter what their size, slows down the page's loading time. Keep an eye on your page's download time and, if necessary, break hefty pages into several more sparsely filled pages.

For the FrontPage-less Web designer, thumbnails take a lot of time to produce. But for you, blessed with FrontPage as you are, thumbnails take only moments to create. Follow these steps:

1. **In the page, insert the picture that you want to turn into a thumbnail.**

2. **Click the picture, and then click the Auto Thumbnail button on the Pictures toolbar.**

    Note: If the Auto Thumbnail button appears dimmed, then you cannot use the selected picture as a thumbnail. Here are the no-no's: pictures that are already hyperlinked, pictures that have text labels, pictures whose original dimensions are smaller than the thumbnail, and image maps. (I introduce you to image maps in Chapter 7.)

    After you click the Auto Thumbnail button, the picture shrinks, and a colorful border appears around the picture, indicating it is now a graphic hyperlink.

To see the thumbnail in action, preview the page and click the thumbnail.

You can control the dimensions, the border thickness, and the bevel setting that FrontPage uses to create thumbnails. To access FrontPage's thumbnail settings, choose Tools➪Page Options to display the Page Options dialog box. In the dialog box, click the Auto Thumbnail tab.

The next time you save the page, the Save Embedded Files dialog box appears prompting you to save any thumbnail images you've created. Click OK to save the files. See Chapter 2 for more details on how this dialog box works.

Creating a Photo Gallery

Imagine sharing your travel photos with friends across the world or keeping Grandma up to date on your toddler's antics. With a FrontPage Photo Gallery, you can easily add a professional-looking digital photo album, like the one shown in Figure 6-10, to your Web site. This may quickly become your favorite FrontPage goody. It's certainly mine.

Figure 6-10: A FrontPage Photo Gallery.

Think of Photo Galleries as thumbnails on caffeine. (If you're not sure what a thumbnail is, read the previous section of this chapter.) You select the photos that you want to appear in your Photo Gallery, and FrontPage generates thumbnails, lays them out nicely (in some cases with captions and descriptive text), and links the thumbnails to the full-sized photos.

First things first: How do you get your photos onto your computer? If you use a digital camera, the process is as easy as transferring the photo files from your camera's memory card to your computer's hard drive.

Film camera users must *scan* their photos — devices called *scanners* create a digital file from a photo print. If you happen to own a scanner, that's great. If not, you can take your photos to a well-stocked copy shop (most have scanning services), or you can send your film to a developer who scans the photos and sends you the digital files as well as the prints.

Digital cameras and scanners can save photo files as Web-friendly JPEGs. If your photos are saved in another graphic format, you'll need to convert them to JPEG in order to use them in your Web site. FrontPage converts files automatically, or you can convert the files using a separate graphics program. (I talk about file conversion earlier in the chapter.)

After you've saved your photos as JPEGs on your hard drive or network, you're ready to begin. To create a photo gallery, follow these steps:

1. **Create a new page, or open the existing page into which you want to insert a Photo Gallery.**

   If you're starting by creating a new page, save time by using the Photo Gallery page template. This template creates a page containing a Photo Gallery plus a placeholder heading and introductory text. If you use the Photo Gallery template, in the page, double-click the Photo Gallery to display the Photo Gallery Properties dialog box and then skip ahead to Step 7. If you're not sure how to create a new page based on a template, refer to Chapter 2.

2. **In the page, place the cursor where you want the Photo Gallery to appear.**

3. **Click the Web Component button on the Standard toolbar or choose Insert⇨Web Component.**

   The Insert Web Component dialog box appears.

4. **In the dialog box's Component Type list box, click Photo Gallery.**

5. **In the Choose a Photo Gallery Option list box, click the icon that corresponds to the page layout you want.**

   Don't worry — you can change your mind later.

6. **Click Finish.**

   The Insert Web Component dialog box closes and the Photo Gallery Properties dialog box appears with the Pictures tab visible, as shown in Figure 6-11. This dialog box enables you to select the photos that will appear in the Photo Gallery; choose design details such as the thumbnail size, caption and descriptive text; and, if you like, select a whole new layout for the Photo Gallery.

7. **In the dialog box, click Add, and choose Pictures from Files from the drop-down menu.**

   I'm assuming here that your photos are stored on your hard drive or network. If your digital camera or scanner is connected to your computer and the photos are stored in that device's memory, instead, choose Pictures from Scanner or Cameras to grab the images directly.

   After you choose Pictures from Files, the File Open dialog box appears, enabling you to navigate your hard drive or network and select the photos that you want to appear in the Photo Gallery.

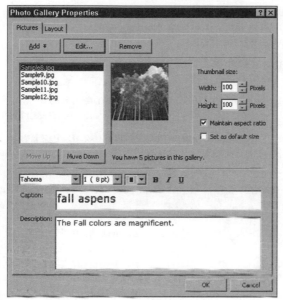

Figure 6-11:
The Photo
Gallery
Properties
dialog box.

8. **In the dialog box, navigate to the location of your photo files, select them, and then click Open.**

You can select more than one file at a time by holding down the Shift or Ctrl key while clicking file icons.

After you click Open, the File Open dialog box closes and the Photo Gallery Properties dialog box becomes visible again. The filenames for the photos you've selected appear in the dialog box's file list, and thumbnail previews of the photos appear alongside the filenames.

To change the size of the thumbnail image that appears in the Photo Gallery, change the numbers in the Width and Height boxes (be sure Maintain Aspect Ratio is checked or the thumbnails will appear distorted when you change their dimensions). Click Set As Default Size if you'd like FrontPage to use the current thumbnail dimensions in future Photo Galleries.

To change the order of the photos as they appear in the Photo Gallery, click the photo's filename in the file list, and then click Move Up or Move Down.

You can also edit the full-sized photos. To do so, click the photo's filename in the file list, and then click Edit. The Edit Picture dialog box appears. This dialog box contains options that allow you to change the photo's resolution, rotate, or crop the photo. When you're done editing the photo, click OK to close the Edit Picture dialog box and return to the Photo Gallery Properties dialog box.

9. **To add a caption and a description to each picture, click the picture's filename in the file list, and then type a caption and a description in the corresponding text boxes.**

   You can format the text in either of these boxes using the formatting options in the dialog box.

   Note: If the Description text box appears dimmed, the layout you've chosen for your Photo Gallery doesn't display a text description.

10. **To change the Photo Gallery's layout, click the dialog box's Layout tab, and then choose a new layout from the Choose a Layout box.**

    You may also control the number of photos that appear in one row by changing the number in the Number of Pictures Per Row list box.

11. **When you're finished, click OK.**

    The Photo Gallery Properties dialog box closes, and the Photo Gallery appears in the page.

You can change the Photo Gallery's settings any time. In the page, double-click anywhere inside the Photo Gallery to open the Photo Gallery Properties dialog box.

Using Background Images

You can use a picture as the background of your page, with the page's text sitting on top. How the background image appears as viewed with a browser depends on the dimensions of the graphic file itself. The Web browser *tiles* the picture, repeating the picture over and over until it fills the browser window, which creates a consistent background for the text.

You can also turn your background into a *watermark*. Watermarks are the same as regular backgrounds, except that watermarks appear fixed in place if viewed with a Web browser — when a visitor scrolls around the screen, the text appears to float above the fixed background. (With regular background images, the background and text move together when a visitor scrolls around the page.) As of this writing, Microsoft Internet Explorer is the only browser that can display watermarks.

Each FrontPage theme contains a background pattern that you can use in your pages. (I show you how to work with themes in Chapter 11.) You can also download backgrounds from the Web, or you can create your own backgrounds in a graphics program.

If you decide to use a background image, choose one that harmonizes with the colors in your site. If the picture is too busy, the background may obscure the text, making the page difficult to read. Additionally, background images, like regular pictures, add time to your page's total download speed. The smaller and simpler your background image is, the faster the page loads.

To insert a background image, follow these steps:

1. **With a page open in Page View, choose Format⇨Background.**

   The Page Properties dialog box appears, with the Background tab visible.

   Note: If the page uses a theme, this menu option is unavailable, because all background options are determined by that theme.

2. **In the dialog box, click the Background Picture check box.**

3. **In the corresponding text box, type the graphic file's path.**

   Or click Browse to select the file from a list of files on your computer, on your local network, or in the Media Gallery.

4. **If you want the background to appear fixed, click the Watermark check box.**

5. **Click OK to close the dialog box.**

   The background image appears in your page.

If the background image is stored in a location other than in the currently open Web site, then the Save Embedded Files dialog box offers to import the graphic file to your Web site the next time you save the page. Click OK to import the file.

You can choose a solid color as your page background instead of a picture. Solid background colors load instantly and are often easier to coordinate with the color scheme of the page. To specify a background color, choose Format⇨Background to display the Page Properties dialog box. Choose a color from the Background list box (or choose More Colors to pick a color from the More Colors dialog box) and then click OK.

Alternatively, you can base the page's background color or image on that of another page in your Web site. I explain how in Chapter 5.

Working with Drawn Graphics

If you've read the earlier parts of this chapter, forget everything you've learned. *Drawn graphics* differ from bitmap graphics in more ways than they are similar, and, as such, are subject to a different set of rules.

Drawn graphics, such as lines, shapes, and bits of fancy text, are more flexible than bitmaps. Whereas bitmaps can be edited only in minimal ways, you can manipulate a drawn graphic however you like. You can change its shape, color, size, or orientation. You can apply special effects, such as shadows and 3-D. You can group drawn graphics together and then make changes to the group as a unit.

The drawback to using drawn graphics is browser compatibility. Although FrontPage compensates for browser differences in some ways, drawn graphics aren't always consistent across different browser flavors and versions. So, if you use drawn graphics in your Web pages, be sure to preview the page using several browsers.

Awesome AutoShapes

No need to hunt around the Web for clip art when you simply want to draw a shape in your page! AutoShapes are commonly used presentation shapes, such as lines, arrows, basic shapes, flowcharts, callouts, and banners.

Inserting AutoShapes into your page

You can draw your own shapes, or you can plop ready-made AutoShapes into your page with a few quick clicks. To do so, follow these steps:

1. **Click anywhere inside the page, and then choose Insert➪Picture➪ AutoShapes.**

   The AutoShapes and Drawing toolbars, shown in Figure 6-12, appear in the FrontPage window. The AutoShapes toolbar contains the same options as the AutoShapes button on the Drawing toolbar, so I'll focus on the Drawing toolbar.

Figure 6-12:
The
AutoShapes
and
Drawing
toolbars.

2. **To use a ready-made AutoShape, click the AutoShapes button on the Drawing toolbar.**

   A menu pops up listing the different categories of AutoShapes available to you.

3. **Choose the category of AutoShape you want, and from the corresponding menu that appears, choose the AutoShape you want.**

   You can float any of the AutoShape menus to make them visible all the time. To do so, move your cursor over the solid line at the top of the menu, and when it changes color, click and drag the menu to another place on your screen.

   After you select your AutoShape, the cursor changes from a pointer into a drawing crosshatch.

4. **Move the cursor to the location in the page where you want the AutoShape to appear, and then click and drag to draw the AutoShape. When you're happy with what you see, release the mouse button.**

   The AutoShape appears in your page. If you drew the AutoShape over existing text or content in the page, the AutoShape sits on top of that content. I explain how to change the AutoShape's placement (and color, size and other attributes) in a moment.

The Drawing toolbar contains shortcut buttons to the most commonly used AutoShapes: lines, arrows, rectangles, and ovals. To use the shortcut buttons, in Step 2 of the previous set of steps, click the appropriate button, and then skip ahead to Step 4.

Changing how AutoShapes look

If you're not satisfied with your AutoShape's attributes, you can change them easily enough. Here are some tips for making the following changes to AutoShapes (all the buttons mentioned in this section are on the Drawing toolbar):

- ✔ **Moving:** Click and drag the AutoShape to a new location on the page. To move the AutoShape just a tiny bit, click the AutoShape; choose Draw⇨Nudge; and then choose Up, Down, Left, or Right.

- ✔ **Placing the AutoShape on top of or below other content on the page:** Click the AutoShape; choose Draw⇨Order; and then choose Bring to Front, Send to Back, Bring Forward, or Send Backward.

- ✔ **Changing the dimensions:** Click the AutoShape to display its size handles. Click and drag any of the size handles until the shape is the size you want. Some AutoShapes have a yellow handle that modifies the AutoShape's shape as well.

- ✔ **Rotating:** Click the AutoShape to display its size handles. Click and drag the green handle to rotate the AutoShape freely. Alternatively, you can choose Draw⇨Rotate or Flip and then choose Rotate Left, Rotate Right, Flip Horizontal, or Flip Vertical.

- ✔ **Changing the fill color:** Click the AutoShape, and then click the Fill Color button. To display a menu of color options, click the arrow next to the Fill Color button, and choose the fill color you want.

- ✔ **Changing the color of the line surrounding the AutoShape:** Click the AutoShape, and then click the Line Color button. To display a menu of color options, click the arrow next to the Line Color button, and then choose the fill color you want.

- ✔ **Changing the style of the line surrounding the AutoShape:** Click the AutoShape, and then click the Line Style button. From the menu that pops up, choose the line style you want. If you prefer a dashed to a solid line, click the Dash Style button.

Part II: Creating Envy-Inducing Web Pages

✔ **Changing the arrow style:** If the AutoShape contains arrows or pointing lines, you can change the arrow style (or turn a plain line into an arrow) by clicking the AutoShape and then clicking the Arrow Style button. Choose an arrow style from the menu that pops up.

✔ **Adding a shadow or 3-D effect:** Click the AutoShape and then click the Shadow Style or 3-D Style button. From the menu that pops up, choose the style you want.

✔ **Placing text on top of an AutoShape:** Move the cursor over the AutoShape until the cursor looks like an I-Beam, click, and start typing. You can format the text — change its color and size, for example. Some AutoShapes don't accept text placement, in which case you need to place a text box on top of the AutoShape. I explain how to create a text box later in this chapter.

✔ **Applying any effect to more than one AutoShape:** While holding down the Shift key, click the AutoShapes to select them, and then click the corresponding Drawing toolbar button. If you group the AutoShapes together to turn them into a single unit, you can select the AutoShapes and choose Draw⇨Group.

✔ **Aligning AutoShapes or Distributing the space between them evenly:** Select the AutoShapes you want to align or distribute; choose Draw⇨ Align or Distribute; and then choose Align Left, Align Center, Align Right, Align Top, Align Middle, Align Bottom, Distribute Horizontally, or Distribute Vertically.

For even more control over an AutoShape's attributes, double-click the AutoShape to display the Format AutoShape dialog box (see Figure 6-13). This dialog box contains all the options described in the previous list, plus a few more. Don't be afraid to experiment. The trusty Undo button is always within reach.

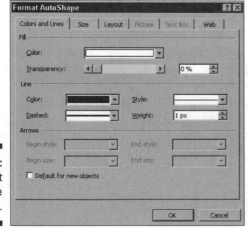

Figure 6-13:
The Format
AutoShape
dialog box.

Working with WordArt

At times, plain old text just doesn't cut it, especially if you're creating a page heading or banner. These times call for WordArt, the Microsoft Office feature that lets you choose from a gallery of flashy effects you can apply to text. Figure 6-14 shows you just one of the effects you can create using WordArt.

Figure 6-14: WordArt at work.

To insert WordArt into your page, do the following:

1. **In the page, place the cursor where you want the WordArt to appear, and then choose Insert⇨Picture⇨WordArt. Or click the Insert WordArt button on the Drawing toolbar.**

   The WordArt Gallery dialog box appears.

2. **In the dialog box, double-click the graphic that most closely approximates how you want the text to look (you can more finely tune the graphic's appearance in a moment).**

   The WordArt Gallery dialog box closes, and the Edit WordArt Text dialog box appears with the WordArt text highlighted.

3. **Type your desired WordArt text.**

   You can also change the text's font, size, and attributes using the options in the Edit WordArt Text dialog box.

4. **When you like what you see, click OK.**

   The Edit WordArt Text dialog box closes, and the WordArt appears on your page.

As with AutoShapes, you can change the shape of and rotate the WordArt by clicking and dragging its size handles. WordArt is placed in line with text and other page content by default. You can change WordArt positioning by using the settings in the Format WordArt dialog box (read on for details).

After you insert WordArt into your page, the WordArt toolbar appears, as shown in Figure 6-15, offering even more options for changing how the WordArt looks. Have fun experimenting with the buttons on this toolbar. For finer control, click the Format WordArt button to display the Format WordArt dialog box. This dialog box contains options for changing the WordArt's attributes, including its layout. I explain how to use the options in the dialog box's Layout tab in Chapter 12.

Figure 6-15:
The
WordArt
toolbar.

Creating a drawing

You can bunch your AutoShapes and WordArt together into a composition of sorts. Rather than place individual drawn graphics inside your page, you can create a *drawing*. A drawing is essentially an empty space (called a *canvas*) into which you place as many drawn graphics as you like. You can then format the canvas itself by changing its size, layout, color, and other attributes.

To create a drawing, follow these steps.

1. **In the page, place the cursor where you want the drawing to appear, and then choose Insert⇨Picture⇨New Drawing.**

   An empty box appears on your page. This is the drawing canvas. At the same time, the Drawing Canvas toolbar appears.

2. **Insert the drawn graphic of your choice into the drawing canvas, and make any changes to the graphic you wish.**

   To do so, follow the steps for working with AutoShapes and WordArt earlier in the chapter.

You can change the shape of the canvas by dragging any of its size handles, or by clicking the Fit or Expand buttons in the Drawing Canvas toolbar.

To change the drawing canvas's attributes, right-click inside the empty area of the canvas, and from the pop-up menu that appears, choose Format Drawing Canvas. In the Format Drawing Canvas dialog box, make any changes you like.

Chapter 7

Creating an Image Map

In This Chapter

▶ Understanding what image maps do

▶ Choosing the right graphic

▶ Creating and working with hotspots

*I*mage maps look like regular pictures, but act like a collection of text hyperlinks. In this chapter, I show you how to transform a picture into an image map.

What Is an Image Map?

An *image map* is a picture that contains more than one hyperlink. Unlike a regular graphic hyperlink, which leads to a single destination, an image map can lead to several destinations. Visitors activate different hyperlinks by clicking different places inside the picture (see Figure 7-1).

Figure 7-1:
The
"buttons"
on this
image map
show
visitors
where to
click to
activate a
hyperlink.

The clickable areas of the picture are called *hotspots*. Hotspots work just like regular hyperlinks; they can link to an e-mail address, a downloadable file, or another location in the Web site or on the Internet. Most often, however, image maps contain links to other places inside the Web site.

FrontPage contains simple tools you use to "draw" hotspots on the picture of your choice. Hotspots are visible to you as you work with the image map in FrontPage, but when visitors view your page with a Web browser, hotspots are invisible. (Visitors see only the image map graphic.)

If you use an image map in your Web site, consider including a corresponding list of text hyperlinks somewhere else in the page. Visitors who surf the Web with their browsers' image-loading function turned off (or who use text-only browsers) cannot see regular pictures or image maps and, therefore, must rely on the text hyperlinks to move around. If you're not sure how to create a text hyperlink, refer to Chapter 5.

Choosing the Right Picture

You don't want to turn just any old picture into an image map. Because hotspots are invisible to the visitor, the picture you choose should clearly indicate where to click, either with the help of a visual metaphor (the example pictured in Figure 7-1 uses buttons) or with text labels. The ideal image map picture doesn't require explanation; the clickable areas should be obvious.

Don't worry if you can't get your hands on the perfect image map graphic. Even though image map hotspots are invisible when visitors view your page with a Web browser, the pointer changes shape and the hotspot's destination address appears in the browser's status bar when a visitor hovers the pointer over a hotspot. These clues are enough to prompt most visitors to click.

After you choose your picture, open the page in which you want the image map to appear and then insert the picture into the page. (Refer to Chapter 6 if you're not sure how to insert a picture.)

Creating Hotspots

After you find the right picture and insert it in your page, you're ready to draw the hotspots. Read on to find out how to create and work with hotspots.

Drawing hotspots

You use tools available on the Pictures toolbar to draw hotspots. You can draw rectangles, circles, and multisided shapes (polygons) around the areas you want to make clickable.

Don't confuse drawing hotspots with the graphic shapes you can create using FrontPage's drawing tools. I explain how to work with drawing tools in Chapter 6.

To draw hotspots on a picture, follow these steps:

1. **Open the page containing the image map graphic and then click the picture.**

   The Pictures toolbar appears.

2. **Click the Rectangular Hotspot, Circular Hotspot, or Polygonal Hotspot button on the Pictures toolbar.**

   Pick the shape that resembles the shape of the area you want to turn into a hotspot. You can always move or reshape the hotspot later, or delete the hotspot and start again.

3. **Move the pointer over the picture.**

   The pointer turns into a little pencil.

4. **Click the hotspot area and drag the cursor until the resulting hotspot surrounds the area.**

   The best place to click depends on the shape you chose. Here's what to do for the following shapes:

   - **Rectangle:** Click the corner of the hotspot area and drag the rectangle until the shape surrounds the area.

   - **Circle:** Click the center of the hotspot area and drag. (The circle expands from its center point.)

   - **Polygon:** Creating a polygonal hotspot is like playing connect the dots, only you decide where the dots are: Click the first point, release the mouse button, and then drag the pointer. (This action produces a line.) Stretch the line to the second point — click, stretch, click, stretch — until you enclose your hotspot area. After you've finished defining the hotspot, click the hotspot's starting point, and FrontPage closes the hotspot for you.

   You can overlap hotspots. If you do so, the most recent hotspot is on top, which means this hotspot takes priority if you click the overlapped area.

   After you draw the hotspot, the hotspot border appears on top of your picture, and the Insert Hyperlink dialog box appears, enabling you to associate a hyperlink with the hotspot.

5. **Create a link for the hotspot, just as you would a regular hyperlink.**

   Refer to Chapter 5 if you're not sure how to create hyperlinks.

6. **Keep creating hotspots until you define all the clickable areas inside the picture.**

   Areas not covered by a hotspot don't do anything if clicked unless you specify a *default hyperlink.* (I show you how to do this later in this chapter.)

7. **When you're finished, click anywhere outside the picture to hide the hotspot borders.**

 For a quick look at all the hotspots inside the picture, click the Highlight Hotspots button on the Pictures toolbar. The picture becomes blank, and only the hotspot borders are visible. To return to the regular display, click the Highlight Hotspots button again.

If you later want to change a hotspot's hyperlink, click the picture to make the hotspots visible and then double-click the hotspot to open the Edit Hyperlink dialog box. Make any changes you want and then click OK to close the dialog box.

Drawing labeled hotspots

Hotspots are most effective when the area of the picture that visitors are supposed to click is obvious. If the clickable area isn't readily apparent, you may need to label a hotspot with descriptive text. To draw a labeled hotspot, do this:

1. **In the page, click the picture.**

   The Pictures toolbar appears.

 2. **Click the Text button on the Pictures toolbar.**

   A rectangular hotspot with a flashing insertion point appears in the center of the picture.

3. **Type a descriptive text label.**

4. **Click anywhere outside the hotspot to deselect it.**

   Now you need to specify the hotspot's hyperlink.

5. **Double-click the text hotspot.**

   The Insert Hyperlink dialog box appears.

6. **Create a link for the hotspot and, when you're finished, click anywhere outside the picture.**

To change the text label, click the hotspot to select it, click inside the text label, and then type new text. You can also format the text by using any of the text tools on the Formatting toolbar or in the Font dialog box (available by choosing Format⇨Font).

Because a text hotspot is essentially a rectangular hotspot with some text on top, you can resize the hotspot as you would a non-labeled rectangular hotspot. (Read on for more about resizing hotspots.)

Moving hotspots

If the placement of a hotspot isn't just so, move the hotspot by following these simple steps:

1. **Click the image map to make its hotspots visible.**

   It's okay — image maps aren't modest.

2. **Click the hotspot you want to move.**

   You can tell whether you selected a hotspot, because size handles that look like little square points appear on its border after you select the hotspot.

3. **Drag the hotspot to a new location inside the picture and drop it there.**

Resizing hotspots

Hotspots are as malleable as taffy. Adjusting their shapes and sizes is easy. Just follow these steps:

1. **Click the image map to make its hotspots visible.**

2. **Click the hotspot you want to resize.**

   Size handles appear on the hotspot border.

3. **Click a size handle and drag the handle until the hotspot is the size or shape you want.**

Size handles act differently depending on the shape of the hotspot. Working with handles is not a precise science. Just keep clicking, dragging, and stretching until you're happy with the results.

Deleting hotspots

Sometimes, no amount of coaxing gets a stubborn hotspot into shape. Time to delete the troublemaker and draw a new one. Just follow these steps:

1. **Click the image map to make its hotspots visible.**

2. **Click the hotspot you want to delete.**

3. **Press the Backspace or Delete key.**

Setting the Default Hyperlink

The final (and optional) step in creating an image map is setting the image map's *default hyperlink*. Visitors jump to the destination of the default hyperlink if they click anywhere on the image map not covered by a hotspot. If you forgo the default hyperlink, clicking an undefined area does nothing. To set an image map's default hyperlink, follow these steps:

1. **Right-click the image map and then choose Picture Properties from the pop-up menu that appears.**

   The Picture Properties dialog box appears with the Appearance tab visible.

2. **In the dialog box, click the General tab to make the options on the tab visible.**

3. **In the Default Hyperlink area of the tab, type the default hyperlink's URL in the Location text box.**

   If you can't remember the URL, click the Browse button to display the Edit Hyperlink dialog box. Chapter 5 explains how to use this dialog box.

   After you specify the URL, click OK to close the Edit Hyperlink dialog box. The Picture Properties dialog box becomes visible again, with the default hyperlink's URL appearing in the Location text box.

4. **Click OK to close the dialog box.**

   FrontPage applies the default hyperlink to the image map.

To test-drive the image map, preview your page. (Refer to Chapter 2 if you're not sure how.) Alternatively, in FrontPage, hold down the Ctrl key and click one of the hotspots. In a moment, the destination page opens in Page View.

Chapter 8

You Don't Have to Take Wood Shop to Build a Table

· ·

In This Chapter

▶ Figuring out how tables are useful

▶ Creating an empty table

▶ Building a table around existing text

▶ Inserting text, pictures, or even another table into a table

▶ Changing how a table looks

▶ Modifying cells, columns, and rows

▶ Adding color with backgrounds, borders, and the AutoFormat command

· ·

*P*ut away that hacksaw! True, after you finish this chapter, you can build a table — but not the kind at which you play cards with your buddies. No, in this chapter, I introduce you to the wonders of the Web page table, a lovable layout tool that shows up in the best-designed pages on the Web.

What's a Table Good For?

Both left- and right-brained Web designers love tables.

Left-brained, organized types use tables to create grids of information, which are similar in layout to a spreadsheet. Tables cordon off individual bits of data into *cells,* which are arranged in horizontal rows and vertical columns. Figure 8-1 illustrates a typical table.

Right-brained, creative types use tables to structure the layout of the page. Tables without visible borders create a framework into which you can place chunks of text, pictures, and even other tables (see Figure 8-2). The result is a layout similar to what you can achieve by using a desktop-publishing program. Invisible tables are a boon for designers who feel constrained by the traditional one-paragraph-after-another Web page layout.

Figure 8-1:
A traditional
table.

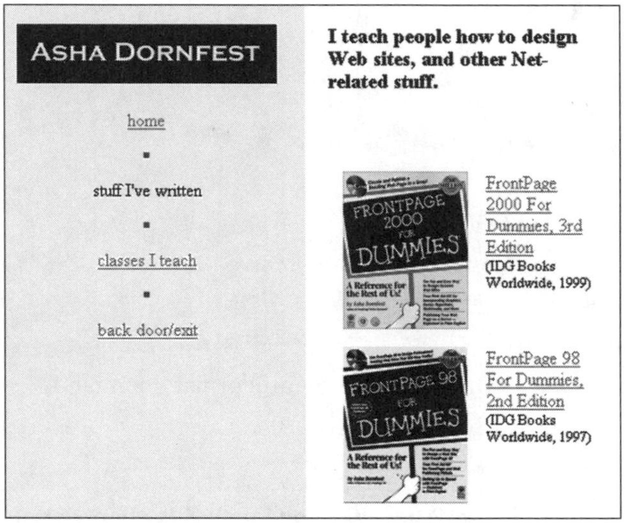

Flavor of the week

Monday	Vanilla
Tuesday	Butter Brickle
Wednesday	Mint Chip
Thursday	Rocky Road
Friday	Strawberry

Figure 8-2:
I use tables
to create
columns of
text and
pictures in
my Web
site.

For an excellent example of how invisible tables can be used to structure page layout, take a look at one of the many FrontPage page templates. In Chapter 2, I show you how to use a template to create a new Web page.

The HTML coding required to build tables can get convoluted, causing newbie Web publishers to shy away from using tables in their pages. FrontPage eliminates all cause for alarm, because table creation in FrontPage is a snap. And the only power tool you need is your mouse.

Tables work well as a page-layout tool. *Positioning* is another option. FrontPage positioning features enable you to place elements in your page with more precision than is possible with an invisible table. However, only advanced Web browsers are able to display positioned elements, whereas most browsers are able to display tables. I talk more about positioning in Chapter 12.

Creating a Table

FrontPage bends over backward to make tables accessible to the neophyte Web publisher. FrontPage offers no less than four methods for creating a table. Choose the table creation method that suits your personality:

- ✓ **You like instant gratification.** Use the Insert Table button.

- ✓ **You are a perfectionist.** Use the Table⇨Insert⇨Table command.

- ✓ **You are creative.** Use table-drawing tools.

- ✓ **You would rather be using a word-processing program right now.** Convert regular text into a table.

Using the Insert Table button

The Insert Table button suits people who want fast results. Two clicks of the mouse, and you have a perfectly good table. Try this:

1. **Place the cursor in the page where you want the table to appear.**

   If the cursor location doesn't exactly correspond to where you want the table to sit inside your page, just do the best you can; you can more precisely position the table later by using alignment options (described later in this chapter) or positioning (described in Chapter 12).

2. **On the Standard toolbar, click the Insert Table button.**

   A grid of white boxes representing table rows and columns appears underneath the button.

3. **Click and drag your pointer on the grid until the number of highlighted boxes equals the number of rows and columns that you want your table to contain (see Figure 8-3).**

   As you highlight boxes, the table dimensions appear at the bottom of the grid. If you drag past the last box in a column or row, the grid expands.

   If you don't know exactly how many rows or columns you need, just pick something close. You can always add or delete rows and columns later.

4. **Release the mouse button.**

   A new, empty table appears in your page.

Figure 8-3:
Highlight the
squares that
correspond
to the table
dimensions
you want.

Using the Insert Table command

If you like everything to be just so, you may prefer to create your table by
using the Table⇨Insert⇨Table command. With this method, you first set all
the table's attributes — number of rows and columns, border size, width, and
so on — and *then* stick the table inside the page. To do so, follow these steps:

1. **Place the cursor in the page where you want the table to appear and
   then choose T̲able⇨I̲nsert⇨T̲able.**

   The Insert Table dialog box appears.

2. **In the dialog box, specify the table's size, layout, and width.**

   I explain each attribute later in this chapter.

3. **Click OK.**

   The dialog box closes, and the table appears in the page.

Drawing a table

If you view table creation as an inspirational act, you can sketch your table's
layout by using drawing tools. To draw a table, follow these steps:

1. **Choose T̲able⇨Dra̲w Table.**

   The Tables toolbar appears, and the pointer turns into a pencil.

   Note: The Tables toolbar *floats;* to dock the toolbar at the top of the
   window, double-click the toolbar's title bar.

2. **Click the pointer where you want the table to appear in the page and
   then, while holding down the mouse button, drag the cursor from left
   to right.**

   A dotted line appears, marking out the table's external boundary.

3. **Release the mouse button.**

   A one-celled table appears in the page.

Next, you add the rows and columns. Follow these steps:

1. **Click inside the table and then drag the pencil pointer to the left or right.**

   A horizontal dotted line appears, marking out a row boundary.

2. **Release the mouse button.**

   A new row appears.

3. **Click inside the table and then drag the pencil pointer up or down.**

   A vertical dotted line appears, marking out a column boundary.

4. **Release the mouse button.**

   A new column appears.

5. **Keep drawing rows and columns until the table looks the way you want it to look.**

6. **When you're finished, click the Draw Table button on the Tables toolbar to turn off table drawing.**

Don't worry if the rows and columns aren't spaced properly. You can adjust the spacing later.

Converting existing text into a table

If you're more comfortable with your trusty word processor than you are with FrontPage, you can convert text separated with tabs, commas, or any other character, into a table. To do so, follow these steps:

1. **In the page, insert the text you want to appear inside the table.**

   Separate each line of text you want to appear in its own row by placing the text inside its own paragraph. Section each row into "columns" by separating the text with tabs, commas, or some other character. Don't worry if the spacing is uneven — when you convert the text into a table it all lines up nicely.

2. **Highlight the text and then choose Table⇨Convert⇨Text to Table.**

   The Convert Text to Table dialog box appears.

3. **Click the option button next to the text separator that you want FrontPage to recognize when it creates columns.**

   If the text separator in your page isn't a tab or comma, click the Other option button and then, in the accompanying text box, type the text separator character.

4. **Click OK.**

   The dialog box closes, and a table materializes around the selected text.

FrontPage can also convert Microsoft Word tables and Excel or Lotus 1-2-3 worksheets into Web page tables. Just cut and paste portions of a Word, Excel, or Lotus 1-2-3 file into an open page in FrontPage.

Inserting Stuff into a Table (Including Another Table)

You can insert anything into a table cell that you can into a regular page: text, pictures, and even other tables. Just click inside a cell and proceed as usual. By default, cell height and width stretch to accommodate whatever you place inside.

Text entered into a cell *wraps* as you type, which means that, when the text reaches a cell boundary, the word being typed jumps down to a new line. You create new paragraphs in a cell by pressing Enter and create line breaks by pressing Shift+Enter.

If you're ready to type text in another cell, press Tab until the cursor ends up in the destination cell and then type away. If you press the Tab key when the cursor is sitting in the last cell in the bottom row of the table, a new table row appears, and the cursor jumps to the first cell in that row so that you can continue to add to the table. To move the cursor backward through a table, press Shift+Tab.

To effortlessly fill a row or column with the same contents as the first cell of that row or column, insert something into the first cell in the row/column, select the row/column, and then click the Fill Down or Fill Right button on the Tables toolbar. (If you're having trouble selecting a row or column, I share the secret later in this chapter.) If the Tables toolbar isn't visible, choose View⇨Toolbars⇨Tables.

Table Tinkering

After you plug stuff into your table, you can tinker with the table's layout until the thing looks just the way you want it to look.

Aligning a table on the page

You can left-align, right-align, or center a table on the page. Just follow these steps:

1. **Right-click the table and choose Table Properties from the pop-up menu that appears.**

   The Table Properties dialog box appears (see Figure 8-4).

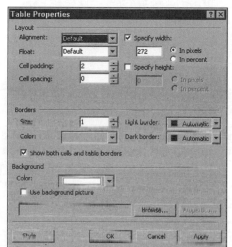

Figure 0-4:
Tho Table
Properties
dialog box.

2. **In the dialog box, choose an option from the Alignment list box.**

   Your choices are Default, Left, Right, and Center. The Default option uses the visitor's default browser alignment setting, which is left-aligned.

3. **Click the Apply button to see how the change looks before you close the dialog box.**

   If you like what you see, click OK. If you don't like what you see, choose a new option from the Alignment list box or click Cancel to close the dialog box without making any changes. After you click OK, the dialog box closes, and the table alignment changes accordingly.

Creating a floating table

No levitation occurs during this operation, but the effect is impressive just the same. Similar to a picture, adjacent text can wrap around the right or left side of a table. This effect is referred to as *floating*. Figure 8-5 shows an example of a floating table.

Third Quarter Report

Sales	+15%
Growth	+30%
Profit	Lots

We're pleased to report that sales of the new, grape-flavored Sugar Missile have exceeded all expectations. We're now rolling in money, and we can't seem to spend it fast enough.

Our product is especially popular with the nine-to-seventeen year-old market. Older consumers prefer the Champagne flavor.

Figure 8-5:
A floating
table.

To make your table float, do the following:

1. **Display the Table Properties dialog box by right-clicking the table and choosing Table Properties from the pop-up menu that appears.**

2. **In the dialog box, choose an option from the Float list box.**

   The Default setting creates no floating effect. The Left setting causes the table to float over to the left margin, with adjacent text wrapping around its right side. The Right setting causes the table to float over to the right margin, with adjacent text wrapping around its left side.

3. **Click OK to close the dialog box and change the table's floating setting.**

Older browsers aren't able to display floating tables; the table appears left-aligned with no text wrapping.

Padded cells

What do horror-movie mental institutions and tables in Web pages have in common? I'll spare you the answer to that one. All you need to know is that adding space between the contents of table cells and the cell borders is called *cell padding.* Padded cells open up a table by placing white space around the contents of each cell. Figures 8-6 and 8-7 illustrate the difference a little padding makes.

To pad cells, follow these steps:

1. **Display the Table Properties dialog box by right-clicking the table and choosing Table Properties from the pop-up menu that appears.**

2. **In the dialog box's Cell Padding text box, type the desired amount of white space (in pixels) that you want to separate cell contents from cell borders.**

3. **Click OK to close the dialog box and change the cell padding setting.**

Figure 8-6:
A table with
no cell
padding.

Flavor of the week

Monday	Vanilla
Tuesday	Butter Brickle
Wednesday	Mint Chip
Thursday	Rocky Road
Friday	Strawberry

Figure 8-7:
A table with
5 pixels
of cell
padding.

Flavor of the week

Monday	Vanilla
Tuesday	Butter Brickle
Wednesday	Mint Chip
Thursday	Rocky Road
Friday	Strawberry

Adding space between cells

Cell spacing determines how much space exists between cells and also affects the appearance of table and cell borders. Figures 8-8 and 8-9 illustrate how changes in cell spacing affect the look of a table. To change cell spacing, follow these steps:

1. **Display the Table Properties dialog box by right-clicking the table and choosing Table Properties from the pop-up menu that appears.**

2. **In the dialog box's Cell Spacing text box, type the desired amount of space (in pixels) separating table cells.**

3. **Click OK to close the dialog box and change the cell spacing setting.**

Figure 8-8:
A table with
a one-pixel
border and
no cell
spacing.

Flavor of the week

Monday	Vanilla
Tuesday	Butter Brickle
Wednesday	Mint Chip
Thursday	Rocky Road
Friday	Strawberry

Flavor of the week

Monday	Vanilla
Tuesday	Butter Brickle
Wednesday	Mint Chip
Thursday	Rocky Road
Friday	Strawberry

Figure 8-9:
A table with
a one-pixel
border and
five pixels of
cell spacing.

Changing the borders

In FrontPage, tables are born with 1-pixel-thick, beveled borders. Within certain limitations, you can change how the borders look. If you turn off the borders, you transform the table from a traditional grid into an invisible framework that you can use to arrange text, pictures, and other elements in your page.

Tables have two types of borders: those surrounding individual cells and those surrounding the entire table. Cell borders can be a maximum of 1 pixel thick. Table borders can be of any thickness. To change a table's border setting, follow these steps:

1. **Display the Table Properties dialog box by right-clicking the table and choosing Table Properties from the pop-up menu that appears.**

2. **In the dialog box's Size text box, type the desired border thickness in pixels.**

   The number you type refers to the thickness of the border surrounding the table; the borders inside the table remain at 1 pixel. If you want to make table and cell borders invisible, type **0** in the Size text box.

3. **To turn off border bevelling, unmark the Show Both Cells and Table Borders check box.**

   This setting eliminates the raised look of table and cell borders, and turns them into solid lines. FrontPage creates this effect by applying cascading style sheet (CSS) commands to the table, which means that the effect doesn't show up in older browsers that don't recognize CSS. Also, the table looks different in different browsers (even those that *do* know how to deal with CSS). Be sure to preview your table in several browsers for an accurate idea of what your visitors will see on the Web.

4. **Click OK to close the dialog box and change the border setting.**

If you turn off your table's borders, the solid border lines shown in Page View are replaced with dotted lines. These lines appear only in FrontPage — when viewed with a Web browser, the borders are invisible.

You can also control which table borders appear by experimenting with the Borders button on the Formatting toolbar. To do so, select the part of the table you want to affect (or select the entire table), and then click the arrow next to the Borders button to display a menu of options. Choose the option you want and see how your table changes.

Keep in mind that FrontPage creates these border effects using cascading style sheets. Although the CSS coding that FrontPage adds to your page's HTML is perfectly valid, browsers display the effects inconsistently. At the risk of sounding like a broken record . . . preview, preview, preview.

FrontPage gives you more options for changing your table's borders, and I elaborate on those options later in the chapter.

Setting table height and width

You have two options for controlling the dimensions of your table: You can give the table *absolute measurements* (a fixed size) or *proportional measurements* (the particulars of which are based on the size of the visitor's browser window).

You may be tempted to opt for absolute measurements so that you can retain total control over the table size. Consider, however, the unfortunate visitor who must view your page inside a tiny or low-resolution monitor. That visitor may need to scroll all over the place to see the table in its entirety and may curse the inconsiderate person who created such a table.

By using proportional measurements, you enable the visitor's browser window to determine the dimensions of the table. You give up precise control, but your visitor gets to see the entire table inside the browser window, no matter what the monitor or window size.

Which option is best? The choice depends on how you intend to use your table. If the table's overall structure is more important than the precise placement of its contents, use proportional measurements. If you require control, use absolute measurements.

Another option is to forgo specifying the table's height and width altogether. If you do this, the table stretches to accommodate the dimensions of whatever sits inside the table's cells, and no more.

A good middle ground is to specify the dimensions of each column instead of the dimensions of the table as a whole. In this way, you can give some columns an absolute width and others a proportional width, creating a more flexible table. I show you how to change column dimensions later in this chapter.

To eyeball your table's absolute dimensions, click one of the outer table borders and drag the border to the desired size.

Otherwise, follow these steps:

1. **Display the Table Properties dialog box by right-clicking the table and choosing Table Properties from the pop-up menu that appears.**

2. **In the dialog box, mark the Specify Width check box, and in the corresponding text box, type the width of the table.**

   To specify a proportional width, type the width of the table as a percentage of the width of the browser window. For example, if you type **50**, FrontPage sets the width of the table at 50 percent, or half the width of the browser window.

   To specify an absolute width, type the table width in pixels.

   To turn off table width specifications, unmark the Specify Width check box.

3. **Click the option button that corresponds to the measurement you specified in Step 2.**

   If you specified a proportional width, choose the In Percent option button. If you specified an absolute width, choose the In Pixels option button.

4. **If you want to specify a table height, mark the Specify Height check box; in the corresponding text box, type the table's height in pixels or as a percentage value, and then click the corresponding option button.**

5. **Click OK to close the dialog box and change the table size.**

Splitting a table

FrontPage knows how to split a table into two — no karate chops necessary. Just follow these steps:

1. **Click inside the table at the location where you want the split to occur.**

   The row in which you click will become the top row of the second table.

2. **Select Table⇨Split Table to do the deed.**

Fiddling with Cells, Columns, and Rows

In addition to tinkering with the table as a whole, you can fiddle with the layout and structure of individual table cells, rows, and columns.

Many of the operations in this section take advantage of buttons on the Tables toolbar, shown in Figure 8-10. To make the Tables toolbar visible, choose View⇨Toolbars⇨Tables.

Figure 8-10:
The Tables
toolbar.

Selecting table parts

Selecting table parts. . . . It sounds like something you do at a hardware store. I'm not about to discuss buying lumber or wood screws; I talk about how to highlight, or select, different parts of your table in order to format those parts in some way.

At times throughout the rest of the chapter, I instruct you to select different parts of the table. Here's how you select the following table parts:

- **Cells:** To select a cell, click inside the cell and then choose Table⇨Select⇨Cell. To select more than one cell, select the first cell and then press and hold down the Shift key as you click other cells.

- **Columns:** To select a column, click inside the column and then choose Table⇨Select⇨Column. Or, pass the cursor over the table until the cursor hovers just above a column. The cursor turns into a stubby down-pointing arrow. Click once to select the column. To select more than one column, select the first column and then drag until you highlight the area you want.

- **Rows:** To select a row, choose Table⇨Select⇨Row or pass the cursor over the left side of the table until the cursor hovers just to the left of a row. The cursor turns into a stubby arrow pointing to the right. Click once to select the row. To select more than one row, select the first row and then drag until you highlight the area you want.

- **Entire table:** Choose Table⇨Select⇨Table.

Adding new columns, rows, and cells

Here's how to add a new column to your table:

1. **Place the cursor anywhere inside the column to the right of where you want the new column to appear.**

 2. **Click the Insert Columns button on the Tables toolbar.**

   A new column appears to the left of the selected column.

Adding new rows involves a similar procedure. To add a new row to an existing table, follow these steps:

1. **Place the cursor anywhere inside the row that is beneath where you want the new row to appear.**

2. **Click the Insert Rows button on the Tables toolbar.**

   A new row appears above the selected row.

If you want to add a single cell rather than an entire row or column, you can do that, too. Just follow these steps:

1. **Click inside the cell to the right of where you want the new cell to appear.**

2. **Choose Table⇨Insert⇨Cell.**

   A new cell appears.

When you insert a single cell, the cell dislocates the other cells in the row, creating a somewhat lopsided table. Not a problem if that's the effect you're looking for. However, if you want to add a cell to a table and, at the same time, maintain the table's grid-like structure, consider splitting an existing cell into two. I show you how to do this later in the chapter.

Deleting columns, rows, and cells

Want to shave a cell, row, or column off your table? No problem. Just follow these steps:

1. **Select the cell(s), row(s), or column(s) you want to consign to oblivion.**

2. **Click the Delete Cells button on the Tables toolbar.**

   The selected cells, rows, or columns and their contents disappear. (Had you pressed the Delete key instead, only the cell contents would have disappeared; the cells would have remained in place.)

Aligning cell contents

You can control the vertical (up and down) and horizontal (left and right) alignment of the stuff inside table cells. By selecting several cells, a row or column, or even the entire table, you can apply alignment controls to a group of cells in one fell swoop.

To change vertical alignment, select the cells, rows, or columns you want to format, and then click the Align Top, Center Vertically, or Align Bottom button on the Tables toolbar.

To change horizontal alignment, select the cells, rows, or columns you want to format, and then click the Align Left, Center, or Align Right button on the Formatting toolbar.

The Cell Properties dialog box contains an extra vertical alignment option that lines cell contents up along the baseline (the invisible line on top of which text sits) and an extra horizontal alignment option that justifies cell contents. To access the Cell Properties dialog box, right-click the selected cells and choose Cell Properties from the pop-up menu that appears.

Changing cell, row, and column dimensions

Controlling the dimensions of table cells (and by extension, columns and rows) is similar to working with table dimensions, because you can set an absolute size in pixels or a proportional size based on the size of the entire table. If you want to use absolute measurements, the easiest way to adjust the dimensions of cells, rows, and columns is to click a border and drag it to a new position.

To use proportional measurements to adjust the height and/or width of a cell, column, or row (or for more control over the absolute dimensions), follow these steps:

1. **Select the cells, columns, or rows you want to format.**

2. **Right-click the selection and choose Cell Properties from the pop-up menu that appears.**

   The Cell Properties dialog box appears, as shown in Figure 8-11.

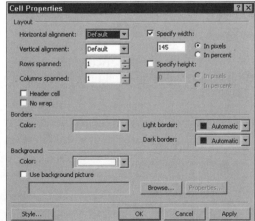

Figure 8-11: The Cell Properties dialog box.

3. **In the dialog box's Specify Width text box, type the desired width.**

   (If the text box appears dimmed, be sure the Specify Width check box is marked.)

   If you are specifying a proportional width, type the width of the cell or column as a percentage of the width of the table. For example, if you type **50**, FrontPage sets the width of the cell or column at 50 percent, or half the width of table.

   If you are specifying an absolute width, type the width in pixels.

   To turn off width specifications, click to deselect the Specify Width check box. (If you do this, the size of the selected area is determined by the size of its contents.)

4. **Click the option button that corresponds to the measurement you specified in Step 3.**

   If you are specifying a proportional width, click the In Percent option button. If you are specifying an absolute width, click the In Pixels option button.

5. **Click the Specify Height check box; in the corresponding text box, type the desired height in pixels or as a percentage value and then click the corresponding option button.**

   To turn off height specifications, unmark the Specify Height check box.

6. **Click OK to close the dialog box and change the dimension settings.**

To distribute the rows and/or columns equally in the table, select the row or column and then click the Distribute Rows Evenly or the Distribute Columns Evenly button.

To adjust the dimensions of columns and rows to fit their contents precisely, click inside the table and then click the AutoFit button.

Merging and splitting cells

When you merge cells, you erase the borders between the cells, creating one big, combined cell. Splitting cells divides one cell into two or more cells that are arranged in rows or columns.

To merge cells, select the cells you want to merge and then click the Merge Cells button.

Or, click the Eraser button and swipe over the borders you want to erase.

Tables and tribulations

FrontPage contains a bug (or is this quirk actually a feature?) that makes it possible to set the width of table columns to a number not equal to the total width of the table. For example, if you set the width of a two-column table to 100 pixels, you can also set the width of the table's columns to a number totaling more or less than 100.

FrontPage's display also gets confused if you set different widths for individual table cells (as opposed to entire columns of cells), especially if the table is complex.

The solution is to keep your tables relatively simple. At the very least, preview your page in a Web browser (preferably more than one model) to see how your table looks to your visitors.

To split cells, follow these steps:

1. **Select the cell (or cells) you want to split and then click the Split Cells button.**

   The Split Cells dialog box appears.

2. **Click the Split into Columns option button to split the cell(s) vertically, or click the Split into Rows option button to split the cell(s) horizontally.**

   Depending on which option you click, the diagram next to the option buttons shows a representation of how the cell will look after it is split.

3. **In the Number of Columns text box (or Number of Rows text box, depending on your selection in Step 2), type the number of cells into which you want to divide the selected cell(s).**

4. **Click OK to close the dialog box and split the selected cells.**

Merging cells is different than using the Table AutoFormat command to render the border between cells invisible. When you merge cells, you actually transform more than one cell into a single cell (merging the cell contents as well). When you use the Table AutoFormat command, some of the cell borders become invisible, but the cells themselves remain distinct. I describe the Table AutoFormat command in detail later in this chapter.

Adding a caption

You can easily add a caption — a bit of descriptive text that sits just above or below the table — to your table. To add a caption, follow these steps:

1. **Click anywhere inside the table and then choose Table⇨Insert⇨Caption.**

   The cursor hops to an empty space above the table.

2. **Type the caption text.**

If you want the caption to appear beneath the table, do this:

1. **Right-click the caption and choose Caption Properties from the pop-up menu that appears.**

   The Caption Properties dialog box appears.

2. **Click the Bottom of Table option button and then click OK.**

   The cursor moves to an empty space beneath the table.

Adding Color to a Table

Here's a nifty design effect: You can apply color to the background of your table, down to the individual cell. You can also change the color of table and cell borders.

Changing the background

You can apply a solid background color or a background image to a table or cell, just as you can to an entire page. (I show you how to change your page's background in Chapter 6.)

To add a background color to a table or cell, follow these steps:

1. **Select the cells you want to color (or select the entire table).**

 2. **Click the down-arrow next to the Fill Color button and then select the color you want.**

   The Fill Color button works just like the Text Color button, which I describe in Chapter 4.

To add a background image to a table or cell, follow these steps:

1. **If you're changing the background of the entire table, right-click the table and choose Table Properties from the pop-up menu that appears.**

   If, instead, you're changing the background of selected cells, choose Cell Properties from the pop-up menu. Depending on your choice, the Table Properties or Cell Properties dialog box appears.

2. **In the dialog box, click the Use Background Picture check box.**

3. **In the accompanying text box, type the location of the background image.**

   If you don't remember the file's location, click Browse to display the Select Background Picture dialog box. (Refer to the steps outlined in Chapter 6 if you're not sure how to select a graphic file from this dialog box.) After you select the file, the dialog box closes, and the picture's location appears in the text box of the Table Properties (or Cell Properties) dialog box.

4. **Click OK to close the dialog box and apply the background setting.**

Only advanced browsers, such as Internet Explorer (Version 3.0 or greater) or Netscape Navigator (Version 4.0 or greater), are able to display table background color and images.

Changing border color

You can also change the color of table and cell borders. Keep in mind, however, that the same caveat applies to border colors as to background colors: Only advanced browsers, such as Internet Explorer (Version 3.0 or greater) or Netscape Navigator (Version 4.0 or greater), can display these effects.

To further complicate things, these versions of Explorer and Navigator display border colors differently — be sure to preview your page in each browser (plus a browser that can't display colored borders) for the most accurate representation of what visitors will see after you publish your site.

You can use color to create two different visual effects: a flat table with solid borders or a raised table, in which you use light and dark colors to simulate shadows.

To change the color of your table border, follow these steps:

1. **Display the Table Properties dialog box by right-clicking the table and choosing Table Properties from the pop-up menu that appears.**

2. **Choose a border color from the list boxes in the Borders area of the dialog box.**

   Note: If the page uses a theme, these list boxes are unavailable, because table border colors are determined by that theme.

   To create a flat table, choose a color from the Color list box. To create a raised table, choose colors from the Light Border and Dark Border list boxes.

   If, in any of the list boxes, you choose More Colors, the More Colors dialog box appears. I explain the workings of this dialog box in Chapter 4.

3. **Click OK to close the dialog box and apply the border color.**

To change the border color of cells, follow these steps:

1. **Select the cells, columns, or rows you want to format.**

2. **Right-click the selection and choose Cell Properties from the pop-up menu that appears.**

   The Cell Properties dialog box appears.

3. **Choose a border color from the list boxes in the Borders area of the dialog box.**

   As with table border color, you may choose either a solid border color or light and dark border colors.

4. **Click OK to close the dialog box and apply the border color.**

Using the Table AutoFormat command

With the Table AutoFormat command, you can slap attractive sets of colors, border styles, and alignment options onto your table. Instant table gratification.

Problem is, the special effects created by this command only appear when viewed with browsers that know how to process cascading style sheets (CSS). To make matters more confusing, even those browsers that understand CSS render the effects differently, making for cross-browser variations.

Table AutoFormat effects show up most reliably in (surprise) Microsoft Internet Explorer 5.0 and later. Netscape Navigator (even the later versions) displays some effects and ignores others. What to do? Preview your pages, and accept that your table will look prettier to some users than others.

To use the Table AutoFormat command, just follow these steps:

1. **Click inside the table, and then choose Table⇨Table AutoFormat.**

   The Table AutoFormat dialog box appears, as shown in Figure 8-12.

2. **In the dialog box, select the format you want to use.**

   You can choose a preset option in the Formats list box, turn on and off options in the Formats to Apply and Apply Special Formats sections, or both.

3. **When you're happy with the format you see in the Preview box, click OK to close the dialog box and apply the format to your table.**

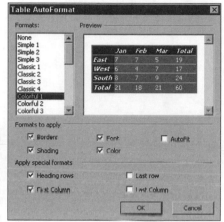

Figure 8-12:
The Table
AutoFormat
dialog box.

Deleting a Table

Building the perfect table takes some work, but deleting a table is effortless. You can either preserve the table's contents by converting the contents to regular paragraphs, or you can erase the table completely.

To convert the contents of a table into regular paragraphs, click inside the table and then choose Table⇨Convert⇨Table to Text.

To *really* delete a table, select the table by choosing Table⇨Select⇨Table, and then press the Backspace or Delete key.

Chapter 9

Forms Aren't Only for the IRS

*W*hat's the first thing that pops into your mind when I say *forms?* Bureaucracy-perpetuating pieces of paper? Multipage monstrosities in triplicate? Well, put those thoughts aside for a moment, because I'm going to introduce you to the wonders of the *interactive form.* Interactive forms transform your Web site from a showpiece into a workhorse. Here are a few things you can do with forms:

✔ Survey your visitors and ask for their opinions.

✔ Enable visitors to search the contents of your site for keywords.

✔ Host a discussion group in which visitors post their thoughts on a continuously updated Web page.

✔ Promote community by providing a guest book that visitors "sign" by submitting a form.

All this, and you don't need to hire an accountant.

How Do Forms Work?

Before you build a form, understanding the basics of how forms work can help. If this stuff seems a little tricky, don't worry. FrontPage takes care of the hard part. All you need to do is decide how you want to use forms in your Web site.

Like paper forms, interactive forms collect different types of information. Web site visitors fill in *fields,* either by typing information or selecting an item from a list. After visitors complete the form, they click a button to submit the information. The form shown in Figure 9-1 illustrates how this works.

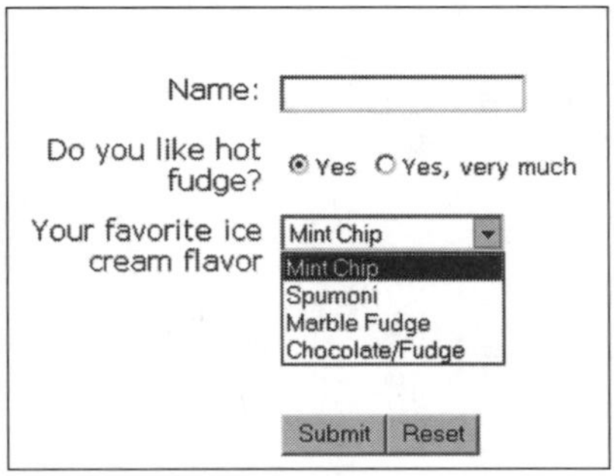

Figure 9-1:
A typical
Web page
form.

The information submitted from forms is organized into a list of *field names* (also known as *variable names*) and *field values.* The *field name* is a unique identifying descriptor assigned to each field in your form. The field name is invisible to your visitors; it exists inside the form's HTML and is visible only to the person (or computer) receiving the information submitted from the form. The pieces of text that you see in Figure 9-1 — Name, Your favorite ice cream flavor, and so on — are not field names; they are bits of regular text sitting inside the page, prompting the visitor to fill in the accompanying field.

The *field value* is the information that the visitor submits. Depending on the type of field, the value is either the stuff that the visitor types or an item that the visitor chooses from a list you define. (In Figure 9-1, for example, the value of the third field is Mint Chip.)

What happens to that information after a visitor submits the completed form depends on the type of *form handler* assigned to the form. A form handler is a program that resides on the host Web server. This program receives the form data and then does something with it. Depending on the type of form handler, the program may save the data (also known as the *form results*) in a text file, format the results as a Web page, or even send the information back to the site administrator in an e-mail message.

Creating a Form

After that rah-rah introduction, no doubt you're pumped up and ready for some serious form creation. FrontPage is happy to oblige with three different methods: You can use a prefab form page template, you can tag along with the Form Page Wizard, or you can build your own form.

Using a form page template

FrontPage contains the following templates for forms that often show up in Web sites:

- ✔ **Feedback Form:** This template creates a simple form that visitors use to send comments, questions, or suggestions.

- ✔ **Guest Book:** This template also collects comments, but it saves the submissions in a public Web page that other visitors can read.

- ✔ **User Registration:** The User Registration template creates a registration page that enables you to track or restrict who visits the Web site. With a registration system in place, visitors can choose their own access user names and passwords, and you decide what level of access these visitors have to your site. (With regular permissions, which I discuss in Chapter 15, you choose the user names and passwords for your site's visitors.) FrontPage registration systems have fairly specific server requirements; for details, refer to the FrontPage Help system by choosing Help➪Microsoft FrontPage Help.

To create a form by using a form page template, follow the directions in Chapter 2 for creating a new page based on a template.

Inside pages created by using form templates, the form consists of all the stuff inside the space surrounded by dotted lines, also known as the *form area*. The colorful comments at the top of the page give you hints about how to customize the form. The rest of what appears on-screen is a regular old Web page. Treat the entire page (including text inside the form area) just as you would any Web page: Format the text, insert graphics — whatever you want.

Using the Form Page Wizard

The Form Page Wizard possesses magical powers — at least, that's what I thought when I discovered how easy this wizard makes creating a form. The wizard walks you through the entire process of creating a form, including choosing form fields, suggesting questions to prompt visitors for different types of information, setting up the layout of the page, choosing a form handler, and deciding how to format form results.

Unless you have a Web form or two under your belt, you may not understand some of the Form Page Wizard's options at first glance. For that reason, before you activate the wizard, you might want to skim the rest of this chapter to familiarize yourself with forms. The form-creation process makes more sense after you do so, and you'll realize just how ingenious the Form Page Wizard really is.

To create a form with the help of the Form Page Wizard, follow these steps:

1. **Choose File⇨New⇨Page or Web.**

   If it's not already visible, the Task Pane appears on the right side of the FrontPage window.

2. **In the New from Template section of the Task Pane, click Page Templates.**

   The Page Templates dialog box appears.

3. **In the dialog box's list of templates, double-click Form Page Wizard.**

   The dialog box closes, and the Form Page Wizard launches. The wizard's initial dialog box explains what the wizard is about to do. As with all wizards, click Next to advance to the next screen or Back to return to a previous screen. You can also click Cancel at any time to close the wizard.

4. **In the Form Page Wizard dialog box, click Next.**

   The next dialog box appears. Here, you decide what kind of information to include in your form.

5. **Click the Add button.**

   In the Select the Type of Input to Collect for This Question list box, the wizard lists several categories of information commonly collected with forms (as shown in Figure 9-2). Scroll down the list to see all your options.

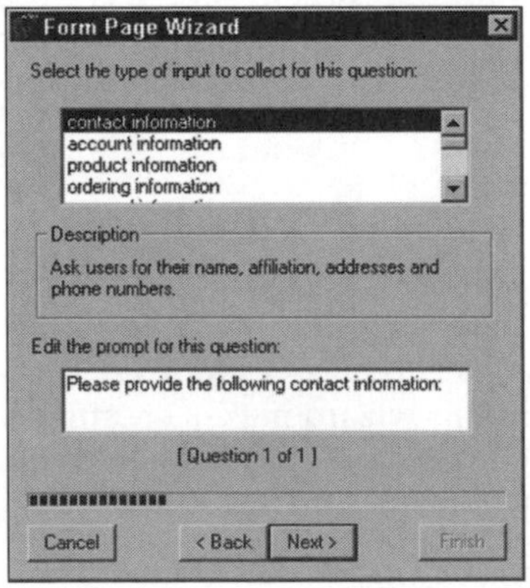

Figure 9-2:
The Form Page Wizard helps you decide what kind of information to collect.

6. **In the list box, click the first category of information you want your form to contain.**

   A description of the category appears inside the Description area. The text question that prompts visitors to fill in the field appears in the Edit the Prompt for This Question text box.

7. **If you like, change the wording of the text question in the Edit the Prompt for This Question box, and then click Next.**

The dialog box that appears next depends on the category you selected in Step 6. In this dialog box, you choose the specific types of information that you want the form to collect (see Figure 9-3). If some options don't seem to make sense to you yet, keep this book close at hand as you work and skim the rest of this chapter to clear things up.

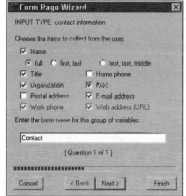

Figure 9-3:
Specify the information you want the form to contain.

8. **After you choose the items you want the form to contain, click Next.**

You return to the section of the wizard in which you add more questions to the form. The question you chose in the previous steps appears inside the list box. To add more questions to your form, click Add and repeat Steps 6 through 8. To change the order in which questions appear inside the form, click an item in the list and then click Move Up or Move Down. To modify or remove any item in your form, select the item and then click Modify or Remove. To erase everything and start again, click Clear List.

9. **When you finish adding questions, click Next.**

The Presentation Options dialog box appears. Here, you decide how you want FrontPage to arrange the questions and fields on the page: as a series of paragraphs or as a list of items. (Refer to Chapter 4 for a description of each type of list.) You can also include in the form page a Table of Contents that contains links to each section of the form. Finally, you can tell the wizard to use an invisible table to align the form fields. (Chapter 8 tells you all about tables.)

10. **Click the option button next to the presentation options you want to use and then click Next.**

The Output Options dialog box appears. Here, you decide what happens to the information contained in form submissions. (I explain each output option — plus a couple of options not included in the wizard — later in this chapter.) You also choose a filename for the file in which the information submitted from forms will eventually be stored.

11. **Choose an output option and then click Next to advance to the final dialog box of the Form Page Wizard.**

12. **Click Finish to create the form page.**

    The wizard disappears after it generates a new page containing a form based on your specifications.

Adding a form to an existing page

A form is nothing more than a particular type of HTML that sits inside a page. You can, therefore, add a form to any Web page. To do so, you can rely on the assistance of the Form Page Wizard, or you can create a form from scratch.

If you want the help of the Form Page Wizard but want to add the resulting form to an existing page, follow the steps in the preceding section to create a new form, and then copy and paste the form (including the form area) into an existing page.

To build your own form, follow the directions in the next section of this chapter.

Working with Form Fields

If the FrontPage form templates and Form Page Wizard don't create the kind of form you want, you can easily build your own form by adding individual form fields to a page.

Form fields are the collection plates into which visitors drop bits of information. The kinds of fields you include in your form depend on the kinds of information you want to gather. Do you want visitors to select from a predefined list of choices? Would you rather let them fill in whatever information they like? The answers to these questions determine the types of fields you should use in your form.

To create your own form, you add one or more fields to a page and then customize the fields so that they look and act the way that you want them to. By *customize,* I mean that you assign the field a name — in some cases, a value — and you adjust how the field looks. (I explain what field names and values are earlier in this chapter.) You can also create data entry rules for certain fields that restrict the kind of information visitors can enter there.

The first time you add a form field to a page, FrontPage sets aside a space for the form (indicated by a box surrounded by dotted lines) and inserts Submit and Reset buttons. (Visitors click these buttons to submit completed forms and to clear form contents; I talk more about how these buttons work later in this chapter.) You add fields to the form by inserting one or more fields inside the form area. You can add as many fields as you like to your form. You can cut, copy, and paste fields. You can also drag and drop fields to different locations.

To add fields to your page, you use the Insert⇨Form command. You can build a field-laden form more quickly by *floating* the Insert⇨Form menu — that is, transforming the menu into a toolbar. To do so, choose Insert⇨Form, and then move your pointer over the thin stripe at the top of the menu that appears. When the stripe appears highlighted, click and drag the menu elsewhere inside the FrontPage window.

When you add fields to a form, you must insert the fields *inside* the form area. If you insert a form field outside the form area, FrontPage thinks that you want to create a second form and creates a new form area, complete with its own Submit and Reset buttons. These two forms will then work independently of each other. Although technically, one Web page can contain multiple forms, I assume that your intention is to create a single form.

As you create your form, be sure to preview the page to get a more accurate picture of how the page will look after it's published. If you're not sure how to preview a page, refer to Chapter 3.

Finally, I've held off on explaining two types of form fields in this section: the list form and the list field. These fields are specific to a site that's published on a Web server that supports SharePoint Team Services. I talk briefly about SharePoint in Chapter 15.

Text boxes

Text boxes are plain-vanilla fields into which visitors type a single line of text. Use a text box when you want to collect small bits of information, such as a name or an e-mail address. Figure 9-4 shows a filled-in text box as it appears in a Web browser.

Figure 9-4:
A text box field.

Name: Asha Dornfest

Creating a text box

To add a text box to your page, follow these steps:

1. **Place the cursor in the page where you want the field to appear (for a new form, anywhere in the page, or to add a field to an existing form, inside the form area) and then choose Insert⇨Form⇨Textbox.**

   A text box appears on your page.

2. **In the page, double-click the text box.**

   The Text Box Properties dialog box appears.

3. **In the dialog box's Name text box, type the field name.**

   Choose a one-word, generic name that describes the information that the text box collects. If, for example, you're creating a text box to collect a visitor's e-mail address, type **E-mail** or **E-mail_address**.

   Always keep your field names restricted to one word. (You can use the underscore character to cheat a bit, as I did in the preceding example.) Some Web servers aren't able to process forms with longer field names. The name you choose does not need to match the text descriptor you insert in the page to identify the field to visitors.

4. **If you want the text box field to appear with default text inside (instead of empty), type the text in the Initial Value text box.**

5. **In the Width in Characters text box, type the visible width of the text box field.**

   The number you type affects the visible size of the text box, not the amount of text a visitor can type in the text box. To limit the amount of text a visitor can type into a text box, use a validation option, as described in the following section.

   If you prefer to adjust the width of a text box by hand, skip this step. Instead, after you're finished defining the text box's properties, click the text box in the page and then drag the field's size handles until you're satisfied with its new width.

6. **Optionally, type a number in the Tab Order text box.**

   The *tab order* is the order in which the cursor advances to the next field when a visitor presses the Tab key. By default, the tab order is sequential; the visitor fills out the first form field and then presses Tab to advance to the next field in the form. By entering a number in the Tab Order text box, you can control the sequence in which the cursor moves. For example, type **1** in the Tab Order text box if you want the current field to be the first field in which the cursor appears, even if that field isn't the first field on the page.

   As of this writing, only Internet Explorer (Version 4.0 or later) can display changes in tab order. In other browsers, the tab order is sequential, starting with the first field in the form.

7. Specify whether the text box is a password field.

Password fields are no different from regular text boxes except that, if viewed with a browser, text that someone types into a password field appears on-screen as dots or asterisks. These characters prevent nosy passersby from seeing the characters that you type.

Including a password field in your form *does not* automatically add password protection to your Web site. I show you how to work with passwords in Chapter 15.

8. To restrict the type of information visitors can enter into the text box, click the Validate button.

The following section explains how to use validation options. If you don't want to restrict the information visitors can enter, skip this step.

9. Click OK.

The dialog box closes, and any default text you specified appears inside the text box. If you changed the width of the text box, it stretches or shrinks accordingly.

Form design tips

Here are a few tricks to make your homegrown forms easy for visitors to fill out:

✔ Place helpful descriptors next to each field. If, for example, you include a field in your form for the visitor's e-mail address, use the text descriptor F-mail address (username@server.com) to make absolutely clear what information you want.

✔ Help visitors provide you with the correct information. If your form contains mandatory fields or fields that require information to be entered in a certain way, include a note that demonstrates the correct format or at least that reads *This field is required.*

✔ Use an invisible table to keep the form's layout neat and tidy. (Chapter 8 explains how to build a table.) Insert the first form field in the page. Inside the form area, create a two-column invisible table, and then drag and drop the field into the top-right table cell. Next, place text descriptors in the left column and more form fields in the right column.

✔ Pay attention to the order of the fields. Most Web browsers enable visitors to use the Tab key to advance to the next field. You, therefore, should arrange fields in sequential order.

✔ Use default text in text box fields (also known as the field's initial value) to save visitors' time and effort. For example, if your form asks the visitor's country of origin and most of your visitors are American, use *USA* as the field's default text.

✔ Consider rewarding your visitors for taking the time to fill out the form. Enter them in a drawing (with their permission) or give them access to free downloadable goodies.

Validating information entered into a text box

FrontPage enables you to make certain form fields mandatory. Unless visitors complete these fields, they can't submit the form. You can also control the format of information that visitors type into text boxes. This control is especially helpful if you want to standardize the format of form results.

Before you use FrontPage validation features, you must first specify how you want FrontPage to create the data rules. See the sidebar "Setting up FrontPage form validation," later in this chapter, for details.

After you click the Validate button in the Text Box Properties dialog box, the Text Box Validation dialog box appears, as shown in Figure 9-5.

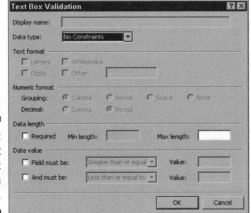

Figure 9-5:
The Text
Box
Validation
dialog box.

To validate information entered into text boxes, follow these steps:

1. **To restrict the type of data that can be entered into the text box, choose an option from the Data Type list box.**

   Choose one of the following options: No Constraints (no restrictions on data type), Text (letters, characters, or numerals), Integer (whole numbers only), or Number (all numbers, both whole and decimal).

2. **Depending on the option you chose in Step 1, choose an option from either the Text Format or the Numeric Format area of the dialog box.**

   If you chose the Text data type, choose from the following options in the Text Format area of the dialog box:

   • **Letters:** This check box creates a text box that can contain only alphabetic characters.

   • **Digits:** This check box creates a text box that can contain only numeric characters.

- **Whitespace:** This check box creates a text box that can contain white space (such as spaces, tabs, and line breaks).

- **Other:** If you want to allow other types of characters (such as commas or hyphens, for example), click the Other check box and type the characters in the corresponding text box.

If you chose the Integer or Number data type, choose from the following options in the Numeric Format area of the dialog box:

- **Grouping:** These option buttons enable you to control how visitors punctuate numbers greater than or equal to 1,000: with a comma (1,000), with a period (1.000), or with no punctuation (1000).

- **Decimal:** These option buttons enable you to choose which punctuation character visitors can use as a decimal point: a period or a comma.

3. **To control the amount of information typed into a text box or to make a text box mandatory, choose options from the Data Length area of the dialog box.**

   Click the Required check box to make the text box mandatory.

   Type a number of characters in the Min Length and Max Length text boxes to control the length of information entered into the text box.

4. **To place restrictive conditions on the content of text box data, choose options from the Data Value area.**

   If you choose the Text or No Constraints data type, these options compare the information that visitors type into the text box against the order of the alphabet. If you specify that the field must be greater than *E*, for example, all information entered into the text box must start with the letter *F* or any other letter later in the alphabet (such as *H*, *Q*, or *Z* — but not *A*, *C*, or even *E*). I can't imagine why anyone would use this option, but there it is.

   If you choose the Integer or Number data type, these options make a numerical order comparison. If you specify that the field must be less than or equal to 10, for example, a visitor may type *10* or any lesser number in the text box.

5. **Click OK to close the dialog box.**

If a visitor enters information that doesn't stick to the validation rules, a *validation warning message* appears. The warning message identifies the offending field to the visitor by using the field name you entered in the Name text box in the Text Box Properties dialog box. If the field name you used wouldn't make sense to a visitor (say, the field collects phone numbers and you chose field name *phon_num*), you can specify a friendlier display name (such as *Phone Number*) for the purposes of the validation warning. To do so, type the display name text in the Display Name text box, which is at the top of the Text Box Validation dialog box.

Group boxes make your forms friendlier

You build a long form. It contains numerous fields. Your users have visions of the 1040, tax day, and associated unpleasantness.

Don't like where this image is heading? Take it from me, neither do your visitors. When you include a form in your site, you must give your visitors every reason to fill it out. A surefire way to scare away your respondents is to load your form with lots of time-consuming fields.

Group boxes can ease the sting of a long form by creating visual groupings of related form fields. Group boxes are empty, captioned rectangles into which you can insert form fields. Group boxes don't *do* anything per se, but, if your form must contain lots of fields, group boxes do visually divide your form into palatable chunks of information. For example, imagine users must fill in a lengthy form in order to register for your site. Instead of bombarding your visitors with 30 empty fields, you can group related details (such as contact information, interests, and referral information) inside group boxes to break the form into more manageable pieces.

See if your form can benefit with the addition of a group box or two. Adding group boxes is easy; just follow these steps:

1. **Click anywhere inside the form area and then choose Insert⇨Form⇨Group Box.**

   A group box appears inside your form.

2. **Insert the fields of your choice inside the group box, or drag existing fields into the group box.**

   You can do anything inside the group box that you can do inside the form area — add descriptive text, format text, align the form fields using a table, and more.

3. **To change the group box caption, select the caption and type new text.**

4. **To change the caption alignment, right-click inside the group box and choose Group Box Properties from the pop-up menu that appears.**

   The Group Box Properties dialog box appears.

5. **Choose an option from the Align list box and then click OK to close the dialog box.**

You can nest group boxes (place group boxes within group boxes), you can format the caption text, and you can format the box itself by accessing cascading style sheet (CSS) commands using the Style button in the Group Box Properties dialog box. (See Chapter 12 for more about the capabilities of a CSS.) Note that group boxes look different in different browsers (and may not appear at all in older browsers).

Text areas

Text areas are just like text boxes, except that this type of field holds more than one line of text. (See Figure 9-6 for an example of what a text area looks like in a Web browser.) Text areas are perfect for verbose visitors who want to send lots of comments.

Figure 9-6:
A text area
field.

To create a text area, follow these steps:

1. **Place the cursor in the page where you want the field to appear (for a new form, anywhere in the page, or to add a field to an existing form, inside the form area) and then choose Insert⇨Form⇨Text Area.**

   A text area field appears on the page.

2. **In the page, double-click the field.**

   The TextArea Box Properties dialog box appears, as shown in Figure 9-7.

Figure 9-7:
The
TextArea
Box
Properties
dialog box.

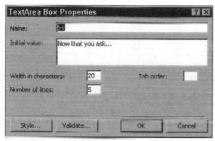

3. **In the Name text box, type the text area's field name.**

   The name you choose does not need to match the text descriptor that you insert in the page to identify the field to visitors.

4. **If you want the text area to appear with default text inside, type that text in the Initial Value text box.**

5. **In the Width in Characters text box, type the visible width of the text area.**

6. **In the Number of Lines text box, type the number of lines of text that the text area can hold.**

   Effectively, this option controls the field's height. You can also adjust the height and width by hand (after you finish defining the field's properties) by clicking the text area and dragging the size handles until the field is the size you want.

7. **Optionally, type a number in the Tab Order text box.**

   You can find out more about the tab order under Step 6 in the section "Creating a text box," earlier in this chapter.

8. **To restrict the type of information that visitors can type into the text area, click the Validate button.**

   Before you use FrontPage validation features, you must first specify how you want FrontPage to create the data rules. See the sidebar "Setting up FrontPage form validation" for details.

   Refer to the preceding section, "Validating information entered into a text box," for details on how to use validation options. If you don't want to restrict this information, skip this step.

9. **Click OK.**

   The dialog box closes, and any default text you specified appears inside the text area. If you changed the size of the text area, it stretches or shrinks accordingly.

Check boxes

Check boxes are like teenagers: They're independent but still prefer to hang around in groups. (Figure 9-8 shows an example of what a group of check boxes looks like in a Web browser.) Use check boxes if you want visitors to select as many items from a predefined list as they want. You can include one check box or several in your form.

Figure 9-8:
A gang of check boxes.

Check the items about which you want more information:	☐ This week's bubble gum flavors ☐ Nutritional analysis of Choco-Bombs ☐ Candy factory tour schedule

To insert a check box, follow these steps:

1. **Place the cursor in the page where you want the field to appear. (For a new form, place the cursor anywhere in the page; to add a field to an existing form, place the cursor inside the form area.) Then choose Insert➪Form➪Checkbox.**

   A check box appears on your page.

2. **In the page, double-click the check box.**

   The Check Box Properties dialog box appears.

3. In the Name text box, type the check box's field name.

The name you choose does not need to match the text descriptor that you insert in the page to identify the field to visitors. You should, however, stick to one word.

4. In the Value text box, type a word or two that describes what the marked check box means.

For example, suppose you're using a check box to enable visitors to request more information about a particular product. Using the first check box in Figure 9-8 as an example, *flavors* is a good name choice, and *more info* is a good value choice, because if visitors mark that check box, their choice means "I want more information about bubble gum flavors."

5. If you want the check box to appear marked initially, click the Checked option button.

6. If you want to specify a tab order, type a number in the Tab Order text box.

You can find out more about the tab order under Step 6 in the section "Creating a text box," earlier in this chapter.

7. Click OK to close the Check Box Properties dialog box.

To add more check boxes, repeat the preceding steps until you have all the check boxes you want.

Option buttons

If check boxes are independent teens, *option buttons* are a giddy high school clique. Option buttons are never seen alone and base their identity solely on the others in the group.

Use a group of option buttons to present visitors with a list of options from which only one option may be chosen. Figure 9-9 shows an example of what a group of option buttons looks like in a Web browser.

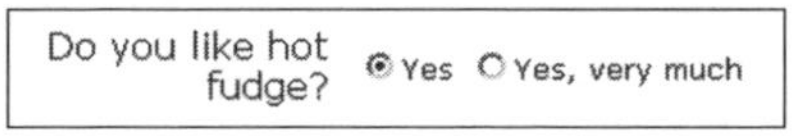

Figure 9-9:
A gathering
of option
buttons.

Do you like hot fudge? ⦿ Yes ◯ Yes, very much

Setting up FrontPage form validation

If you use FrontPage form validation, FrontPage takes down all the data-entry requirements you specify as a set of rules. You can tell FrontPage to store these data rules in one of two locations: either as a script that sits inside the HTML of your Web page, or as a script stored on the host Web server. Why do you care? Because, if you choose the wrong method, a few of your visitors may be able to slip past your data rules. Here's why.

By default, FrontPage stores the data rules as a script inside the Web page. The advantage to this method is the speed at which the browser is able to check the information. If a visitor enters information that doesn't conform to a data rule, a pesky dialog box pops up right away prompting the visitor to change the entry. Unfortunately, this approach comes with a big downside: If a visitor using an older browser fills in the form, the validation doesn't work, because the browser doesn't know how to process the script and simply ignores the data rules.

The other option is to tell FrontPage to store the data rules on the host server. If you choose this method, after a visitor fills in the form and clicks the Submit button, the form handler checks the submission against the data rules. If everything checks out, the server sends back a response letting the visitor know all is well. If not, the visitor gets an error message and is returned to the form to try again. This method is clunkier for visitors, but it ensures that all visitors, regardless of browser choice, must comply with the form's data rules. The only requirement is that you publish your Web site on a host Web server that has FrontPage Server Extensions installed.

To choose the method or scripting language that FrontPage uses to create data rules, follow these steps:

1. **Choose Tools⇨Web Settings.**

   The Web Settings dialog box appears.

2. **At the top of the dialog box, click the Advanced tab.**

3. **From the Client list box, choose the appropriate option.**

   To store data rules inside the Web page, choose JavaScript or VBScript. (Only Internet Explorer 3.0 or later understands VBScript, whereas recent versions of both Internet Explorer and Netscape Navigator understand JavaScript.)

   To store the data rules on the host Web server, choose <None>.

4. **Click OK to close the dialog box.**

   The Microsoft FrontPage dialog box appears, prompting you to recalculate the Web site.

5. **Click Yes.**

   The dialog box closes, and FrontPage recalculates the site. You can now set up data rules for your form.

To create an option button group, follow these steps:

1. **Place the cursor in the page where you want the field to appear (for a new form, anywhere in the page, or to add a field to an existing form, inside the form area) and then choose Insert⇨Form⇨Option Button.**

   A single option button appears on your page.

2. **In the page, double-click the option button.**

   The Option Button Properties dialog box appears.

3. **In the Group Name text box, type a name that applies to the entire group (even though you've created only one option button so far).**

   In the example shown in Figure 9-9, the Group Name is *LikeFudge*.

   The group name you choose does not need to match the text descriptor that you insert in the page to identify the list of option buttons to visitors.

4. **In the Value text box, type the value for the individual option button.**

   In the example shown in Figure 9-9, the value for the first option button is Yes.

5. **If you want the option button to appear unmarked initially, click the Not Selected option button.**

   By default, the first option button in a group appears selected.

6. **If you want to specify a tab order, type a number in the Tab Order text box.**

   You can find out more about the tab order under Step 6 in the section "Creating a text box," earlier in this chapter.

7. **If you want to require visitors to choose one of the items in the list of option buttons, click the Validate button.**

   Before you use FrontPage validation features, you must first specify how you want FrontPage to create the data rules. See the sidebar "Setting up FrontPage form validation" for details.

   (In this case, validation applies only to an option button group in which none of the option buttons appears initially selected.) In the Option Button Validation dialog box that appears, click the Data Required check box. If you want the validation warning message to identify the option button group by a name other than the group name that you specified in Step 3, type a display name in the Display Name text box. (The "Validating information entered into a text box" section, earlier in the chapter, explains the purpose of the display name.) Click OK to close the Option Button Validation dialog box.

8. **Click OK to close the Option Button Properties dialog box.**

Now you must create at least one more option button to complete the group. To do so, follow these steps:

1. **Place the cursor inside the form area (ideally, near the first option button field) and then choose Insert➪Form➪Option Button.**

   A second option button appears on the page, to the right of the first one.

2. **In the page, double-click the second option button.**

The Option Button Properties dialog box appears. The Group Name is the same as for the first option button. (I told you they stick together.) All you need to do is give the second option button a unique value. In the example shown in Figure 9-9, the value for the second option button is Very Much.

3. **Choose the option button's initial state.**

   If you want the second option button to appear initially selected, click the Selected option button. (By default, the first option button in a group appears selected. If you choose this option, the first option button in the group appears initially empty.) If you want the second option button to appear empty, click the Not Selected option button.

4. **If you want to specify a tab order, type a number in the Tab Order text box.**

5. **Click OK to close the Option Button Properties dialog box.**

Validation options apply to the entire option button group, so whatever you specify for the first option button applies to all the option buttons in that particular group.

Drop-down boxes

Drop-down boxes are so named because, after you click the field, a list of choices "drops down." Figure 9-10 shows how a drop-down box works when viewed with a Web browser. Like option button groups, drop-down boxes let visitors choose from a predefined group of options. In some cases, drop-down boxes have some advantages over option button groups, such as the following:

✔ Drop-down boxes save space on your page by popping open only after a visitor clicks the down arrow next to the option.

✔ You can set up a drop-down box to accept more than one choice at a time.

Figure 9-10:
A drop-down box.

Your favorite ice cream flavor

Mint Chip
Spumoni
Marble Fudge
Chocolate/Fudge

To create a drop-down box, follow these steps:

1. **Place the cursor in the page where you want the field to appear (for a new form, anywhere in the page, or to add a field to an existing form, inside the form area) and then choose Insert⇨Form⇨Drop-Down Box.**

   A drop-down box field appears on your page.

2. **In the page, double-click the drop-down box.**

   The Drop-Down Box Properties dialog box appears, as shown in Figure 9-11.

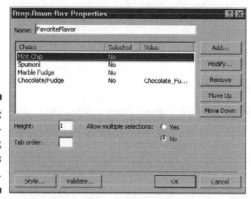

Figure 9-11:
The Drop-Down Box Properties dialog box.

3. **In the Name text box, type the field name.**

   In the example in Figure 9-10, the name is FavoriteFlavor.

   The name you choose does not need to match the text descriptor you insert in the page to identify the field to visitors.

4. **To add menu choices, click the Add button.**

   The Add Choice dialog box appears, as shown in Figure 9-12.

Figure 9-12:
The Add Choice dialog box.

5. **In the Choice text box, type the text that you want to appear in the drop-down box.**

   In the example in Figure 9-10, the choices are Mint Chip, Spumoni, and so on.

6. **If you want the choice's value to be something other than the information you type in the Choice text box, click the Specify Value check box and then type the value in the accompanying text box.**

   For example, if you transfer the form results from the example in Figure 9-10 into a database and the database program is unable to process the / character (as in the Chocolate/Fudge menu choice), you can instead specify a value of Chocolate_Fudge. That way, visitors select an item from the drop-down box that reads Chocolate/Fudge, but the database receives the value Chocolate_Fudge.

7. **If you want the choice to appear initially selected, click the Selected option button.**

8. **Click OK to close the Add Choice dialog box.**

9. **Repeat Steps 4 through 8 to add more menu choices until the drop-down box is complete.**

   You can rearrange, modify, or remove menu items by selecting the item in the list and then clicking the Move Up, Move Down, Modify, or Remove button.

10. **In the Height text box, type the number of menu choices that are visible before a visitor clicks the drop-down box and causes it to "drop down."**

    You can also manually adjust the height and width of a drop-down box (after you're finished defining the field's properties) by clicking the drop-down box in your page and dragging its size handles.

11. **To enable visitors to select more than one item from the list, click the Yes option button in the Allow Multiple Selections area of the dialog box.**

    When visitors view the form with a Web browser, they select more than one option by pressing and holding the Ctrl key or the Apple Command key (⌘) as they click their selections.

12. **If you want to specify a tab order, type a number in the Tab Order text box.**

    You can find out more about the tab order under Step 6 in the section "Creating a text box," earlier in this chapter.

13. **If you want to restrict choices in the drop-down box or make choosing an item mandatory, click the Validate button.**

    The Drop-Down Box Validation dialog box appears.

Before you use FrontPage validation features, you must first specify how you want FrontPage to create the data rules. See the sidebar "Setting up FrontPage form validation" for details.

To require that visitors choose an item from the list, click the Data Required check box. (In the case of multiple-selection lists, you can specify a minimum and maximum number of choices.) To disallow the first list choice as a valid selection (if, for example, the first item on your list reads *Choose one*), click the Disallow First Item check box. Click OK to close the Drop-Down Box Validation dialog box.

14. **Click OK to close the Drop-Down Box Properties dialog box.**

The first menu choice becomes visible in the drop-down menu in your page. (If you specified that more than one menu choice is initially visible, the drop-down menu expands to display the specified number of choices.)

Specifying What Happens to Form Results

All the action occurs *after* a visitor submits the form. What happens to the form results is up to you; you decide how and where the information eventually ends up. The FrontPage Server Extensions come with a brilliant built-in form handler that can format the information visitors submit and then dump the information into a text file, a Web page, or an e-mail message. If, for some reason, the FrontPage form handler doesn't fit the bill, you can use FrontPage to hitch your form to a custom form-handling script.

Adding Submit and Reset buttons

When you first insert a form field into a page, the field appears along with two hangers-on: the *Submit button* and the *Reset button*. The Submit button is the linchpin of the entire operation. After visitors click this powerful tool, their browsers activate the form handler program, which takes over from there, processing the form results.

If a gray Submit button is too boring for your taste, you can replace it with a *picture field*. Rather than a staid button, you can insert a snazzy picture. Clicking the picture submits the form results, just as a Submit button would.

The Reset button is another handy form tool. After visitors click the Reset button, their browsers clear all the information they entered into the form so that they can start over fresh. Alas, Reset buttons cannot be replaced by picture fields and are fated to look like plain gray rectangles.

FrontPage automatically places a Submit button and a Reset button inside every form you create. In case you accidentally delete the buttons, here are instructions for manually inserting the buttons (as well as a picture field).

Inserting a Submit or Reset button

To insert a Submit button or a Reset button, follow these steps:

1. **Place the cursor inside your form and then choose Insert⇨Form⇨ Push Button.**

   A push button field appears on your page.

2. **In the page, double-click the push button field.**

   The Push Button Properties dialog box appears.

3. **In the Name text box, type** Submit **or** Reset, **depending on the kind of button you're creating.**

4. **If you want the text on top of the button to read something other than the word Button, type new text in the Value/Label text box.**

   How about something vivid? A Submit button could read *Come to Mama!* and a Reset button could read *I changed my mind.*

5. **In the Button Type area, click the Submit or Reset option button.**

6. **If you want to specify a tab order, type a number in the Tab Order text box.**

   You can find out more about the tab order under Step 6 in the section "Creating a text box," earlier in this chapter.

7. **Click OK to close the Push Button Properties dialog box.**

Another push button field type sits quietly inside the Push Button Properties dialog box: the Normal push button. You can program this type of button to do just about anything. You can, for example, include a button in your Web page that plays a sound clip or opens a new Web page when a visitor clicks the button.

For such a feature to work, however, you need to write an associated script (a mini-program that gets embedded into the page's HTML code) using a client-side scripting language such as JavaScript. Intrigued? Check out *JavaScript For Dummies,* 3rd Edition, by Emily A. Vander Veer (IDG Books Worldwide, Inc.) to find out more.

What about the Advanced Button option, which you can find by choosing Insert⇨Form⇨Advanced Button? This option creates a push button field that looks and acts similarly to the Normal push button described earlier. Unfortunately, most browsers don't yet recognize the HTML tag required to create an advanced button, so this feature is not worth using, at least not right now.

Take my file, please

With the *file upload field*, visitors can send you much more than just their feedback. They can actually upload files (real, honest-to-goodness files such as Web pages, Microsoft Word documents, or any other type of file) to a special folder in your Web site.

Say you're working on an online family tree. Instead of managing a bunch of unwieldy e-mail attachments, your relatives can instead upload their files and photos to a common folder in your Web site. All the files are in one place, nice and tidy.

Adding a file upload field to your form is easy, but a few extra steps are required to get the process underway. File upload fields also have special browser and server requirements. I'll leave you in the very capable hands of the FrontPage Help System, which explains, step-by-step, how to proceed. To jump straight to the appropriate topic, type **file upload** in the Type a Question for Help box in the upper-right corner of the FrontPage window, and then press Enter.

Inserting a picture field

To use a picture field in place of a Submit button, follow these steps:

1. **Choose Insert⇨Form⇨Picture.**

   The Picture dialog box appears, because you can use any graphic file as the basis for a picture field.

2. **Insert the picture of your choice into your page.**

   If you're not sure how to use this dialog box, refer to Chapter 6.

3. **In the page, double-click the picture field.**

   The Picture Properties dialog box appears with the Form Field tab visible.

4. **In the Name text box, type a field name (such as** Submit**).**

5. **Click OK to close the dialog box.**

Designating where form results go

The Submit button is useless unless it knows where and in what form to send the form results. In the following sections, I describe the ways in which you can save the information submitted from your form.

The built-in FrontPage form handler described in the next few sections works only if the host Web server on which you publish your site supports FrontPage Server Extensions. If your host Web server doesn't support FrontPage Server

Extensions, jump ahead to the section called "Sending form results to a custom form-handling script." If you're not sure what FrontPage Server Extensions are, see Chapter 16.

Saving form results as a file in your Web site

By default, FrontPage saves form results in a text file stored in your Web site. The first time a visitor submits a form, FrontPage creates the file and stores the information inside that file. From then on, each time a new visitor submits a form, FrontPage appends the new form results to the file.

After visitors submit the form, they are greeted by a *confirmation page* (a page that tells them that the form was successfully submitted) or a *validation failure page* (a page that appears if data they entered into the form didn't obey a server-based data rule), in which case they must return to the form and enter new information.

To control how FrontPage saves form results in a file, follow these steps:

1. **Right-click inside the form area and choose Form Properties from the pop-up menu that appears.**

   The Form Properties dialog box appears (see Figure 9-13).

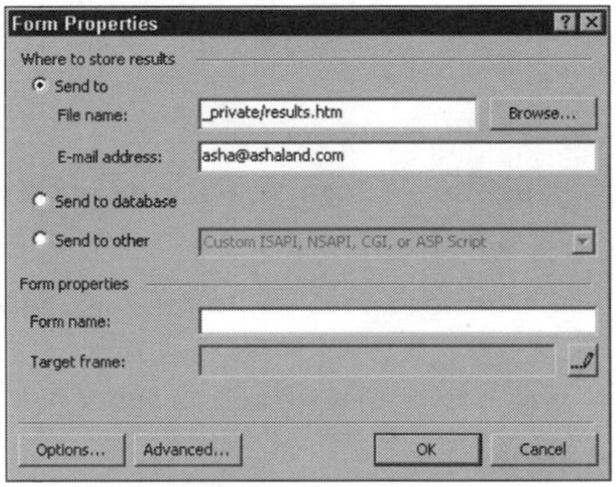

Figure 9-13: The Form Properties dialog box.

In this dialog box, the Where to Store Results area contains options that let you choose where you want form results to go.

2. **In the File Name text box, type the name of the results file.**

   You can type the filename for a text file (for example, `results.txt`) or a Web page (for example, `results.htm`). If you want the results file to be stored inside a Web site folder, type the folder name followed by a slash (/) and the filename (for example, `_private/results.htm`).

Documents stored in the _private folder remain hidden from Web browsers and from the Web Search component (a Web component that you find out about in Chapter 13). Don't forget that underscore (_) when you specify the _private folder's path.

Alternatively, click the Browse button to choose a file that already exists inside your Web site. If you choose an existing file, FrontPage appends the form results to the bottom of the file each time a form is submitted.

3. In the dialog box, click the Options button.

The Saving Results dialog box appears, with the File Results tab visible (see Figure 9-14). This dialog box enables you to customize the results page.

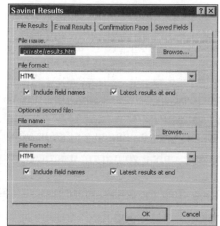

Figure 9-14:
The Saving
Results
dialog box.

4. In the File Format list box, choose your desired page format.

You can save the results file as an HTML file (that is, as a Web page) or as a text file. You can format HTML files as definition lists, bulleted lists, numbered lists, or formatted text. (Refer to Chapter 4 for descriptions of each type of list.) You can save text files as formatted plain text (a nicely laid-out list of field names and values) or as a file with commas, tabs, or spaces separating names and values. (The latter format is handy if you want to import the data into a database or spreadsheet later.)

Be sure the results filename that is visible in the File Name text box uses the filename extension that corresponds to the file type you choose here. HTML files should be named with the filename extension .htm or .html, and text files should be named with the extension .txt.

5. If you want the field names as well as the field values to appear in the results file, check the Include Field Names check box.

6. **If you want the most recent form results to appear at the bottom of the file instead of the top, check the Latest Results at End check box.**

   Note: If the results file is a new file, this check box appears dimmed.

7. **If you want to save form results in a second file as well, type the file path in the File Name text box in the Optional Second File area, or click the Browse button to choose a file in your Web site.**

   This option is handy if, for example, you want FrontPage to generate one file for importing info into a spreadsheet and another file for your own private viewing.

8. **At the top of the dialog box, click the Confirmation Page tab.**

   The Confirmation Page tab becomes visible. (I skipped the E-mail Results tab because I cover it in the next section.)

   This tab enables you to specify custom confirmation and validation failure pages. (You discover how to create confirmation pages later in this chapter.) If you leave this section empty, FrontPage automatically creates generic pages (and you can skip ahead to Step 11).

9. **In the URL of Confirmation Page text box, type the location of the confirmation page (or click Browse to choose a page in your Web site).**

10. **In the URL of Validation Failure Page text box, type the validation failure page location (or click Browse to choose a page in your Web site).**

    Note: This text box is available only if your form uses server-based data validation rules.

11. **At the top of the dialog box, click the Saved Fields tab.**

    If you want only the results of certain form fields to appear in the results page, you can say so in this tab. You can also save additional information in the results file.

12. **In the Form Fields to Save text box, delete the names of the fields for which you don't want results saved.**

13. **In the Date and Time area, choose options from the Date Format and Time Format list boxes.**

    By doing so, you tell FrontPage to affix a date and/or time stamp to each form submission.

14. **In the Additional Information to Save area, click the check boxes next to the other types of information that you want the results file to contain.**

    FrontPage can track the visitor's network user name, the name of the computer from which the form was submitted, and the type of Web browser the visitor was using at the time.

15. **Click OK to close the Saving Results dialog box.**

16. **Click OK to close the Form Properties dialog box.**

Keep in mind that FrontPage will create and save the results file you just specified on the host server on which you publish your Web site, *not* on your local computer's hard drive.

Sending form results to an e-mail address

Sometimes, keeping track of form results as they arrive in your e-mail inbox is easier and more fun than checking a separate results page. FrontPage makes routing form results directly to yourself (or anyone else) as e-mail messages easy.

Before you proceed, check with your ISP or system administrator to be sure that the host Web server on which you will eventually publish your site is set up to handle e-mail form submissions.

You can set up your form to send results via e-mail by following these steps:

1. **Right-click inside the form area and choose Form Properties from the pop-up menu that appears.**

   The Form Properties dialog box appears.

2. **In the E-mail Address text box, type the e-mail address of the person who will receive form results.**

   Presumably that person is you. If so, type your e-mail address here. (It should look like this: username@domain.com.)

   If both the File Name and the E-mail Address text boxes are filled in, FrontPage saves form results in the specified file *and* sends individual submissions via e-mail.

3. **In the dialog box, click the Options button.**

   The Saving Results dialog box appears.

4. **At the top of the dialog box, click the E-mail Results tab.**

   The E-mail Results tab appears. These options enable you to customize the particulars of the e-mail message format.

5. **In the E-Mail Format list box, choose the desired e-mail format.**

   The default value is formatted text, but you can choose other document formats as well.

6. **If you want the field names as well as the field values to appear in the e-mail message, check the Include Field Names check box.**

7. **In the Subject Line text box, type the text that you want to appear in the Subject line of the e-mail message.**

   You might want to choose something descriptive such as *Web Site Visitor Fan Mail.*

If you check the Form Field Name check box, you can specify a field name here instead of static text. That way, visitors can specify what appears in the subject line of the e-mail message by filling out the corresponding form field inside the Web page. For example, say you add a text field to your form and name the field *Subject*. In this step, you would click the Form Field Name check box and type **Subject** in the Subject Line text box.

 8. **In the Reply-to Line text box, specify the information that you want to appear in the reply-to line of the e-mail message.**

Here's where using a form field name really makes sense, especially if you use your form to collect visitor feedback. For example, you can tell FrontPage to replace the reply-to line in the form results e-mail message with the contents of a form field that collects visitors' e-mail addresses. Then, when you receive a form result message, you simply reply to that message, and it goes directly to the person who sent you the feedback (assuming that person entered her e-mail address correctly in the appropriate field).

 9. **Click OK to close the Saving Results dialog box.**

 10. **Click OK to close the Form Properties dialog box.**

After you click OK, you may see the very intimidating dialog box pictured in Figure 9-15.

Figure 9-15:
This dialog box may appear when you set up your form to submit results to an e-mail address.

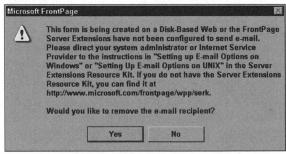

Don't be alarmed. This dialog box pops up because FrontPage noticed you are creating a form that requires certain conditions on the host Web server to be able to work (namely, that the Web server has FrontPage Server Extensions installed, and that the Web server knows how to process form results as e-mail messages). If you haven't already, check with your ISP or system administrator to be sure that the host Web server can handle e-mail form submissions. If the answer is yes, you can ignore this dialog box (click No to close the dialog box and proceed on your merry way).

If the answer is no, you're out of luck; click Yes to close the dialog box and remove the e-mail recipient from your form.

Sending form results to a custom form-handling script

If your host Web server doesn't support FrontPage Server Extensions or if you need special data-processing capabilities that the FrontPage form handler can't accommodate, you can process form results by using a custom *form-handling script.* A custom script does the same job as the form handler included with FrontPage Server Extensions: It receives and processes form data and then outputs the results. The script's internal programming determines how form results are formatted and where they are sent.

Chances are good that your ISP or system administrator has a form-handling script already in place on the Web server. (After all, folks were submitting Web forms long before FrontPage was born!) Speak to your ISP or administrator to discover the script's capabilities and find out where the script is located on the server (that is, the script's URL).

To write a custom form-handling script, you need programming experience or a programmer friend who owes you a big favor.

To use a custom script as your form handler, follow these steps:

1. **Right-click inside the form area and choose Form Properties from the pop-up menu that appears.**

   The Form Properties dialog box appears.

2. **Click the Send to Other option button.**

   The corresponding list box comes into view, with the Custom ISAPI, NSAPI, CGI, or ASP Script option visible.

   If you must know, ISAPI stands for Internet Server Application Programming Interface, NSAPI stands for Netscape Server Application Programming Interface, CGI stands for Common Gateway Interface, and ASP stands for Active Server Pages.

3. **In the dialog box, click the Options button.**

   The Options for Custom Form Handler dialog box appears.

4. **In the Action text box, type the URL of the form handler.**

   If you don't know the URL, ask your ISP or system administrator.

5. **If it's not already visible, choose POST from the Method list box.**

   The majority of Web forms use this method to submit data to a script.

6. **Leave the Encoding Type text box alone.**

7. **Click OK to close the Options for Custom Form Handler dialog box.**

8. **Click OK to close the Form Properties dialog box.**

Creating a Confirmation Page

A *confirmation page* is a Web page that appears after visitors submit a form. This page lets visitors know that the form submission was successful and (depending on how you set up the page) confirms the information that visitors entered in the form. A confirmation page is a nice way to reassure visitors that the information they just sent didn't float off into the ether after they clicked the Submit button.

For all forms except those submitted to custom scripts, FrontPage automatically generates plain-Jane confirmation pages. If you want your confirmation page to blend in nicely with the rest of your site's design, you can create your own page. (If you submit your form to a custom script, the script's programming determines whether it can work in conjunction with a confirmation page. Your ISP or system administrator can fill you in on the script's capabilities.)

The confirmation page can be as simple as a polite acknowledgment and a hyperlink back to the Web site's home page ("Thank you for filling out our survey. Return to the Acme home page."). Alternatively, the page can display some or all of the information that visitors entered into the form, so that the visitors can note the information for future reference. How does the confirmation page know to display visitors' form entries? Because you can insert little jewels called *confirmation fields* into the confirmation page.

Confirmation fields are simple references to the existing fields in your form. If used as part of a Web page, confirmation fields display the information that the visitor typed into the corresponding form fields.

As always, FrontPage steps in to help with a handy Confirmation Form template. You can also create your own confirmation form by adding confirmation fields to an existing Web page.

Using the Confirmation Form template

The Confirmation Form template is a good place to begin building your own confirmation page.

Before you create a confirmation page based on the Confirmation Form template, you must know the names of the form fields that you want to confirm.

To create a confirmation page based on this template, follow these steps:

1. **Choose File⇨New⇨Page or Web.**

   If it's not already visible, the Side Pane appears on the right side of the FrontPage window.

2. **In the New from Template section of the Side Pane, click Page Templates.**

   The Templates dialog box appears.

3. **In the dialog box's template box, double-click Confirmation Form.**

   A generic confirmation page opens in Page View. This page is a boiler-plate confirmation page for a feedback form.

4. **Change the page to suit your needs.**

   This Web page is just like any other; you can format and rearrange the page any way you like. Add or change text, change the color scheme, and add your own graphics.

   The words that appear inside brackets (such as [UserEmail] and [UserTel]) are the page's confirmation fields. The word inside the brackets corresponds to the name of a form field. (The confirmation fields in this template correspond to the field names in the form created by using FrontPage's Feedback Form page template.)

5. **To change a confirmation field so that it corresponds to a field in your form, double-click the confirmation field on the page.**

   The Confirmation Field Properties dialog box appears.

6. **In the Name of Form Field to Confirm text box, type the name of the field you want to confirm.**

   Pay attention to uppercase and lowercase letters while typing the field name.

7. **Click OK to close the dialog box.**

   The word inside the selected confirmation field changes to the specified field name.

 8. **On the Standard toolbar, click the Save button to save the page.**

After you create a custom confirmation page, you must specify its URL when you choose the form's handler. Refer to the section, "Designating where form results go," earlier in this chapter, for details.

Building a custom confirmation page

Chances are the generic template-based confirmation page won't fit into your site's design very well. So, instead, create your own confirmation page. You can add confirmation fields to any page in your Web site and then use that page as your form's confirmation page. To do so, follow these steps:

1. **Create or open the Web page that you want to use as your confirmation page.**

2. **Place the cursor at the point in the page where you want the first confirmation field to appear.**

3. **Click the Web Component button on the Standard toolbar.**

   The Insert Web Page Component dialog box appears.

4. **In the dialog box's Component Type list box, click Advanced Controls.**

5. **In the Choose a Control list box, double-click Confirmation Field.**

   The Confirmation Field Properties dialog box appears.

6. **In the Name of Form Field to Confirm text box, type the name of the field that you want to confirm.**

   Pay attention to uppercase and lowercase letters while typing the field name.

7. **Click OK to close the dialog box.**

   The confirmation field appears in the page.

8. **On the Standard toolbar, click the Save button to save the page.**

After you create a custom confirmation page, you must specify its URL when you choose the form's handler. Refer to the section "Designating where form results go," earlier in this chapter, for details.

Making Sure Your Form Works

After you finish your form, you may as well check to see if the darn thing works. Unfortunately, if you preview the page in a Web browser, fill out your form fields, and then click the Submit button, FrontPage dings you with an error message.

Because forms require a form handler to be able to work, you must go a step beyond simply previewing the page: You must call upon the services of a Web server. To do so, you must publish your Web site and then preview and test the "live" version of the form. (For directions on how to publish your site, see Chapter 16.)

Chapter 10

I've Been Framed!

*O*f the newfangled design effects to arrive on the Web publishing scene, few have changed the face of the Web more than frames. Frames don't just make something happen on a page — frames change the way that visitors experience the Web site as a whole.

In this chapter, I show you how to create a framed Web site. I also show you how to insert an inline frame into a Web site that doesn't contain frames.

What Are Frames?

Frames are dividers that separate the Web browser window into sections. Each section contains a separate Web page, enabling you to display more than one page at the same time, as shown in Figure 10-1.

In this example, the browser window contains three frames, each of which displays a separate page. The top frame contains a banner-like heading, the left frame contains a list of navigational hyperlinks, and the frame on the right contains the site's main content.

Sure, frames look slick. Looks are the least of it, however, when compared to frames' navigational power. Behold — in the site shown in Figure 10-1, when you click a hyperlink in the left frame, the link's destination page appears in the right frame. In this way, you can use frames to keep certain elements visible all the time (as the decorative heading and navigational links are in Figure 10-1), while the rest of the site's content changes based on where the visitor wants to go.

Figure 10-1:
A typical framed Web site.

Inline frames (also known as *floating* frames) work differently than regular frames. Whereas regular frames change the fundamental structure of the Web site, inline frames can be inserted into a Web site that doesn't contain frames. Inline frames are scrollable boxes that can display the contents of another page — for example, the scrollable box shown in Figure 10-2. I explain how to create inline frames at the end of the chapter.

You should know that not all Web browsers can display frames, regular or inline. Netscape Navigator (Version 2.0 or later) and Microsoft Internet Explorer (Version 3.0 or later) are frames-capable, but older or frames-challenged browsers can't even display an approximation of a framed site; the visitor sees only a blank page. The good news is that most Web surfers use a frames-capable browser. For those who don't, FrontPage sidesteps the problem by creating an alternative for browsers that can't display frames.

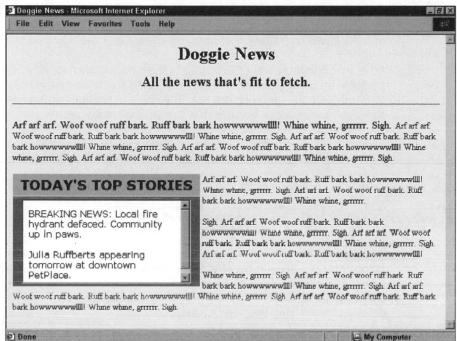

File   Edit   View   Favorites   Tools   Help

Doggie News

All the news that's fit to fetch.

Arf arf arf. Woof woof ruff bark. Ruff bark bark howwwwwwllll! Whine whine, grrrrr. Sigh. Arf arf arf. Woof woof ruff bark. Ruff bark bark howwwwwwllll! Whine whine, grrrrr. Sigh. Arf arf arf. Woof woof ruff bark. Ruff bark bark howwwwwwllll! Whine whine, grrrrr. Sigh. Arf arf arf. Woof woof ruff bark. Ruff bark bark howwwwwwllll! Whine whine, grrrrr. Sigh. Arf arf arf. Woof woof ruff bark. Ruff bark bark howwwwwwllll! Whine whine, grrrrr. Sigh.

TODAY'S TOP STORIES

BREAKING NEWS: Local fire hydrant defaced. Community up in paws.

Julia Ruffberts appearing tomorrow at downtown PetPlace.

Arf arf arf. Woof woof ruff bark. Ruff bark bark howwwwwwllll! Whine whine, grrrrr. Sigh. Arf arf arf. Woof woof ruff bark. Ruff bark bark howwwwwwllll! Whine whine, grrrrr.

Sigh. Arf arf arf. Woof woof ruff bark. Ruff bark bark howwwwwwllll! Whine whine, grrrrr. Sigh. Arf arf arf. Woof woof ruff bark. Ruff bark bark howwwwwwllll! Whine whine, grrrrr. Sigh. Arf arf arf. Woof woof ruff bark. Ruff bark bark howwwwwwllll!

Whine whine, grrrrr. Sigh. Arf arf arf. Woof woof ruff bark. Ruff bark bark howwwwwwllll! Whine whine, grrrrr. Sigh. Arf arf arf. Woof woof ruff bark. Ruff bark bark howwwwwwllll! Whine whine, grrrrr. Sigh. Arf arf arf. Woof woof ruff bark. Ruff bark bark howwwwwwllll! Whine whine, grrrrr. Sigh.

Done   My Computer

Figure 10-2:
An inline frame.

Creating a Framed Web Site: The Game Plan

Creating a framed site involves the following three basic steps:

- ✔ Creating the frames page
- ✔ Filling the frames with content pages (and, if necessary, modifying the pages to work inside the frames)
- ✔ Adjusting the overall layout and properties of each individual frame

A *frames page* is a special type of Web page that defines the size, placement, and properties of the site's frames. A frames page can display as many frames as you want, in whatever layout you want.

After you create a frames page, you fill the frames with *content pages*. Content pages are regular old Web pages that appear inside each frame as a visitor views the frames page with a Web browser. (The frames page itself is transparent, except for the placement of each frame.) *Initial pages* are the first content pages that appear as a visitor views the frames page with a Web browser.

You can either use an existing Web page as a frame's initial page, or fill the frame with a new, blank page. You then must adjust the layout and properties of the individual frames so that the site functions the way you want.

After you finish creating the framed site, you save and preview the whole package by using the FrontPage Preview or a frames-capable browser. By previewing your site, you can see how the site's hyperlinks and frames work together, and you can be sure that the links work correctly.

Ah, but I get ahead of myself. The best place to begin is at the beginning . . . with the frames page.

Creating the Frames Page

The hardest part about creating a framed Web site can be deciding on the layout of the frames in the first place. FrontPage anticipates this problem by providing templates for popular frames page layouts. After you create the frames page by using a template, you can modify the page's layout by adding, deleting, or resizing the page's frames.

To create a new frames page, follow these steps:

1. **Choose File⇨New⇨Page or Web.**

   If it's not already visible, the Task Pane appears on the right side of the FrontPage window.

2. **In the New from Template section of the Task pane, click Page Templates.**

   The Page Templates dialog box appears.

3. **In the dialog box, click the Frames Pages tab to display FrontPage's frames page templates, as shown in Figure 10-3.**

4. **In the template list, click one of the template icons.**

   A description of the frames page template appears in the Description area, and a mini-preview of the frames page layout appears in the Preview area.

5. **After you find a template that resembles the frame layout you want, click OK.**

   If no template looks exactly the way that you want your frames page to look, choose the closest approximation — you can adjust the layout later.

   The Page Templates dialog box closes, and a new frames page appears in Page View, as shown in Figure 10-4.

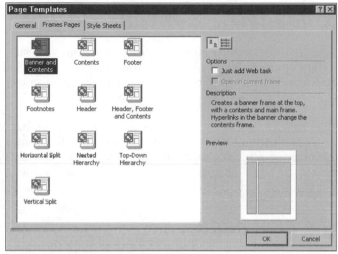

Figure 10-3:
FrontPage
provides
plenty of
templates
for frames
pages.

In addition to the frames page, two new options appear at the bottom of the
Page View window: No Frames and Frames Page HTML. You use the No
Frames button to create a message for those of your visitors whose browsers
can't display frames. (I explain how to do this later in this chapter.) The
Frames Page HTML button displays the frames page's HTML code. (The
HTML button displays the HTML code for the site's content pages.)

Now you need to fill the frames page with content pages.

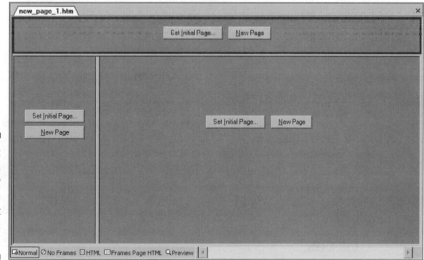

Figure 10-4:
A new,
empty
frames
page, as it
appears in
Page View.

Filling Frames with Content Pages

As with frames around fine paintings, the frames in your Web site exist only to enhance the contents. Right now, the frames page is empty, and you need to fill each frame with an *initial page*. You can either create a new, blank page or choose one of the pages already sitting in your Web site.

If you would rather adjust the frames page layout *before* working with content pages, skip ahead to the section called "Tweaking the Frames Page," later in this chapter. After you've made your changes, return to this section for instructions on how to insert content pages into each frame.

Using a new page

To fill a frame with a new page, click the New Page button in one of the frames. A new, empty page appears inside the frame.

To add stuff to the new page (text, graphics, and anything else you would add to a regular Web page), click inside the page and proceed as usual. If the page is sitting inside a narrow frame and you feel cramped, right-click the page and choose Open Page in New Window from the pop-up menu that appears. FrontPage pops open a new, full-sized window so that you can have a little elbow room while adding content to the page. After you've finished working on that page, close the window to see how the page looks inside its frame.

Using an existing page

To fill the frame with an existing page, follow these steps:

1. **In one of the frames, click the Set Initial Page button.**

   The Insert Hyperlink dialog box appears.

   The appearance of the Insert Hyperlink dialog box makes sense because, on the HTML level, you're actually creating a special type of hyperlink between the frames page and the content page.

2. **In the dialog box, select the page that you want to use as the frame's initial page.**

   If the initial page you want to use is stored elsewhere on the World Wide Web, type the page's URL in the Address text box.

3. **Click OK.**

   The dialog box closes, and the page appears inside the frame.

To edit the page, click inside the page and proceed as usual, or right-click the page and choose Open Page in New Window from the pop-up menu that appears, to display the page in a full-sized window.

Tweaking the Frames Page

The FrontPage frames page templates represent the most popular frame layouts in use on the Web today. That's great if you're the type who sticks to tried-and-true conventions. But if you're a renegade, you're probably itching to rearrange the frames page. In this section, I show you how.

Adding new frames

To add new frames to a frames page, you actually need to split existing frames. Just as splitting a table cell divides the cell in two, splitting a frame divides the frame in two. (Refer to Chapter 8 for information about tables.)

A word to the wise: More is not better when it comes to frames. Framed sites containing four or more frames can be difficult to navigate and visually overwhelming. Lots of convoluted frames not only obscure your site's design, but also annoy your visitors to no end (many of whom may not return). I'm not stating an indisputable fact here; I simply encourage you to value simplicity and design your site with your visitors in mind.

To split a frame, you hold down the Ctrl key, click a frame border (including the outer borders), drag the border to a new position, and then release the mouse button. As soon as you release the mouse button, a new, empty frame appears.

If you create a frames page that you'd like to use for future Web sites, save the page as a FrontPage page template. (I explain how to do this in Chapter 2.)

Deleting frames

If the frames page looks too convoluted, delete a frame or two. By deleting a frame, you don't delete the content page inside; you simply remove the frame from the frames page. The content page remains untouched. To delete a frame, click inside the frame and then choose Frames⇨Delete Frame.

Changing frame properties

In addition to changing the overall layout of the frames page, you can change the following details:

- ✔ Frame name
- ✔ Presence of scrollbars
- ✔ Frame size
- ✔ Amount of space separating frame content from frame borders
- ✔ Presence of frame borders
- ✔ Amount of space between frame borders

To change any or all of these properties, follow these steps:

1. **Right-click inside the frame you want to edit and choose Frame Properties from the pop-up menu that appears.**

   The Frame Properties dialog box appears (see Figure 10-5).

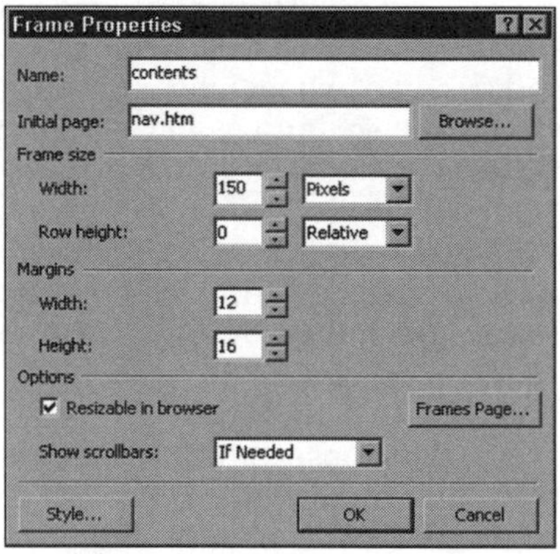

Figure 10-5:
The Frame Properties dialog box.

Note: The following steps describe how to change every frame property. Choose only those steps that apply to the property you want to adjust.

2. **In the Name text box, type a frame name that makes sense to you.**

   The frame's name acts as an identifying label. If the frame will contain a table of contents page, for example, you could type the name **TOC**. Or, if you prefer to identify the frame by its position, you can type something like **Left** or **Top**.

3. **To change the initial page, type a new page filename, path, or URL in the Initial Page text box or click Browse to select the page you want from a file list.**

4. **In the Width and Row Height boxes, type dimension measurements.**

   As with table dimensions, you can specify an absolute pixel value or a relative percentage based on the size of the browser window. (Refer to Chapter 8 for information about how table dimensions work.)

   You can choose Relative if you want the browser to set the frame's dimension relative to the other frames in the page. For example, if the frames page contains two frames, and the width of the first frame is set to 100 pixels, and the width of the second frame is set to Relative, the second frame expands to fill the rest of the browser window, whatever the window's size.

5. **In the Width and Height boxes, type the number of pixels with which you want to separate the content page text from the frame borders.**

   The effect works in a similar way to cell padding inside a table. (See Chapter 8 for details.)

6. **If you want to lock the position of the frame so that visitors can't resize the frame as they view the site, be sure that the Resizable in Browser check box is unmarked.**

   If this check box is marked, when visitors view the framed site with a Web browser, they can adjust the position of frame borders to work with the size of their monitors. By doing so, they don't affect the frames page, just how the framed site appears on their screens. If this check box is unmarked, the frame position is locked in place.

7. **In the Show Scrollbars list box, choose an option that describes when you want the scrollbars to appear inside the frame.**

   You have the following options:

   - **If Needed:** If the visitor's browser window is too small to display the entire contents of a frame, scrollbars appear so that visitors may move around inside the frame.

   - **Always:** Scrollbars are visible at all times, even when they aren't necessary.

   - **Never:** Scrollbars never appear, no matter what.

8. **Click the Frames Page button.**

   The Page Properties dialog box appears, with the Frames tab visible. When you change the settings inside this tab, the changes apply to the entire frames page.

9. **In the Frame Spacing box, type the frame border width (in pixels).**

   This option works similarly to cell spacing in tables. By changing this setting, you change the appearance of the frame borders. (Refer to Chapter 8 for more information about tables.)

10. **To make frame borders invisible, unmark the Show Borders check box.**

11. **Click OK.**

   The Page Properties dialog box closes, and the Frame Properties dialog box becomes visible again.

12. **Click OK to close the Frame Properties dialog box.**

   The dialog box closes, and the selected frame's settings change accordingly.

Changing the target frame

Each frames page template assigns a *target frame* to the content page sitting inside each frame. The target frame is the frame in which hyperlink destination pages appear. In Figure 10-1, for example, after a visitor clicks a navigational link inside the left frame, the corresponding page appears in the right frame. The right frame, therefore, is the target frame for the links in the left frame.

Each frame page template contains default target frame settings. (To determine a frame's default target frame, in Page View, click a hyperlink inside the frame while holding down the Ctrl key. The frame in which the destination page appears is that frame's default target frame.) In the following sections, I show you how to change the target frame setting.

Changing the target frame for all the hyperlinks in a page

To change the target frame for all the hyperlinks in a page (also referred to as changing the *default target frame*), follow these steps:

1. **Right-click inside the frame and choose Page Properties from the pop-up menu that appears.**

   The Page Properties dialog box appears, with the General tab visible. The Default Target Frame text box contains the name of the current target frame. (If the text box is empty, hyperlink destination pages appear inside the same frame.)

2. In the dialog box, click the Change Target Frame button.

The Target Frame dialog box appears, as shown in Figure 10-6.

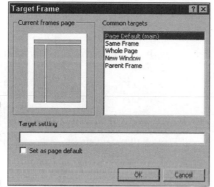

Figure 10-6:
The Target
Frame
dialog box.

3. In the Current Frames Page section of the dialog box, click the frame you want to target, or, in the Common Targets area, click the name of the target you want to use.

(I describe what each Common Target option does in the nearby sidebar called "Special target frame options.")

The frame name appears in the Target Setting text box.

4. Click OK to close the dialog box.

The Page Properties dialog box becomes visible again.

5. Click OK to close the Page Properties dialog box.

Changing the target frame for a single hyperlink

If you want to change the target frame setting for only a single hyperlink (leaving the other links in the page using the default target frame setting), follow these steps:

1. In the content page, create a new hyperlink or click an existing hyperlink, and then click the Insert Hyperlink button on the Standard toolbar.

The Insert Hyperlink or Edit Hyperlink dialog box appears. (Refer to Chapter 5 if you're not sure how to create a new hyperlink.)

2. In the dialog box, click the Target Frame button to choose a frame from the Target Frame dialog box.

Refer to the steps in the preceding section, "Changing the target frame for all the hyperlinks in a page," for detailed instructions on how to use the Target Frame dialog box.

3. Click OK to close the dialog box.

Special target frame options

You can use the following four common target frame options (available in the Target Frame dialog box) to create different effects:

✔ **Same Frame:** This setting causes the hyperlink destination page to open inside the same frame in which the hyperlink source page is located.

✔ **Whole Page:** This setting causes the hyperlink destination page to replace the frames page in the browser window.

✔ **New Window:** This setting causes the hyperlink destination page to open inside a new Web browser window.

✔ **Parent Frame:** If you really want to get fancy, you can use a second frames page as the content page for one or more frames in your site. The result is a *nested frames page:* A secondary level of frames appears inside one of the frames in the top-level (or parent) frames page. When you choose the Parent target frame setting, links in the secondary frames page load inside the parent frame. If you use nested frames, be sure to keep the site simple enough to navigate easily.

Specifying the target frame for form results

If one of your content pages contains a form, you can specify a target frame for form results. (If you're not familiar with forms, take a look at Chapter 9.)

To specify a target frame for form results, follow these steps:

1. **Right-click inside the form and then choose Form Properties from the pop-up menu that appears.**

   The Form Properties dialog box appears.

    2. **In the dialog box, click the Change Target Frame button to choose a frame from the Target Frame dialog box.**

   Refer to the steps in the previous section, "Changing the target frame for all the hyperlinks in a page," for detailed instructions on how to use the Target Frame dialog box.

3. **Click OK to close the dialog box.**

Specifying the target frame for image maps

If one of your content pages contains an image map, you can specify a default target frame for the image map's hotspots. (If you're not sure what an image map or a hotspot is, refer to Chapter 7.)

To do so, follow these steps:

1. **Right-click the image map and then choose Picture Properties from the pop-up menu that appears.**

   The Picture Properties dialog box appears, with the Appearance tab visible.

2. **In the dialog box, click the General tab to make those options visible.**

 3. **In the dialog box, click the Change Target Frame button to choose a frame from the Target Frame dialog box.**

   Refer to the steps in the previous section, "Changing the target frame for all the hyperlinks in a page," for detailed instructions on how to use the Target Frame dialog box.

4. **Click OK to close the dialog box.**

You can also specify a target frame for individual hotspots inside the image map. To do so, double-click a hotspot to display the Edit Hyperlink dialog box. Then follow Steps 2 and 3 listed in the previous section called "Changing the target frame for a single hyperlink."

Creating an Alternative for Browsers That Don't "Do" Frames

Web Truism #2 states that your visitors use different types of Web browsers. (The four Web Truisms are listed in Chapter 3.) The majority of your visitors surf the Web by using frames-capable browsers, but a few people use browsers that can't display frames.

How do you accommodate such visitors? With a *No Frames message*. When visitors with frames-impaired browsers attempt to view the frames page, they see the No Frames message instead. The No Frames message looks and acts like a separate Web page — it can contain text, graphics, hyperlinks, and so on — but, in reality, the message is a chunk of HTML sitting inside the frames page.

To create a No Frames message, click the No Frames button in Page View, and then proceed as though you are creating a regular Web page.

 FrontPage's default No Frames message, "This page uses frames, but your browser doesn't support them," states the obvious but doesn't help the visitor solve the problem. A friendlier No Frames message offers an alternate method for exploring the site, such as providing hyperlinks to the site's content pages. A polite invitation to download a frames-capable browser (plus links that lead straight to the download sites) would be a nice touch, too.

Frames forethought

If you want to give visitors the choice of viewing your site with or without frames, you must place a hyperlink that points to the frames page in another page in your site. Or you can specify the frames page as the site's home page so that the frames page is the first thing visitors see when visiting your site. (To do this, in the Page View Folder List, right-click the icon for the frames page and choose Set As Home Page from the pop-up menu that appears. FrontPage takes care of updating hyperlinks and renaming your old home page so it won't be overwritten.) Because FrontPage knows how to set up a No Frames alternative for browsers that can't handle frames, you're in the clear. Almost.

You need to make sure that visitors who are viewing the site without frames can still get around. To understand what I mean, imagine if the site in Figure 10-1 had no frames and a copy of the main body page was used as the No Frames message. How would visitors navigate the site when that page contains no navigational links?

You can make sure that your visitors can navigate your site by reproducing in the main body page all the links found in the navigational page. Or you can create a separate set of pages for browsers that can't display frames. *Or* you can create a No Frames message that requires visitors to use a frames-capable browser to view your site and provides links to the download sites of these browsers. Whatever you decide, test, test, and test again to be sure that your site is accessible to *all* your visitors.

Saving a Framed Web Site

When you work with a framed Web site, you can easily forget that you're working with several Web pages at the same time — the frames page plus its content pages. Because of this page-juggling, saving a framed Web site involves a couple of extra steps. To save a framed Web site, follow these steps:

 1. **Click the Save button.**

   The Save As dialog box appears, as shown in Figure 10-7. The right side of the dialog box contains a diagram of the frames page. If the content pages are new, one of the frames in the frames diagram appears highlighted. The highlighted frame indicates which content page you are currently saving.

2. **Type a filename in the dialog box's File Name text box.**

3. **If you like, change the page's title by clicking the Change Title button to show the Set Page Title dialog box, typing a new title, and then clicking OK to close the dialog box.**

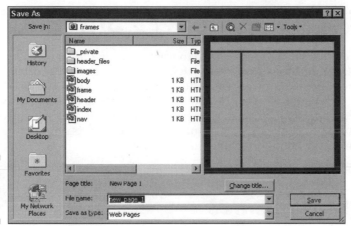

Figure 10-7:
The Save As
dialog box.

4. Click Save.

The dialog box closes, and FrontPage saves the content page. In a moment, the Save As dialog box appears again, this time with a different frame in the frames diagram highlighted.

5. Repeat Steps 2 through 4 for each content page.

After you save the last content page, the Save As dialog box appears a final time, this time with the entire frames page diagram highlighted, indicating that you are now saving the frames page itself.

6. Type a filename and choose a page title.

In a framed site, the title of the frames page is the only one visible as a visitor views the site with a Web browser. The titles of the individual content pages don't appear. Make sure that you choose a descriptive title for the frames page.

7. Click Save.

The dialog box closes, and FrontPage saves the frames page.

In the future, when you click the Save button, FrontPage saves all changes to the frames page and the content pages. To save changes in a single content page, click the page's frame and then choose Frames⇨Save Page.

Previewing a Framed Web Site

 After your site is in order, be sure to preview your site by checking out the Preview tab or by clicking the Preview in Browser button. (For more information about how to preview your site, see Chapter 2.) Test the links in each frame to be sure they work the way you expect them to. If you preview your site by using a Web browser, change the browser window size to see how the frames rearrange themselves. If something is amiss, return to FrontPage and keep tweaking until everything works.

Using Inline Frames

Inline frames give your site some of the utility of regular frames without requiring a complete site overhaul. You can add an inline frame to any page, just as you would add a graphic or other effect.

Inline frames are useful when you want to make the content of another page available to your users without requiring them to leave the current page. For example, you could insert an inline frame to display another page that contains frequently updated content, such as news stories, sports scores, or stock quotes.

 If you like the notion of included content, but you don't want that content to appear inside a scrolling box, investigate the Included Content components, which I describe along with other Web components in Chapter 13.

To insert an inline frame into a page, place the cursor where you want the inline frame to appear, and then choose Insert➪Inline Frame. An empty inline frame appears in the page.

For the most part, from here, working with an inline frame is similar to working with a regular frame, so I'll leave the step-by-step instructions to the earlier sections in this chapter. You begin by filling the inline frame with a content page (either a new or existing page). You can make changes to the content page directly from inside the inline frame, or you can open the content page in its own full-sized window. To do so, right-click inside the inline frame and then choose Open in New Window.

To adjust the inline frame's properties, move your cursor over the inline frame's border until the cursor becomes a pointer. Then right-click, and choose Inline Frame Properties from the pop-up menu that appears. The Inline Frame Properties dialog box appears (see Figure 10-8). Most of the options in this dialog box directly correspond to those in the Frame Properties dialog box (skim the earlier sections of this chapter for details).

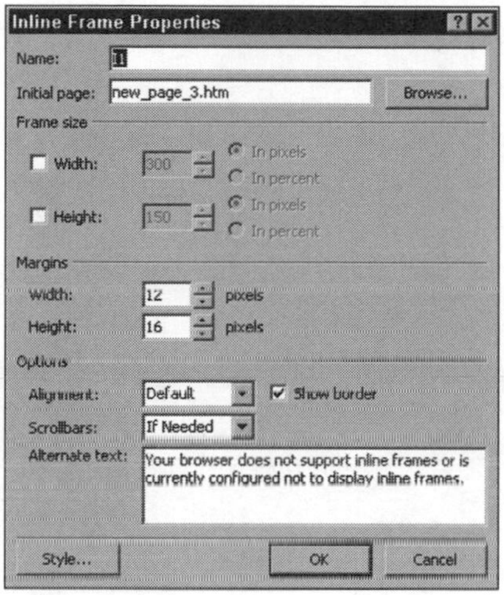

Inline Frame Properties ? X

Name: I
Initial page: new_page_3.htm   Browse...

Frame size
☐ Width: 500 ⬍ ● In pixels
                  ○ In percent
☐ Height: 150 ⬍ ● In pixels
                  ○ In percent

Margins
Width: 12 ⬍ pixels
Height: 16 ⬍ pixels

Options
Alignment: Default ▾   ☑ Show border
Scrollbars: If Needed ▾
Alternate text: Your browser does not support inline frames or is
                 currently configured not to display inline frames.

Style...   OK   Cancel

Figure 10-8:
The Inline
Frame
Properties
dialog box.

One option in the Inline Frame Properties dialog box bears explanation: The Alternate Text box. In this box, you type a message that appears to visitors who are using browsers that are unable to display inline frames (similar to the No Frames message for regular frames). Make sure your message is meaningful, because inline frames are only visible in certain browser flavors and versions.

Part III
Nifty Web Site Additions

The 5th Wave   By Rich Tennant

@RICHTENNANT

"FRANKLY, I'M NOT SURE THIS IS THE WAY TO ENHANCE OUR COLOR GRAPHICS."

In this part . . .

After you build a sturdy, attractive Web site, you may feel the urge to add on to it. Perhaps you want to embellish your Web site with a graphical theme or enable visitors to search your site for keywords. All are easy to construct with FrontPage, and you don't need to hire a contractor.

Chapter 11

Playing in the FrontPage Theme Park

● ●

In This Chapter

▶ Applying a theme to your Web site

▶ Modifying themes

● ●

*I*f you've spent much time on the Web, you can probably tell the difference between a professionally designed Web site and a home-grown operation. Professionally designed sites look smooth and polished, with matching graphics and custom fonts. Web sites built by nondesigners are no less worthwhile, but are sometimes, um, lacking in the looks department. Face it: Most people don't have the expertise to create their own graphics, the time to track down individual pieces of clip art, or the money to pay a designer. Nor should someone need these things to create an attractive Web site.

The FrontPage programmers agree with me, and they got together with professional designers to create *themes*. Now, after a few mouse-clicks, your Web site can have a little of the style and distinction usually reserved for big-budget Web sites.

Touring the Themes Dialog Box

Themes transform a Web site by applying a coordinated set of text and link colors, fonts, background graphics, table borders, link bar buttons, horizontal lines, and bullets to the site's pages. Each theme generates a different look or feel: For example, the Sumi Painting theme projects peace and serenity, and the Expedition theme creates an earthy, safari look.

For a hint at what themes can do, look at Figures 11-1 and 11-2. Figure 11-1 shows a rather dowdy page — perfectly functional but visually uninteresting. Figure 11-2 shows the same page after a theme makeover. Not bad. Themes can't do magic, but they can give you quick, easy access to home page decoration.

Figure 11-1:
A
serviceable,
but plain,
Web page.

Figure 11-2:
The same
Web page,
after the
application
of a theme.

You can check out FrontPage themes by touring the Themes dialog box (see Figure 11-3). To display the Themes dialog box, choose Format⇨Theme.

The Themes dialog box lets you preview the many themes that are included with FrontPage. To preview a theme, click a name in the themes list. A representation of the theme's elements appears in the Sample of Theme area. The preview contains text fonts and colors, bullets, a custom horizontal line, hyperlink colors, link bar buttons, a background graphic, and a page banner.

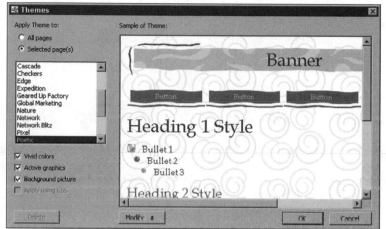

If you're not familiar with some of the elements I just mentioned, flip through the following chapters for more information: Text color, text font, bullets, and horizontal lines are covered in Chapter 4; link bars and hyperlink colors are covered in Chapter 5; background graphics are covered in Chapter 6; and page banners are covered in Chapter 13.

Three check boxes sitting underneath the themes list give you a little control (but not much) over the standard appearance of theme elements:

- ✔ **Vivid Colors:** Mark this option if you want to use a slightly brighter set of text, links, and graphic colors. Unmark this check box if you prefer more muted colors.

- ✔ **Active Graphics:** Active graphics add a bit of spunk to your site. In the Active Graphic set, FrontPage creates link bar buttons that change color or shape when clicked. Some themes also contain different page banners and animated bullets instead of stay-still graphic bullets.

    Some of the active graphic effects in FrontPage are powered by JavaScript and, therefore, don't show up in older Web browsers. Visitors who use browsers that don't understand JavaScript see a static version of the active graphic.

- ✔ **Background Picture:** This option lets you turn on or off the theme's background graphic.

Later in the chapter, I show you how to modify the theme's colors, graphics, and text styles.

You can check out hundreds of free and fee-based themes on the Web. A good place to start: www.frontpagestuff.com/themes_add_ons.htm. I also include a few themes on the CD that comes with this book. See Appendix B for a complete list of CD contents.

Applying a Theme to Your Web Site

So now you're excited to use a theme in your Web site, right? Follow me.

When you apply a theme to your Web site, the theme changes your site's formatting. You can always remove the theme later, but just keep this reformatting in mind as you proceed.

Furthermore, when you use themes, FrontPage copies all the theme's graphics into your Web site's file system, which increases the amount of storage space your Web site takes up. This makes no difference to your visitors, but it may concern you if you have limited storage space available on your host Web server.

You can apply a theme to your entire Web site or to a single page. To do so, follow these steps:

1. **Open the Web site you want to change. If you want to apply a theme to a single page in the Web site, open that page.**

   To apply a theme to more than one page without having to open each page, in the Views bar on the left side of the FrontPage window, click Folders to display the Folders View. Then, while pressing the Ctrl key, click the pages to which you want the theme applied.

2. **Choose Format⇨Theme.**

   The Themes dialog box appears.

3. **In the dialog box's Apply Theme To area, click the appropriate option button.**

   You can apply the theme to all pages in the Web site or to the selected page(s). (If no pages are selected, this option applies the theme to the page that is currently open in the Page View.)

4. **In the list box, click the name of the theme you want to use.**

   A preview of the theme elements appears in the Sample of Theme box.

5. **Depending on the options you want to use, mark one or more of the Vivid Colors, Active Graphics, and Background Picture check boxes.**

   If you later decide you don't like any aspect of the theme, you can change it. I explain how to modify themes later in the chapter.

6. Optionally, click the Apply Using CSS check box.

If you mark this check box, FrontPage uses cascading style sheet commands to apply the theme to your site. The theme looks no different to your visitors, however the commands change the method that FrontPage uses to apply the theme to your pages. The upside: Style sheets can later be edited outside of FrontPage. In other words, if you later want to modify the theme elements by using a program other than FrontPage (or by hand, assuming you know HTML and style sheet syntax) you can. The downside: Several theme elements don't appear properly in older browsers that don't understand style sheets. I talk in detail about what style sheets are and how they work in Chapter 12.

7. Click OK.

The dialog box closes, and FrontPage applies the theme to your Web site. (This takes a few moments.)

Now for the fun part. Open one of your formerly plain pages to see what a difference a theme makes.

If you don't like what you see, return to the Themes dialog box and change the theme's settings. Or, if you want to remove the theme from your Web site, in the dialog box's list box, click [No Theme], and then click OK to apply the changes to your site.

If you apply themes to your site and then remove the themes later, the theme graphics and elements still take up file space in your Web site. FrontPage can remove unused themes for you. To do so, choose View➪Reports➪ Site Summary to view the Site Summary Report. In the report, click Unused Themes. The Recalculate Hyperlinks dialog box appears making sure you know what you're doing. Click Yes to close the dialog box and remove the unused theme files from your Web site.

The FrontPage/Office program CD comes with a bunch of additional themes; to install them on your computer, double-click [Install Additional Themes] in the Themes dialog box's list box, and then follow the directions that appear on your screen.

Modifying Themes

You can easily modify the colors, graphics, and text styles of any of the FrontPage themes. With a little creativity and a few custom graphics, you can even create your own personalized theme.

The following sections show you how to modify existing FrontPage themes. To create your own theme, you can start with an existing theme, modify it to suit your taste, and then save the theme under a different name. (Read on to find out how.)

Modifying theme colors

To change the theme's color scheme, follow these steps:

1. **Choose Format⇨Theme.**

   The Themes dialog box appears.

2. **In the dialog box's list box, click the name of the theme you want to modify, and then click Modify.**

   New buttons appear inside the Themes dialog box, enabling you to customize different aspects of the theme (see Figure 11-4).

Figure 11-4:
New buttons in the Themes dialog box enable you to modify the theme.

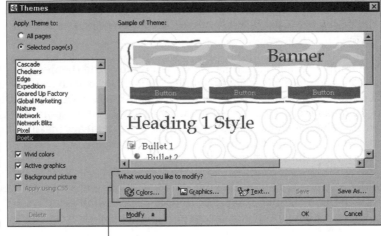

Click a button to modify the theme.

3. **Click the Colors button.**

   The Modify Theme dialog box appears (see Figure 11-5). This dialog box contains options for changing the theme's colors.

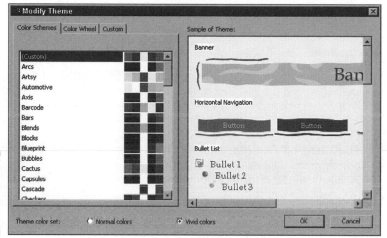

Figure 11-5:
Modifying
the theme's
colors

4. To change the theme's overall color scheme, click the color scheme you like in the dialog box's Color Schemes tab.

After you click a color scheme, you can get an idea for how the theme will look by looking at the preview in the Sample of Theme box. If you prefer a more vivid version of the color scheme, click the Vivid Colors option button at the bottom of the dialog box.

5. To change the theme's hue or brightness, click the Color Wheel tab, and then change the settings of the color wheel or the Brightness meter.

To use the color wheel, click the little circle pointer inside the wheel, and then drag the pointer to an area of the wheel that contains the hue you want. For example, if you want the theme to take on a yellowish hue, drag the circle pointer to the yellow area of the wheel. The Colors in This Scheme grid displays the color change, and, as always, the Sample of Theme box displays how the change looks inside the theme.

To change the theme's brightness, click the Brightness meter and drag it to the left (to decrease brightness) or right (to increase brightness).

6. To change the colors of individual theme elements, click the Custom tab, and then choose options from the Item and Color list boxes.

For example, if you want to change the theme's Heading 1 color, choose Heading 1 from the Item list box, and choose the color you want from the Color list box. Alternatively, you can choose More Colors to display the Color dialog box. (For details on how to use this dialog box, see Chapter 4.)

7. Click OK to close the Modify Theme dialog box.

The Themes dialog box comes into view again.

8. Click OK.

The Microsoft FrontPage dialog box pops open asking if you want to save the changes you just made. If you change your mind, click No, and FrontPage will forget any changes you made. Otherwise . . .

9. Click Yes.

The Microsoft FrontPage dialog box closes, and the Save Theme dialog box appears. Because each FrontPage theme is read-only, the dialog box prompts you to choose a new theme name.

10. In the dialog box's text box, type a new theme name, and then click OK.

The Save Theme and Themes dialog boxes close, and FrontPage saves and applies the theme changes.

If you later decide you want to return to the theme's original color scheme, follow the directions listed in this section, and in Step 4, click the color scheme associated with the theme, and then click OK.

Choosing different theme graphics

You can replace any of the theme's graphics with your own. Say you want a theme to display a page banner of your own design, or a custom horizontal rule graphic. No problem. You can also change the characteristics of the text that appears on top of page banners and link bar buttons. To do so, follow these steps:

1. Choose Format⇨Theme to display the Themes dialog box.

2. In the dialog box's list box, click the name of the theme you want to modify, and then click Modify.

3. Click the Graphics button.

The Modify Theme dialog box appears, this time containing options that control the theme's graphics.

4. From the Item list box, choose the name of the graphic you want to replace.

Based on the graphic you choose, options pertaining to that graphic appear in the dialog box's Picture tab. Also, a sample of the graphic element you selected pops to the top of the theme preview, which is visible in the Sample of Theme box.

5. **At the bottom of the dialog box, click the option button that corresponds to the graphic set you want to modify.**

   You can modify either the Normal graphics set or the Active graphics set.

6. **In the appropriate text box(es), type the filename and location of the graphic you want to use, or click Browse to select a graphic by using the Select Picture dialog box.**

   If you're not sure how to use the Select Picture dialog box, see Chapter 6.

7. **To change the style of the text that appears on top of page banners and link bar buttons, click the Font tab, and then choose the options you want.**

   Note: If the options in the Font tab appear dimmed, then the type of graphic that is visible in the Item list box doesn't have associated text. To make the tab active, from the Item list box, choose an option that has associated text (such as Banner or Global Navigation Buttons) and proceed.

8. **Click OK to close the Modify Theme dialog box.**

9. **In the Themes dialog box, click OK.**

   The Microsoft FrontPage dialog box prompts you to save the changes you just made.

10. **Click Yes.**

    The dialog box closes, and the Save Theme dialog box appears.

11. **In the dialog box's text box, type a new theme name, and then click OK.**

    The Save Theme and Themes dialog boxes close, and FrontPage saves and applies the theme changes.

Changing theme text styles

You can easily change a theme's choices of body and heading text font. To do so, follow these steps:

1. **Choose Format⇨Theme to display the Themes dialog box.**

2. **In the dialog box's list box, click the name of the theme you want to modify, and then click Modify.**

3. **Click the Text button.**

   The Modify Theme dialog box appears, this time containing options that control text style.

4. **From the Item list box, choose the text element you want to change.**

5. **From the Font list box, click the name of the font you want to use for the element visible in the Item list box.**

If you choose an unusual or custom font, keep in mind that only those visitors with that particular font installed on their computers can see the font change. (To the rest, text will appear in the browser's default font.) As a backup, consider choosing a second, similar font that will display if the first font isn't present on the visitor's computer. To do so, in the Font text box, type the first font choice followed by a comma, and then the second font choice (for example, type **Arial, Helvetica**).

6. **Click OK to close the Modify Theme dialog box.**

7. **In the Themes dialog box, click OK.**

The Microsoft FrontPage dialog box prompts you to save the changes you just made.

8. **Click Yes.**

The dialog box closes, and the Save Theme dialog box appears.

9. **In the dialog box's text box, type a new theme name, and then click OK.**

The Save Theme and Themes dialog boxes close, and FrontPage saves and applies the theme changes.

You can, in fact, change any aspect of a theme's text style by clicking the More Styles button in the Modify Theme dialog box. By doing so, you call forth the powerful Styles dialog box, which I explain in Chapter 12.

Chapter 12

Eye-Popping Extras: Multimedia, Dynamic HTML, and Style Sheets

● ●

In This Chapter

▶ Adding video and sound to your Web site

▶ Getting fancy with Dynamic HTML

▶ Positioning objects in your page

▶ Working with style sheets

● ●

*N*ot so long ago, all Web pages looked like flat, gray screens full of text, with maybe a picture or two to liven things up. The most exciting design effect back then was the horizontal line.

Needless to say, times have changed. The Internet, formerly the domain of techies, is now a mainstream information source, shopping mall, and playground all rolled into one. Today's Internet brings sound, video, animation, and stunning design to computer screens the world over.

Unfortunately, cutting-edge design effects generally rely on advanced HTML knowledge and (sometimes) programming expertise, which puts these effects out of reach for most novice Web designers. Even accomplished designers must slog through new and meagerly documented HTML code with little direction and lots of willingness to experiment. Not a task for the faint of heart.

Once again, FrontPage steps in with a slew of design goodies, all usable with a few points and clicks. You can add sound effects and video clips to your Web site, you can tap into the power of Dynamic HTML, and you can even design your pages using style sheets.

As sexy as these extras are, they're entirely optional. The most effective Web sites use special effects to enhance already-strong content and good design. Too many bells and whistles can dull the site's overall impact.

Fun with Multimedia

Multimedia is the ubiquitous term used to lump together the jumble of electronically transmittable media formats. More often than not, when used on the Web, multimedia refers to video and sounds. In this section, I show you how to include both in your Web site.

Keep in mind that only advanced browsers are able to display and play multimedia files. Some older browsers are able to work with multimedia by launching a separate program called a *helper application* to play the file, but other browsers are unable to deal with multimedia at all.

One last detail to remember: Because they pack so much information, multimedia files tend toward chubbiness and, therefore, take a long time to load. For an indication of how much load time each addition tacks onto your page, glance at the Estimated Time to Download box on the right side of the FrontPage status bar.

Fun with video

If a picture says a thousand words, a video clip . . . well, you know.

Even though Netscape Navigator is perfectly able to play multimedia files, the HTML tags that FrontPage adds to your page are specific to Internet Explorer. In the following sections, I describe cross-browser workarounds. The workarounds are tedious but worthwhile as they enable more visitors to enjoy your site in its full glory.

If you want to know more about the video-to-Web process (including how to work with streaming video formats such as RealVideo and Microsoft NetShow), see the Builder.com article "How to Add Video to Your Site" at www.builder.com/Graphics/Video/index.html.

You have two basic options for including video in your site: You can provide users with a hyperlink leading to the video file (causing the video appears in its own window), or you can embed the video in the page, much like a regular picture.

To display the video in its own window, import the video file into your Web site and then create a hyperlink directly to the file. That way, only those visitors who want to see the video will click the link and wait for the download. Chapter 14 explains how to import files, and Chapter 5 shows you how to create hyperlinks.

To embed the video into your page, read on for instructions.

Inserting a video for Netscape Navigator and Internet Explorer users

To embed a video clip that is visible to users of both Internet Explorer (Version 2.0 or later) and Netscape Navigator (Version 3.0 or later), you must use one of FrontPage's so-called Advanced Controls. The control I explain here works for all sorts of multimedia file types that have corresponding *plug-ins* (little programs built into the Web browser) that can play the file. If you insert videos using this method, you can use any video file format that either Web browser is able to display (popular formats include MPEG, AVI, and QuickTime).

1. **Place the cursor in the page where you want the video clip to appear, and then choose Insert⇨Web Component (or, click the Web Component button on the Standard toolbar).**

   The Insert Web Component dialog box appears

2. **In the dialog box's Component Type list box, scroll down to the bottom of the list, and then click Advanced Controls.**

   A list of advanced controls appears in the Choose a Control box on the right side of the dialog box.

3. **In the Choose a Control box, double-click Plug-In.**

   The Insert Web Component dialog box closes, and the Plug-In Properties dialog box appears (see Figure 12-1).

Figure 12-1:
The Plug-In Properties dialog box.

4. **In the dialog box's Data Source text box, type the URL of the video file (or click Browse to locate the file in your Web site, elsewhere on your computer, or on the Web).**

5. **If you want a message to appear in place of the video in browsers without support for that file type, type the message in the Message for Browsers without Plug-In Support text box.**

6. **To adjust the dimensions of the video display area inside the page, type new width and height values (in pixels) in the Height and Width text boxes.**

By default, the original video file dimensions appear in the Height and Width text boxes.

7. **Mark the Hide Plug-In check box if you don't want a plug-in icon to appear in your Web page.**

When viewed with a Web browser, some plug-ins are displayed as icons before the actual plug-in file downloads and is visible. By marking the Hide Plug-in check box, no icon appears.

8. **Choose an option from the Alignment list box.**

Refer to Chapter 6 for a description of each alignment option.

9. **If you want the video to be surrounded by a black border, type the border thickness (in pixels) in the Border thickness text box.**

As of this writing, borders are visible only in Netscape Navigator and Internet Explorer (Version 4.0 or later).

10. **In the Horizontal Spacing text box, type the number of pixels of blank space separating the video from text to its right or left.**

11. **In the Vertical Spacing text box, type the number of pixels of blank space separating the video from text sitting above or below the video.**

12. **Click OK.**

The dialog box closes, and the plug-in icon appears in your page.

To see how the video looks in your Web page, preview your page in a Web browser. (You must have the appropriate plug-in program installed, and your Web browser must be configured to work with the plug-in.)

If the plug-in file is located elsewhere on your computer, the Save Embedded Files dialog box appears the next time you save the page. Refer to Chapter 2 for instructions on how to use this dialog box.

Inserting a video only for Internet Explorer users

The steps in this section explain how to embed a video clip visible only for users of Internet Explorer (Version 2.0 or later). The only time you'd want to use such a browser-specific effect is if you're sure all your visitors use the same browser, as may be the case for a corporate intranet site.

Note: If you insert a video into your page using the following method, your video must be stored as an AVI, ASF, or RealMedia file.

1. **In the page, place the cursor where you want the video to appear.**

2. **Choose Insert➪Picture➪Video.**

The Video dialog box appears. This dialog box works just like the Picture dialog box, which I explain in Chapter 6.

3. **In the dialog box, choose the video file you want to display and then click OK.**

   The dialog box closes, and the video appears in your page. The video doesn't move when viewed in Page View. To see the animation, preview the page using FrontPage's built-in Preview, or use Internet Explorer.

After you insert a video into your page, you can tinker with some of its properties, such as how many times the video repeats and when the video begins playing. To adjust a video's properties, follow these steps:

1. **In the page, right-click the video, and choose Picture Properties from the pop-up menu that appears.**

   The Picture Properties dialog box appears with the Video tab visible (see Figure 12-2).

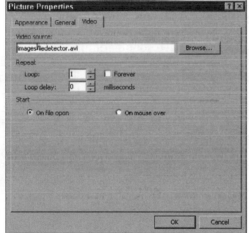

Figure 12-2:
The Video tab of the Picture Properties dialog box.

2. **In the dialog box's Loop box, specify the number of times you want the video to repeat.**

   If you want the clip to keep playing until the visitor leaves the page, mark the Forever check box.

3. **In the Loop Delay text box, specify the number of milliseconds you want the video to pause before repeating.**

   I know that it's hard to conceive of the length of a millisecond. Just do your best. A good reference point: 1,000 milliseconds equals a second.

4. **In the Start area, click the check box next to the event that triggers the video to start playing.**

The On File Open option causes the video to play as soon as a visitor arrives. The On Mouse Over option causes the video to play as soon as the pointer passes over the video. Mark both check boxes to have the video begin playing when the visitor arrives and then repeat as soon as the pointer passes over the video.

5. **Click OK to close the dialog box.**

   To see the video in action, preview your page.

If the video file is stored outside the Web site, the Save Embedded Files dialog box appears the next time you save the page. Refer to Chapter 2 for instructions on how to use this dialog box.

Music to your ears

As with video, you can add music and other audio effects to your site by linking to audio files, or by embedding audio files directly into a page.

To hear sounds, your visitors must have sound equipment (a sound card and speakers) installed on their computers along with an advanced Web browser that is able to play sounds. The two most popular choices are Internet Explorer (Version 3.0 or later) and Netscape Navigator (Version 3.0 and later).

Don't have an audio file to add to your page? No problem. You can download any number of clips, from animal sounds to movie quotes to household noises. A sound archive such as soundamerica.com can get you started. If you want to record your own sounds, see builder.cnet.com/Authoring/Audio for a discussion of the process. This article also explains the difference between conventional audio (in which the entire sound file must be downloaded to the user's computer before it can be played) and streaming audio (in which the sound plays as it downloads).

Most often, you'll include sound in your Web site by linking directly to the sound file. This way, users who want to hear the sound can click the link, and the rest can go about their business. To link to a sound, import the sound file into your Web site and then create a hyperlink directly to the file. Chapter 14 explains how to import files, and Chapter 5 shows you how to create hyperlinks.

Embedded sounds (also known as *background sounds*) play as soon as someone arrives. This feature can be charming if (and only if) you choose a short, pleasant sound bite. Choose wisely, because loud, grating music annoys visitors more than it entertains.

Though Netscape Navigator can play background sounds, the sound-related HTML tags that FrontPage adds to your page are specific to Internet Explorer. In the following sections, I explain how to insert sounds in two ways: The first method creates background sounds that can be heard using both browsers, and the second method is limited to an Internet Explorer-only audience. Choose the method that fits your target audience.

Inserting a background sound for Netscape Navigator and Internet Explorer users

For both Internet Explorer and Netscape Navigator users to be able to hear background sounds, you must first import the sound file into your Web site (see Chapter 14 for instructions). Be sure your sound file is saved using the WAV, AIFF, or AU format, because both Internet Explorer (Version 3.0 or later) and Netscape Navigator (Version 3.0 and later) can play these types of files.

Next, you must add a snippet of HTML code to your page. Just follow these steps:

1. **Place the cursor at or near the bottom of the page, and then choose Insert⇨Web Component (or, click the Web Component button on the Standard toolbar).**

   (Placing the cursor at the bottom of the page enables users to see the page while the background sound file downloads.)

   The Insert Web Component dialog box appears.

2. **In the dialog box's Component Type list box, scroll down to the bottom of the list, and then click Advanced Controls.**

   A list of advanced controls appears in the Choose a Control box on the right side of the dialog box.

3. **In the Choose a Control box, double-click HTML.**

   The Insert Web Component dialog box closes and the HTML Markup dialog box appears.

4. **In the dialog box's HTML Markup to Insert box, type the following bit of code, but replace** sound.wav **with the name and location of your sound file:**

   ```
   <BGSOUND SRC="sound.wav"><EMBED SRC="sound.wav"
            HIDDEN="true" AUTOPLAY="true" AUTOSTART="true">
   ```

   Note: My example assumes the sound file is stored in the same folder as the Web page in which you're inserting the sound. If not (say the sound file is stored in a subfolder), indicate the file location by listing the name of the subfolder followed by a slash and then the filename (for example, foldername/sound.wav). Be sure to update this location in both the BGSOUND and EMBED tags.

5. **Click OK.**

   The dialog box closes, and all is well.

Be sure to preview the page using both browsers to make sure the sound plays properly. (This action works only if you have sound equipment installed on your computer.)

Inserting a background sound only for Internet Explorer users

If you follow the steps in this section, the HTML FrontPage inserts into your page only works when the page is viewed using Internet Explorer. To insert a background sound using this method, follow these steps:

1. **With the page open in Page View, choose <u>F</u>ile⇨Proper<u>t</u>ies.**

   The Page Properties dialog box appears. You specify the page's background sound using options in the Background Sound section of the General tab.

2. **In the dialog box's Location text box, type the filename and location of the sound file you want to use.**

   Or click Browse to choose a sound file from the Background Sound dialog box.

3. **If you want to control how many times the sound plays, click to unmark the Forever check box and type a number in the Loop text box.**

   I don't recommend using the Forever option. Having a sound play over and over drives visitors nuts.

4. **Click OK.**

   The Page Properties dialog box closes.

To hear the sound, preview your page using the FrontPage Preview or Internet Explorer. (This action works only if you have sound equipment installed on your computer.)

If the sound file is located elsewhere on your computer, the Save Embedded Files dialog box appears the next time you save the page. Refer to Chapter 2 for instructions on how to use this dialog box.

Adding Pizzazz with Dynamic HTML

Dynamic HTML enables you to apply effects and animation to just about any object in your page. For example, you can use Dynamic HTML to cause a word to change color when a visitor passes the pointer over the word. Or when a visitor clicks a picture, Dynamic HTML can cause a different picture to appear in its place.

Dynamic HTML effects are impressive. Unfortunately, the effects are visible only in Internet Explorer Version 4.0 or later and Netscape Navigator 4.0 or later. Furthermore, Netscape's interpretation of Dynamic HTML differs in fundamental ways from Microsoft's, resulting in browser-specific differences. If you use Dynamic HTML in your site, be sure to preview using both browsers to make sure everything works as you expect.

To use Dynamic HTML in your site, follow these steps:

1. **In the page, select the object to which you want to apply a Dynamic HTML effect.**

   Highlight a word, click a picture, or select any other object you want to jazz up.

2. **Choose Format⇨Dynamic HTML Effects.**

   The DHTML Effects toolbar appears (see Figure 12-3)

Figure 12-3:
The DHTML
Effects
toolbar.

3. **On the DHTML Effects toolbar, choose the event that triggers the effect from the On list box.**

   Your choices are Click, Double Click, Mouse Over (when the visitor passes the pointer over the object), or Page Load (when the page first opens in the visitor's browser window).

   Note: Only those options that work with the object you selected in Step 1 are visible in the list box.

4. **From the Apply list box, choose the effect you want to apply to the object.**

   The effects visible in this list box change based on the selected object type and trigger event. If you're not sure how an effect looks, try it out. You can always change the setting later.

   If the effect you choose requires additional settings (not all do), the <Choose Settings> list box appears on the DHTML Effects toolbar.

5. **From the <Choose Settings> list box, choose your desired setting.**

And that's it! Save and preview the page to watch Dynamic HTML in action. (Be sure to preview using both Internet Explorer and Netscape Navigator to see how the effect looks in both browsers.)

 To easily distinguish between regular objects in your page and those spiffed up with Dynamic HTML, click the Highlight Dynamic HTML Effects button on the DHTML Effects toolbar. Those objects embellished with DHTML appear color-coded with a light blue background. (This effect is only visible in FrontPage. When viewed with a Web browser, nothing changes.)

To remove Dynamic HTML effects from an object, click the object and then click the Remove Effect button.

 For more information about what Dynamic HTML is and what it can do, visit msdn.microsoft.com/workshop/c-frame.htm#/workshop/author/default.asp.

Positioning Stuff in Your Page

One limitation above all others gets the collective goat of Web designers: the inability to precisely position an object inside a page. If you want to stick, say, a picture in the middle of the page, you either have to wrestle with invisible tables (which are, themselves, rife with limitations), or you have to play fast-and-loose with HTML, commandeering tags to produce effects for which the tags were never intended.

The spirits of the technology heavens heard our prayers (or was it our banging fists?) and came up with a set of positioning commands that control object placement. Objects, be they paragraphs, pictures, or any other thing sitting inside a Web page, will never look the same way again.

 Of course, like other emerging Web design technologies, positioning comes with major strings attached. Positioning requires that the visitor's browser knows how to process a version of cascading style sheet commands known as CSS 2.0. (I talk more about style sheets later in this chapter.) As of this writing, the two most popular choices are Microsoft Internet Explorer (Version 4.0 or later) and Netscape Navigator (Version 4.0 or later). Older browsers ignore the positioning commands and place the object in line with other objects in the page.

Furthermore, Netscape and Internet Explorer interpret certain positioning commands differently, resulting in browser-specific variations. If you use positioning in your Web site, be sure to preview your pages using both browsers, and prepare yourself for different results.

Your fallback is to stick to using invisible tables as layout guides (see Chapter 8 for details about tables). Because more browsers are able to display tables properly, this option works more consistently.

The bottom line is this: Use positioning features at your own risk. As browsers evolve, positioning effects promise to become the standard for layout control inside Web pages, far surpassing tables in flexibility and features. Until then, watch for bugs.

You have several choices for how to position an object. You can use positioning commands to create *floating objects*. You can also position objects *relative* to the object's initial position, or *absolutely* (without regard for the object's initial position).

Creating a floating object

A *floating object* sits in the left or right margin of the page, with surrounding text and page objects wrapping around it. You can float just about anything: a sentence, a paragraph, a picture, or any other object you can insert into a page. Figure 12-4 shows an example of text wrapping around sidebar text

Figure 12-4:
The sidebar in this page is positioned as a floating object.

Sidebar Sidebar

Regular text Regular text

To make an object float, follow these steps:

1. **In the page, select the object you want to position.**

   The object can be some text, a picture, a table, or whatever.

2. **Choose Format⇨Position.**

   The Position dialog box appears, as shown in Figure 12-5.

3. **In the Wrapping Style area of the dialog box, click the option that looks like the wrapping style you want.**

   Left floats the object over to the left margin, with the rest of the page content wrapping around the right side of the object, and Right floats the object over to the right margin, with the rest of the page content wrapping around the left side of the object.

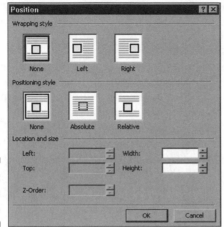

Figure 12-5:
The Position
dialog box.

4. **Click OK.**

   The dialog box closes, and, in the page, size handles appear around the object. (Look closely because they may be hard to see.) The size handles define the *position box* that now surrounds the object. A position box is a like an invisible container inside which positioned objects sit.

5. **In the page, resize the position box by clicking one of the size handles and dragging it until the object is the size you want.**

   If you prefer to use more precise measurements, open the Positioning toolbar by choosing View⇨Toolbars⇨Positioning, and then type pixel values in the toolbar's Width and Height boxes.

The Page View doesn't always display positioned objects correctly. To see positioning in effect, I recommend previewing the page using both Internet Explorer and Netscape Navigator to see how the page looks in both browsers.

Using absolute positioning

When you absolutely position an object, FrontPage uses the page's top and left margins as its reference points. For example, if you tell FrontPage to absolutely position a picture 50 pixels from the top of the page and 100 pixels from the page's left margin, FrontPage places the picture at that location no matter what. If another object already occupies the spot (say the page is filled with text), the picture plops itself on top of the current occupant (see Figure 12-6).

The implications are exciting: Imagine layering several objects, one on top of the other or laying a descriptive paragraph over a picture.

Regular text Regular text Regular text Regular text Regular text Regular text
Regular text Regular text Regular text Regular text Regular text Regular text
Regular text Re   egular text Regular text Regular text Regular text
Regular text Re   egular text Regular text Regular text Regular text
Regular text Re   egular text Regular text Regular text Regular text
Regular text Re   egular text Regular text Regular text Regular text
Regular text Re   egular text Regular text Regular text Regular text
Regular text Regular text Regular text Regular text Regular text Regular text

Regular text Regular text Regular text Regular text Regular text Regular text
Regular text Regular text Regular text Regular text Regular text Regular text
Regular text Regular text Regular text Regular text Regular text Regular text
Regular text Regular text Regular text Regular text Regular text Regular text
Regular text Regular text Regular text Regular text Regular text Regular text
Regular text Regular text Regular text Regular text Regular text Regular text
Regular text Regular text Regular text Regular text Regular text Regular text
Regular text Regular text Regular text Regular text Regular text Regular text

Figure 12-6:
The picture
in this page
is absolutely
positioned.

You can even control the order in which objects stack up (known in Web lingo as the object's *z-index*). By default, the most recently placed object sits on top, but you can easily change the setting.

The easiest way to place an object absolutely is to drag it into place using your pointer. Here's how:

1. **In the page, select the object you want to position.**

2. **If it's not already visible, open the Positioning toolbar by choosing View⇒Toolbars⇒Positioning.**

3. **Click the Position Absolutely button on the Positioning toolbar.**

   A position box with size handles appears around the selected object, and any surrounding objects move to fill in the spot where the selected object previously sat.

   When you absolutely position an object, the object now sits "on top" of the other objects in the page. (It's as though you lifted the object onto a transparent level hovering above the other objects.)

4. **If you like, resize the position box by clicking one of the box's size handles and then dragging it to the desired size.**

5. **Move the pointer over a position box boundary until the cursor turns into a four-pointed arrow, and then click and drag the object to whatever position in the page you want.**

6. **To change the object's z-index, type a value in the Z-Index box or click the Bring Forward or Send Backward buttons on the Positioning toolbar.**

   When you stack objects on top of each other, you can specify which item sits on top of the layering order by specifying the object's z-index. A negative number moves the object deeper in the stack, and a positive number moves the object higher in the stack. A z-index of 0 places the object in the same layer as the rest of the page's content.

If the concept of a z-index is a little too abstract to grasp, click the Bring Forward or Send Backward buttons to achieve the effect you want.

7. When you're finished, click elsewhere in the page to deselect the object.

The Page View isn't always able to display positioned objects correctly. To see positioning in effect, I recommend previewing the page using both Internet Explorer and Netscape Navigator to see how the page looks in both browsers.

Furthermore, be sure to check how the page looks in browser windows of different sizes. The placement of an absolutely positioned object is fixed on the page, but the rest of the page content rearranges itself depending on the size of the browser window. Therefore, you might see effects you don't expect.

To change the positioning properties of an object, select the object you want to change, and then enter new values in the appropriate places on the Positioning toolbar.

Using relative positioning

Relative positioning means that FrontPage determines the placement of an object based on its initial position in the page's text flow instead of based on the margins of the page. An example will help illustrate the concept. The page in Figure 12-7 contains no relatively positioned objects. Like any other Web page, each item sits inside the page after the item before it.

Relative Positioning

Relative Positioning

Regular text Regular text Regular text Regular text Regular text Regular text
Regular text Regular text Regular text Regular text Regular text Regular text
Regular text Regular text Regular text Regular text Regular text Regular text
Regular text Regular text Regular text Regular text Regular text Regular text
Regular text Regular text Regular text Regular text Regular text Regular text
Regular text Regular text Regular text Regular text Regular text Regular text
Regular text Regular text Regular text Regular text Regular text Regular text
Regular text Regular text Regular text Regular text Regular text Regular text

Regular text Regular text Regular text Regular text Regular text Regular text
Regular text Regular text Regular text Regular text Regular text Regular text
Regular text Regular text Regular text Regular text Regular text Regular text
Regular text Regular text Regular text Regular text Regular text Regular text

Figure 12-7:
A Web page with no relatively positioned objects.

In Figure 12-8, however, I applied relative positioning to the first instance in the page of the words *Relative Positioning*. I told FrontPage to move those words 65 pixels down from their original position. Not only did FrontPage nudge the words down, causing them to sit on top of the second instance of the words, it left a blank spot in the page where the words used to sit.

Figure 12-8:
I used
relative
positioning
to make two
lines of text
overlap.

Relative positioning is less flexible than absolute positioning (described in the previous section), but can create interesting visual effects even so.

To relatively position an object, follow these steps:

1. **In the page, select the object you want to position.**

2. **Choose Format⇨Position.**

   The Position dialog box appears.

3. **In the Positioning Style section of the dialog box, click Relative.**

4. **In the Left box, type the number of pixels you want to move the object to the left.**

   If you would rather eyeball the object's position, skip Steps 4 and 5, and later, type values in the Left and Top boxes of the Positioning toolbar.

5. **In the Top box, type the number of pixels you want to move the object down from its original position.**

   A positive number moves the object down, and a negative number moves the object up.

6. **To resize the position box surrounding the object, type new numbers in the Width and Height boxes.**

   Or skip this step and, after you're finished working in this dialog box, resize the position box by hand by dragging the box's size handles.

7. **In the Z-Index box, type a value that moves the object's placement in the layering order.**

    Or when you're finished, change the object's layering order by selecting the object in the page and clicking the Bring Forward or Send Backward buttons on the Positioning toolbar.

8. **Click OK.**

    The dialog box closes, and FrontPage positions the object in the page.

The Page View can't always display positioned objects correctly. To see positioning in effect, I recommend previewing the page using both Internet Explorer and Netscape Navigator to see how the page looks in both browsers.

To change the positioning properties of an object, select the object you want to change, and then enter new values in the appropriate places on the Positioning toolbar.

Working with Style Sheets

I've saved the most powerful extra for last: *cascading style sheets* or *CSS* (in FrontPage, referred to simply as *style sheets*). Style sheets enable you to create new styles and to modify the standard HTML style definitions that come with FrontPage.

If you're a Microsoft Word user, styles may not seem like such a big deal. After all, word-processing styles have been around for years. Styles in Web pages, on the other hand, are relatively new. Until recently, Web designers were stuck with the standard effects produced by HTML. Style sheets open every HTML tag to modification, taking you beyond each tag's inherent abilities.

For example, if you're not satisfied with the staid appearance of the Heading 1 paragraph style (big, bold, plain text), you can use style sheets to define the Heading 1 style however you like. If you want all text formatted with the Heading 1 style to appear as magenta, 36-point, underlined, and blinking text, so be it.

Style sheets are especially useful if more than one author works on a site. Because the site's formatting instructions are stored in the style sheet, individual authors can concentrate on the page's content and can later apply the style sheet to take care of the stylistic details.

Style sheets are capable of much more than I demonstrate here. FrontPage gives you powerful access to style sheets, but to use style sheets to their fullest potential, you must be fluent in both HTML and style sheet syntax. So, think of this section as an introduction to the wonders of style sheets . . . you may very well be seduced into finding out more.

For more information about style sheets, turn to the World Wide Web. Go to www.webreview.com/style/index.shtml (for starters). Also, be sure to look at the style sheet coverage in the FrontPage Help system (available when you choose Help➪Microsoft FrontPage Help).

Creating and modifying styles in the current page

The Style dialog box (shown in Figure 12-9) enables you to embed a style sheet in the page currently open in Page View. You access the Style dialog box by choosing Format➪Style.

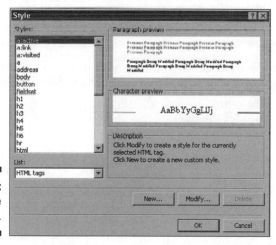

Figure 12-9:
The Style
dialog box.

In the dialog box, the Styles list box contains all the HTML tags you can modify using style sheet commands. I realize you probably don't know HTML, and you're not interested in learning it this very moment. So, in Table 12-1, I list a few of the tags that control the elements you most likely want to change. For example, after you modify the style of the b tag (the tag that creates bold text), FrontPage refers to your style sheet for instructions each time you tell FrontPage to apply bold formatting to text.

Table 12-1	Quickie HTML Tag Reference
This HTML Tag . . .	*. . . Controls This Aspect of the Page*
a	Hyperlink color
b	Bold text
body	Default text color, page background color
h1–h6	Heading 1 through Heading 6 paragraph styles
i	Italic text
ol	Numbered lists
p	Default paragraph text
ul	Bulleted lists

To embed a style sheet inside the page currently open in Page View, follow these steps:

1. **With the cursor sitting anywhere inside the page, choose Format⇨ Style.**

   The Style dialog box appears.

2. **Click the tag you want to modify in the Styles list box, and then click the Modify button. Or, to create a new style, click the New button.**

   Depending on which button you click, either the Modify Style or the New Style dialog box appears. Aside from their names, the dialog boxes are identical, so the instructions that follow apply to both.

3. **In the dialog box's Name (Selector) text box, type a one-word name. (If you are modifying the style of an existing HTML tag, skip this step).**

4. **To define the style, click the Format button, and choose the category of style change that you want to create from the menu that appears.**

   You can choose from the following categories:

   - **Font:** Affects typeface, font size, attributes, letter spacing, and font color
   - **Paragraph:** Affects alignment, indentation, and word/line spacing
   - **Border:** Affects borders, white space around paragraphs, and background and foreground colors
   - **Numbering:** Affects the appearance of bulleted or numbered lists

The category you choose determines the resulting dialog box that appears.

5. **From the dialog box, select the options you want, and then click OK.**

   If you're not sure how to use the dialog box, see Chapter 4; these are the same dialog boxes that appear if you choose corresponding commands in the Format menu.

   After you click OK, the dialog box closes, and the Style dialog box comes back into view.

6. **If you like, define more styles by repeating Steps 2–5, or click OK to close the dialog box.**

   FrontPage applies the new style definitions to the current page.

If you later want to change the style definitions you've set up, choose Format➪Style. In the Styles dialog box, choose User-Defined Styles from the List box. Then, click the style you want to change in the Styles list box, and follow Steps 2–6 in the previous set of steps.

You can also apply style sheet effects to single instances of an object or effect. You may already have noticed the Style button sitting quietly in many of FrontPage's Properties dialog boxes. To apply a style sheet effect to a particular object, right-click the object, and from the pop-up menu that appears, choose the Properties command pertinent to that object (for example, if you right-click a word with the intention of changing its font, choose Font Properties). In the Properties dialog box that appears, click the Style button to bring up the Modify Style dialog box, and then follow the steps above (starting from Step 4).

Applying styles to more than one page in your site

The technique for applying a style sheet to more than one page in your site (or across the entire site) differs from embedding a style sheet inside a single page. In this case, you must create or have access to a separate style sheet file, which you then link to the pages to which you want the style sheet to apply.

Creating the style sheet

If you already have access to a style sheet file — say your company provides a standard style sheet to everyone building company-sponsored pages — import the file into your Web site, and skip to the next section (see Chapter 14 for details on how to import an existing file into a Web site).

If you don't have access to a ready-made style sheet, you don't have to start from scratch. FrontPage contains templates for several style sheets, all of which coordinate with different FrontPage themes. To create a new style sheet by using a template, follow these steps:

1. **Choose File⇨New⇨Page or Web.**

   If it's not already visible, the Task Pane appears on the right side of the FrontPage window.

2. **In the New from Template section of the Task Pane, click Page Templates.**

   The Page Templates dialog box appears with the General tab visible.

3. **In the dialog box, click the Style Sheets tab to display the list of style sheet templates, and then double-click the template you want to use.**

   The dialog box closes, and the style sheet appears in Page View. Also, the Style toolbar (containing a single button: Style) appears floating inside the FrontPage window.

Don't be put off by all the style sheet's codes and brackets; you don't need to type anything into the page at all. You can modify the style sheet using the Style dialog box. (To access the dialog box, click the Style button on the Style toolbar; see the previous section of this chapter for instructions on how to use the Style dialog box.) When you're done, save the page as part of your Web site (the process is the same as saving a regular Web page).

If you know HTML and style sheet syntax, the more straightforward course is to create a new blank page, type up your own style sheet, and save the page as part of your Web site (be sure to specify in the Save As dialog box that FrontPage is to save the file as a Hypertext Style Sheet).

Linking the style sheet to the rest of your site

Now that the style sheet is tucked away in your site, you must link the style sheet to those pages in your site to which you want the style sheet to apply.

To do so, follow these steps:

1. **On the Views bar on the left side of the FrontPage window, click the Folders button.**

   The Folders View becomes visible. (I describe all of FrontPage's views in Chapter 14.)

2. **In the Contents list of the Folders View, while pressing the Ctrl key, click the pages to which you want the style sheet to apply.**

   If you want to apply the style sheet to the entire site, skip this step.

3. Choose Format⇨Style Sheet Links.

The Link Style Sheet dialog box appears.

4. If you want the style sheet to apply to all the pages in your site, mark the All Pages option button in the dialog box.

Otherwise, FrontPage will apply the style sheet to the pages you selected in Step 2.

5. Click the Add button.

The Select Style Sheet dialog box appears.

6. In the dialog box, navigate your Web site's file list until you find the style sheet file, and then double-click the file.

After you double-click the file, the Select Style Sheet dialog box closes, and the Link Style Sheet dialog box comes back into view with the style sheet file listed in the dialog box.

7. Click OK.

The dialog box closes, and FrontPage applies the style sheet to the pages you specified.

You can apply more than one style sheet to selected pages. Here's where the *cascading* part of *cascading style sheets* comes in: FrontPage applies the style sheet definitions, in order and starting with the most recently attached style sheet, to the page. Imagine, for example, that you have two style sheets. The first style sheet contains a background color and a typeface setting, and the second style sheet contains only a different background color setting. If you want to use features from both style sheets, you can apply both to your site. The background color setting from the second style sheet takes precedence (because that style sheet was most recently linked to the Web page), but the typeface setting from the first style sheet appears as well.

Chapter 13

Cool Web Components

In This Chapter

▶ Finding out what Web components can do

▶ Integrating Web components into your site

*N*o longer satisfied with static text and pictures, the Web design community has figured out ways to include interactive features in Web pages. FrontPage harnesses this wave of Web development by transforming complex features into easy-to-use tools called *Web components*. In this chapter, you discover what Web components can do and how to use them in your site.

What's a Web Component?

A Web component is a gizmo that you insert into your Web page to simplify certain Web publishing tasks or to add interactive features to your site.

Before the creation of Web components, if you wanted interactivity, you had to do lots of mucking around with HTML and server-based programs, and you had to coordinate the whole process with your ISP or system administrator. Now you accomplish the same thing in a few mouse clicks.

FrontPage contains the following Web components, each of which performs a different task:

- ✔ **Hover Button:** This Web component creates a button that, when clicked, works like a hyperlink.
- ✔ **Marquee:** This Web component creates scrolling text.
- ✔ **Banner Ad Manager:** If you display banner advertising in your site, this Web component may simplify the process.
- ✔ **Web Search:** Add a keyword search to your site with the help of this Web component.

✔ **Spreadsheets and Charts:** Add functionality to your site with embedded spreadsheets, charts, and PivotTables.

✔ **Hit Counter:** This handy tool helps you keep track of the number of visits a page receives.

✔ **Photo Gallery:** Transform your site into an online digital photo gallery. I explain how to create a Photo Gallery in Chapter 6.

✔ **Included content:** This group of Web components enables you to automate the inclusion of text and pictures into your site.

✔ **Link bars:** These rows of text or graphic hyperlinks help users navigate your site. I explain how to create link bars in Chapter 5.

✔ **Table of Contents:** This Web component generates an automatically updated list of links to all the other pages in your site. (I cover this Web component in more detail in Chapter 5.) Another version can display a list of links to pages based on the pages' categories (I elaborate on this feature in Chapter 15).

✔ **Top 10 List:** This Web component displays interesting information about the people that come to your site, such as the top-10 browser types visitors use, the top-10 search phrases people use to get to your site, and more.

✔ **Additional Web components:** You'll also find Web components that work with Microsoft Web-based services, such as bCentral, MSN, Expedia and MSNBC.

In the following sections, I show you how Web components can simplify your life, and I demonstrate how to put most of the critters to work. Web components aren't without their limitations, which I describe as well. In some cases I suggest alternate ways to include similar functionality.

To work properly, several Web components must team up with a Web server that is outfitted with FrontPage Server Extensions. (I talk about what FrontPage Server Extensions are and what they do in Chapter 16.) I point out specialized server requirements as I go along.

Two additional Web components — List View and Document Library View — work only in Web sites published on Web servers that support Microsoft SharePoint. I talk briefly about SharePoint Team Web sites in Chapter 15.

Inserting a Hover Button

A *hover button* is an animated button that, when clicked, activates a hyperlink. When the visitor moves the pointer over the button before clicking it, the button changes color or shape, and, if you like, can play a sound.

By default, hover buttons are colorful rectangular boxes. If rectangles aren't your style, you can use this Web component to place text on top of a graphic to turn the graphic into a button.

The steps for creating a rectangular versus a graphic button are slightly different, so I describe each task separately in the steps that follow.

Hover buttons are produced using Java applets and therefore require that your visitors use Java-capable browsers.

Creating a rectangular hover button

To create a hover button, follow these steps:

1. **Place the cursor in the page where you want the hover button to appear, and then choose Insert⇨Web Component (or click the Web Component button on the Standard toolbar).**

   The Insert Web Component dialog box appears.

2. **In the Component Type list box, click Dynamic Effects (it may already be selected by default).**

   A list of available effects appears on the right side of the dialog box.

3. **In the Choose an Effect list box, double-click Hover Button.**

   The Insert Web Component dialog box closes, and the Hover Button Properties dialog box appears (see Figure 13-1). Also, a hover button (with the generic label *Button Text*) appears in your page (you might have to move the Hover Button Properties dialog box out of the way to be able to see the hover button).

Figure 13-1:
The Hover
Button
Properties
dialog box.

Hover Button Properties			? ×
Button text:	Button Text		Font...
Link to:			Browse...
Button color:	■ ▼	Background color:	■ Automa ▼
Effect:	Glow ▼	Effect color:	■ ▼
Width:	120	Height:	24
Custom...		OK	Cancel

4. **In the Button Text box, type the text label you want to be visible on top of the button.**

5. **To change the appearance of the label text, click the Font button. (If you don't want to change how the font looks, skip ahead to Step 7.)**

   After you click the Font button, the Font dialog box appears.

6. **Choose your desired font, font style, text size, and text color, and then click OK to close the Font dialog box.**

   (For detailed information about each font effect, see Chapter 4.)

   The Font dialog box closes, and the Hover Button dialog box becomes visible again.

7. **In the Link To text box, type the filename or URL of the page that appears when the hover button is clicked.**

   Or click Browse to choose a page from the Select Hover Button Hyperlink dialog box. This dialog box works exactly like the Create Hyperlink dialog box, which I describe in Chapter 5.

8. **In the Button Color list box, choose a button color.**

9. **In the Effect list box, choose the visual effect you want to appear when the visitor passes the pointer over the button.**

   I won't waste your time describing each effect here. Just pick the effect that sounds like what you want. After you're finished creating the button, you can preview the page to see how the effect looks. If you don't like the effect, you can change this setting.

10. **In the Effect Color list box, choose the color that you want to appear as part of the hover effect.**

11. **Type the button's dimensions in pixels in the Width and Height text boxes.**

    You also can adjust button dimensions by leaving these text boxes alone and resizing the button later by dragging its size handles.

12. **If you want to associate a sound with the hover button, click the Custom button. (If not, click OK to close the dialog box, and you're done!)**

    The Custom dialog box appears.

13. **In the On Click text box, type the filename of the sound file that you want to play after the visitor clicks the button.**

    Or click Browse to choose a sound file using the Select Sound dialog box.

14. **In the On Hover text box, type the filename of the sound file that you want to play after the visitor passes the pointer over the button.**

15. **Click OK.**

    The Custom dialog box closes, and the Hover Button Properties dialog box becomes visible again.

16. **Click OK.**

    The Hover Button Properties dialog box closes, and your hover button is ready to roll.

Creating a graphic hover button

To create a graphic hover button, follow these steps:

1. **Place the cursor in the page where you want the hover button to appear, and then choose Insert⇨Web Component (or click the Web Component button on the Standard toolbar).**

   The Insert Web Component dialog box appears.

2. **In the Component Type list box, click Dynamic Effects (it may already be selected by default).**

   A list of available effects appears on the right side of the dialog box.

3. **In the Choose an Effect list box, double-click Hover Button.**

   The Insert Web Component dialog box closes, and the Hover Button Properties dialog box appears. Also, a hover button (with the generic label *Button Text*) appears in your page (you might have to move the Hover Button Properties dialog box out of the way to be able to see the hover button).

4. **In the Button Text box, type the text label that you want to appear on top of the button.**

   If you don't want text to appear on the button, clear the contents of this text box and skip ahead to Step 7.

5. **To change the appearance of the label text, click the Font button.**

   The Font dialog box appears.

6. **Choose your desired font, font style, text size, and text color, and then click OK to close the dialog box.**

   The Font dialog box closes, and the Hover Button dialog box becomes visible again.

7. **In the Link To text box, type the filename or URL of the page that appears when the hover button is clicked.**

   Or click Browse to choose a page from the Select Hover Button Hyperlink dialog box. (This dialog box works exactly like the Insert Hyperlink dialog box, which I describe in Chapter 5.)

8. **In the Background Color list box, choose a background color for the hover button graphic.**

9. **In the Width and Height text boxes, type the dimensions of the hover button.**

   The hover button feature creates an empty space inside which the button graphic appears. Chances are you want the hover button area to be the same size as the graphic that you're using to create the button. If so, these dimensions should equal the width and height of the graphic.

10. **Click the Custom button.**

    The Custom dialog box appears.

11. **If you want to associate sounds with the button, type the filenames of the sound files that you want to use in the On Click and/or On Hover text boxes.**

    Or click Browse to choose sound files using the Select Sound dialog box.

12. **In the Custom section of the dialog box, type the filename and location of the button graphic in the Button text box.**

    Or click Browse to choose a picture from the Select Picture dialog box.

13. **In the On Hover text box, type the filename of the graphic that you want to appear when the visitor passes the pointer over the button.**

    (Or click Browse . . . and I think you can guess the rest.)

14. **Click OK.**

    The Custom dialog box closes, and the Hover Button Properties dialog box becomes visible again.

15. **Click OK.**

    The Hover Button Properties dialog box closes, and the newly edited hover button appears in the page.

Test your hover button by previewing the page with the Preview tab or by launching your Java-capable Web browser. To edit the hover button in FrontPage, double-click the button in the page to open the Hover Button Properties dialog box.

Creating a Marquee

A *marquee* is a rectangular box that contains scrolling text. Marquees are a fun way to highlight announcements or other important information on your Web pages.

The big bummer is that marquees are visible only in Microsoft Internet Explorer, which limits their utility considerably. If you view a marquee in another browser, the thing just appears as regular text.

I'll go out on a limb here and recommend that you forgo this Web component entirely. Any effect that's so browser-specific is bound to frustrate your visitors, especially effects of the bells-and-whistles variety (as scrolling text is).

Besides, there's more than one way to skin a banana. You can insert a bit of JavaScript code into your page's HTML to add scrolling text to your page. Although JavaScript effects are visible only in newer browsers, at least the use of JavaScript is widespread enough to warrant a wider audience.

To create a JavaScript scrolling text message, you must first copy the JavaScript code (one example is available at `www.javascript-page.com/fbanner.html`). Next, you must paste the code into your page's HTML, and then make changes to the script so the thing looks they way you want.

Of course, this method assumes some level of comfort working with HTML. If you're not HTML-literate, you can purchase a package of JavaScript-based Web components that you can insert in your page using familiar menus and buttons. The two most popular offerings are Webs Unlimited JBOTS (`www.jbots.com`) and A Big Lime's El Scripto (`www.elscripto.com/info/index.htm`). The CD at the back of this book contains an evaluation version of El Scripto — be sure to check it out.

Placing Banner Advertising in Your Site

In the ongoing quest to turn a profit on the Internet, many Web sites help fund operations with *banner ads*. Banner ads are rectangular graphics that encourage visitors to buy a product or service (Figure 13-2 illustrates one example of banner advertising). If your Web site attracts enough daily traffic, you may be able to sell the premium spot at the top of your home page (and other popular pages in your site) to advertisers. Some companies pay a pretty penny for the chance to tout their wares to your visitors.

Figure 13-2: CNN.com sells its top spot to advertisers.

Banner ads also lend a whiff of legitimacy to your site. The clever folks at LinkExchange came up with the idea of letting subscribers swap banner ads with other subscribers in the network. That way, everyone gets the cool look of a rotating banner ad display, plus Web-wide exposure, for free.

FrontPage attempts to help you include banner advertising in your site by providing you with a Web component called the Banner Ad Manager. Helpful in theory, this component creates a rotating display of ads in your site. You control the amount of time each ad appears on the page and the transition effect between ads. In practice however, the Banner Ad Manager doesn't do such a good job. It lacks the crucial ability to link each ad to its own unique Web address, which is why most companies buy ad space in the first place.

More useful is the bCentral Banner Ad component. This Web component hooks you into the LinkExchange Banner Network (now a Microsoft bCentral partner). This Web component not only places the appropriate code into your page's HTML, but also takes you through the process of creating a simple banner graphic for your own site — no experience necessary. In fact, the Web component is so well explained in its various Wizard-style dialog boxes that providing step-by-step instructions here would be redundant. Give this Web component a shot — you'll see just how easy it is to use.

To access the bCentral Banner Network component, choose Insert⇨ Web Component to display the Insert Web Component dialog box. In the dialog box's Component Type list box, click bCentral Web Components, and double-click bCentral Banner Ad in the corresponding list. The dialog box that appears leads you through the rest of the process.

To use the bCentral Banner Ad component, you must have a valid Web address — that is, you must know the address that visitors will enter in their browsers to view your site.

The bCentral Banner Ad Web component integrates you into the world of free banner advertising. If you want to sell advertising space and rotate the display of paid ads, your best bet is to contract the services of a consultant who can create an ad display for you. If you're comfortable working with HTML and server-side scripts (also known as *CGI scripts*), and your Web hosting provider allows CGI script use, you can download and use a free rotating image script. One good option: the Server Side Include Random Image Displayer at Matt's Script Archive (www.worldwidemart.com/scripts/ ssi_image.shtml).

Adding a Keyword Search to Your Web Site

A *keyword search* is to a Web site what a knowledgeable tour guide is to a big city: Both help you bypass the flotsam and get straight to the stuff you want to see. The Web Search component enables you to add a keyword search to your Web site in under a minute.

With the Web Search component nestled in a page in your site, visitors type words or phrases into a text box and then click a button to activate the search. In a moment, a linked list of Web pages matching the search request appears. From there, your visitors just click a link to go to a particular page.

You can add a search form to an existing page or create a separate search page with the help of the Search Page template. See Chapter 2 if you're not sure how to create a new page based on a template.

To use the Web Search component, you must publish your Web site on a host Web server that has FrontPage Server Extensions installed. For more information about FrontPage Server Extensions, see Chapter 16.

FrontPage also comes with a Web component that enables your visitors to perform a search of the entire Web (the World Wide Web, that is) from your site. This Web component doesn't require FrontPage Server Extensions. If you're interested, be sure to check out the Web component called Search the Web with MSN.

To use the Web Search component (the one that creates a keyword site search), follow these steps:

1. **Place the cursor in the page where you want the search form to appear, and then choose Insert⇨Web Component (or click the Web Component button on the Standard toolbar).**

   The Insert Web Component dialog box appears.

2. **In the Component Type list box, click Web Search.**

3. **In the Choose a Type of Search list box, double-click Current Web.**

   The Insert Web Component dialog box closes, and the Search Form Properties dialog box appears.

4. **In the Label for Input text box, type the text label that prompts visitors to type keywords.**

   Search for: is the default label.

5. **In the Width in Characters text box, type the width (in number of characters) of the text box into which visitors type keywords.**

6. **In the Label for "Start Search" Button text box, type the text label that appears on the button that visitors click to start the search.**

   The default label is *Start Search.*

7. **In the Label for "Reset" Button text box, type the label that appears on the button that visitors click to erase the contents of the keyword text box.**

   The default label is *Reset.*

8. **In the dialog box, click the Search Results tab.**

9. **If necessary, specify the scope of the search by typing information in the Word List to Search text box.**

   The default value *All* causes the search to look through every page in your Web site. To restrict the search to a discussion group in your Web site, type the name of the discussion group directory here. (I show you how to create a discussion group — complete with a keyword search — in the bonus chapter called "Can We Talk" on the CD.)

To hide pages from the Web Search component, stow them away in the _private folder. (In Chapter 14, I show you how to move pages into folders.) For example, you may not want the search to extend to pages that aren't yet complete.

10. **Mark the check boxes next to the items you want to appear in the search results list.**

    After a visitor performs a search, the Web Search component returns a linked list of matching pages. You can display additional information in the results page by clicking one or more of the following check boxes: Display Score (Closeness of Match) sorts the pages according to the closeness of the match; Display File Date shows the date that the page was last modified; and Display File Size (in K bytes) shows the page's file size.

11. **Click OK to close the Search Form Properties dialog box.**

    A search form appears in your page.

To preview and test the search form, you must use FrontPage in conjunction with a Web server that is outfitted with FrontPage Server Extensions. To try out the keyword search, you must publish your Web site and then preview the live version of the site.

If, after you test the keyword search, the search results seem out-of-date, save all open pages in FrontPage and then recalculate your Web site's hyperlinks (choose Tools⇨Recalculate Hyperlinks). Now republish your site and try your search again — it should be fit as a fiddle.

Using Office spreadsheets and charts in your Web site

FrontPage comes with three Web components that enable you to add Office functionality to your Web site in the form of working spreadsheets, charts, and PivotTables. These Web components are best reserved for use on an intranet site because they have specific server and browser requirements: the site must be published on a server that has FrontPage Server Extensions installed, and visitors must be using Internet Explorer (version 3.0 and later) *and* have Microsoft Office (version 2000 and later) with Office Web components installed on their computers. If your publishing environment meets these conditions and you'd like to know more, visit the FrontPage Help system for details. To get there, in the upper right corner of the FrontPage window, type **Office Web Component** in the Ask a Question list box, and then press Enter.

Tracking Visits with a Hit Counter

A *hit counter* is an odometer-like row of numbers that sits in your page and records the number of visits or *hits* that the page receives (see Figure 13-3). Each time someone visits the page, the number in the hit counter goes up by one. Hit counters let you brag to visitors about your site's popularity, and watching the numbers increase every day is fun.

Figure 13-3:
A hit counter offers one way to gauge your popularity.

 people have visited this page.

To use a FrontPage hit counter, you must publish your Web site on a host Web server that has FrontPage Server Extensions installed (version 2000 or later). For more information about FrontPage Server Extensions, see Chapter 16.

For more hit counter options (or, if you publish your site on a host Web server that *doesn't* support FrontPage Server Extensions), be sure to check out another Web component — the bCentral FastCounter. This Web component has no server requirements.

To insert a hit counter into your page, follow these steps:

1. **Place the cursor in the page where you want the hit counter to appear, and then choose Insert⇨Web Component (or click the Web Component button on the Standard toolbar).**

   The Insert Web Component dialog box appears.

2. **In the Component Type list box, click Hit Counter.**

   A list of available counters appears on the right side of the dialog box.

3. **In the Choose a Counter Style list box, double-click graphic style you like (if you don't like any of the graphic styles, just double-click any one of the counters; I explain how you can substitute your own graphic for the FrontPage offerings in a moment).**

   The Insert Web Component dialog box closes, and the Hit Coutner Properties dialog box appears.

   You can use your own image in place of FrontPage's preset counter graphics. To do so, click the Custom Picture option button, and then type the image's filename and location in the accompanying text box. You must choose a single graphic that contains the numbers 0–9, and the numbers must be evenly spaced inside the image.

4. **Mark the Reset Counter To check box, and in the accompanying text box, type the counter's starting number.**

   If your Web site is new, leave the number at 0. If your site has already been around for a while, you can start the counter with an approximation of the number of visitors who came by before your counter was installed. (Or you can artificially inflate the number of folks who visit, but I know you weren't even considering that option.)

5. **If you want the counter to appear with a fixed number of digits, mark the Fixed Number of Digits check box and then type the number of digits in the accompanying text box.**

   For example, if you type **5** in the text box, the counter displays hit number 1 as 00001.

6. **Click OK.**

   The dialog box closes, and a placeholder appears in the page (the place-holder looks like this: [Hit Counter]).

To preview and test the hit counter, you must use FrontPage in conjunction with a Web server that is outfitted with FrontPage Server Extensions. To see the hit counter in action, you must publish your Web site and then preview the live version of the site.

Automating Content with Inclusions

Most Web sites contain some sort of repeating information, whether it's a copyright notice along the bottom of each page, or a list of important department announcements that appears on several pages in your site. You can minimize the time spent typing information more than once by taking advantage of *included content* components. When you place an included content Web component into your page, the component replaces itself with content from some source: either a list of entries you define, another Web page, or a picture file. The beauty of this technology shines when you use included content in more than one page: You update the content source, and the change automatically appears wherever that content is included.

Substitution

The Substitution component enables you to display placeholders in your page that replace themselves with bits of information called *configuration variables.* Configuration variables describe certain details about the page or contain snippets of information that you specify.

Displaying standard configuration variables

FrontPage maintains a standard set of configuration variables for each page:

- ✔ **Author** is the user name of the person who created the page.
- ✔ **Modified By** is the user name of the person who most recently edited the page.
- ✔ **Description** is a description of the page.
- ✔ **Page URL** is the current location of the page.

Some Web sites created using FrontPage's Web site templates contain additional standard configuration variables.

To see the values for each configuration variable in a page, right-click the page's icon in any of the FrontPage views and choose Properties from the pop-up menu that appears. The Properties dialog box appears, with the General tab visible. In the dialog box, click the Summary tab. The author's name appears next to Created By on the Summary tab. (If no name appears next to Created By, then the author did not use FrontPage to create the page.) The name of the person who last modified the page appears next to Modified By. The page description appears in the Comments text box. In the General tab, the page's current URL appears in the Location box.

To use the Substitution component to display standard configuration variables, follow these steps:

1. **Place the cursor in the page where you want the substitution to appear, and then choose Insert⇨Web Component (or click the Web Component button on the Standard toolbar).**

   The Insert Web Component dialog box appears.

2. **In the Component Type list box, click Included Content.**

   A list of available content types appears on the right side of the dialog box.

3. **In the Choose a Content Type list box, double-click Substitution.**

   The Insert Web Component dialog box closes, and the Substitution Properties dialog box appears.

4. **In the Substitute With list box, choose the name of the configuration variable that you want to display.**

5. **Click OK to close the dialog box.**

   The value of the configuration variable appears in your page.

If you use the Substitution component to display the Page URL configuration variable, the URL that appears corresponds to the computer on which the page is *currently* located. If you later publish the page on another Web server, the old, incorrect URL remains displayed inside the page.

To solve this problem, after you publish the Web site, open the Web site directly from the Web server on which the site is published (refer to Chapter 1 if you're not sure how) and then open the page displaying the Page URL configuration variable. Click the URL and press the Delete key to delete the Substitution Web component. Now reinsert the Substitution Web component and set it up to display the Page URL configuration variable. (Follow the steps outlined in this section.) The correct URL appears. Save the page to make the change visible to the rest of the World Wide Web.

Creating and displaying your own configuration variables

You can create your own configuration variables to use as placeholders for standard bits of information throughout the Web site. Say, for example, you want to list your mailing address in several Web pages. Instead of typing the address repeatedly, you can create a configuration variable named MyAddress. If you use the Substitution Web component to include the MyAddress configuration variable in your page, your address appears in its place. Even better, if you move down the street, you simply need to update the configuration variable instead of editing your address in every single page.

To create your own configuration variables, follow these steps:

1. **Choose Tools➪Web Settings.**

   The Web Settings dialog box appears, with the Configuration tab visible.

2. **In the dialog box, click the Parameters tab.**

3. **Click the Add button.**

   The Add Name and Value dialog box appears.

4. **Type the name of the configuration variable in the Name text box.**

   Choose a one-word name that is brief and descriptive, such as *MyAddress*.

5. **Type the value of the configuration variable in the Value text box.**

   FrontPage substitutes this text whenever you display the configuration variable in your page. For the MyAddress configuration variable, for example, you type your address here.

6. **Click OK to close the Add Name and Value dialog box.**

   The configuration variable's name and value appear in the box in the Parameters panel.

7. **To add more configuration variables, repeat Steps 3–6.**

   Modify or remove configuration variables by clicking their names in the list and then clicking the Modify or Remove buttons.

8. **After you finish creating configuration variables, click OK to close the Web Settings dialog box.**

To insert the newly created configuration variables in your Web site, follow the steps for displaying standard configuration variables in the previous section.

Include Page

Include Page is a Web component that simplifies the process of inserting the same information in more than one page in your Web site. After you insert an Include Page component into your page, the Web component is replaced by the contents of a second page.

Here's an example: Say you want to display a list of news headlines in several pages in your Web site. Instead of typing the list of headlines into each page, you create a separate page that contains only the headlines. You then use the Include Page component to include the contents of the headlines page in the other pages in your Web site. If you want to change the headlines later, you update the headlines page, and the Include Page component reflects the update throughout the Web site.

The Include Page component works very much like shared borders (for more information about shared borders, see Chapter 5). However, you can insert an Include Page component in the body of your page, whereas shared borders stick to the page's margins.

Inserting the Include Page Web component

To use the Include Page component, follow these steps:

1. **Place the cursor in the page where you want the substitution to appear, and then choose Insert➪Web Component (or click the Web Component button on the Standard toolbar).**

   The Insert Web Component dialog box appears.

2. **In the Component Type list box, click Included Content.**

   A list of available content types appears on the right side of the dialog box.

3. **In the Choose a Content Type list box, double-click Page.**

   The Insert Web Component dialog box closes, and the Include Page Properties dialog box appears.

4. **In the Page to Include text box, type the filename and location of the page in your Web site that you want to include.**

   Or click Browse to choose a page from the Current Web dialog box.

5. **Click OK.**

   The Include Page Properties dialog box closes, and the contents of the included page appear inside the current page.

Try passing your pointer over the included information; the pointer turns into a little hand holding a piece of paper. This special pointer reminds you that the text is there courtesy of the Include Page component.

Because the pages that you include by using the Include Page component are often just fragments of information that only the "host" page needs to access, you may want to hide included pages from Web browsers and from the Web Search component. To do so, store the included pages inside your Web site's _private folder. (Refer to Chapter 14 for descriptions of the different FrontPage folders and how to store pages inside them.)

The _private folder is private only if you publish the Web site on a Web server that supports FrontPage Server Extensions. For more information, see Chapter 16.

Updating included pages

To update a page that you've included inside other pages, simply open the included page in Page View, make your changes, and save the page just as you would any other Web page. When you save and close the page, FrontPage *recalculates* the site's hyperlinks, which updates the inclusion throughout the rest of your Web site. When FrontPage recalculates hyperlinks, it refreshes the site, integrating any changes made to the site's system of hyperlinks. This process usually happens automatically as you update your site (you don't even notice), but you can also specifically tell FrontPage to recalculate your site's hyperlinks.

To do so, choose Tools⇨Recalculate Hyperlinks. The Recalculate Hyperlinks dialog box appears, warning you that recalculating hyperlinks may take several minutes. Click Yes to close the dialog box and proceed with the recalculation.

If remembering to recalculate hyperlinks every time you change an included page is a hassle, you can tell FrontPage to remind you when an included page has changed but hasn't yet been updated throughout the site. To do so, choose Tools⇨Options. The Options dialog box appears with the General tab visible. In the dialog box, click the Warn When Included Web Components Are Out of Date check box, and then click OK to close the dialog box.

Including a page or picture based on a schedule

Scheduled Include Page and Scheduled Picture are Web components that work like the Include Page component, except the inclusion appears only during a specified time period. The Scheduled Include Page component (like the Include Page component) inserts the contents of a page into another page, and the Scheduled Picture component inserts a single picture.

As an example of how the Scheduled Include Page component can help you, suppose that you use your Web site to announce upcoming events. Instead of keeping track of event dates and making sure that you update your Web site before the event occurs, you can create a separate page for the announcements. Then you can use the Scheduled Include Page component to include the contents of the page in other pages in your Web site, specifying the time period during which the announcements apply. After that time period is over, the announcements disappear.

The Scheduled Picture component is handy if, for example, you flag additions to your Web site with a "New!" icon. Because things are new only for a limited time, you can use this Web component to remove the icons after a week or so.

Both Scheduled Web components work the same way, so I describe them together in the following steps:

 1. **Place the cursor in the page where you want the included content to appear, and then choose Insert⇨Web Component (or click the Web Component button on the Standard toolbar).**

    The Insert Web Component dialog box appears.

2. **In the Component Type list box, click Included Content.**

    A list of available content types appears on the right side of the dialog box.

3. **In the Choose a Content Type list box, double-click either Page Based on Schedule or Picture Based on Schedule.**

    The Insert Web Component dialog box closes, and depending on your choice, either the Scheduled Include Page Properties dialog box or the Scheduled Picture Properties dialog box appears.

4. **In the During the Scheduled Time text box, type the filename and location of the page or picture that you want to include.**

    Or click Browse to choose a file from your Web site.

5. **If you want to include a different page or picture before and after the inclusion period, type the filename and location in the Before and After the Scheduled Time text box.**

    If you don't include an alternative page or picture, nothing appears at the location of the Web component before and after the inclusion period.

6. **In the Starting area, choose the date and time you want the inclusion to first appear.**

    Specify the date by selecting options from the Year, Month, and Day list boxes. To specify the time, click the time notation inside the Time scroll box and click the up- or down-pointing arrows at the right side of the box to adjust the time.

7. **In the Ending area, choose the date and time when you want the inclusion to disappear.**

8. **Click OK.**

    The dialog box closes, and the specified page contents or picture appears at the location of the cursor. If the inclusion period begins at a later time, the message [Scheduled Include Page] or [Scheduled Picture] appears in your page — unless you specified an alternative, in which case the contents of the alternative page or the alternative picture appears. The message appears in FrontPage only to remind you that the Scheduled Web component is present. People who view the page with a Web browser can't see the message.

If your host Web server is located in another time zone (which is unlikely but possible if you publish your FrontPage Web sites by using an ISP or company server in another region), the times that you specify must apply to the server's time zone, not yours.

Inserting a page banner

FrontPage knows how to create a decorative *page banner* that you can use in place of a page header. FrontPage superimposes the page's navigation structure label on top of the theme's banner graphic to create the banner (see Figure 13-4). If you're not sure what a navigation structure is or how it works, refer to Chapter 14. To find out more about themes, see Chapter 11.

Figure 13-4:
An example
of the page
banner
graphic
produced by
the Nature
theme.

Here's how to insert a page banner:

1. **Open the page into which you want to insert a page banner.**

   If you haven't already, in the Navigation View, add the page to the navigation structure. (See Chapter 14 for instructions on how to work with the Navigation View.)

2. **Place the cursor in the page where you want the banner to appear, and then choose Insert⇨Page Banner.**

   The Page Banner Properties dialog box appears.

3. **In the dialog box, mark the Picture option button.**

   If you prefer a plain text banner, click the Text option button.

4. **If you want a different text label to appear on top of the banner, type the text in the Page Banner Text box.**

When you change a banner label, FrontPage changes the label in the site's navigation structure and also uses the label as the page title.

5. **Click OK.**

The Page Banner Properties dialog box closes, and the banner appears in the page.

If the message [Add this page to the Navigation View to display a page banner here] appears in place of the page banner, the page in which the banner sits is not yet part of the site's navigation structure. To fix the problem, add the page to the navigation structure in the Navigation View, and then switch back to the Page View. The page banner now appears and displays the correct label.

If you were expecting a picture and a text banner appears instead, your page or site lacks a theme. To apply a theme to your site, choose Format⇨Theme, and then choose a theme from the Themes dialog box (for more information about how to work with themes, see Chapter 11).

To include a page banner in every page in your Web site automatically, take advantage of *shared borders*. I discuss shared borders in Chapter 5.

Inserting a Top 10 List component

I'm not talking about David Letterman or Billboard music charts here. In FrontPage lingo, a Top 10 List is information about your site's visitors. Using the Top 10 List component, you can find out the following things:

✔ The ten most frequently visited pages in your site

✔ The top ten referring domains to your site (that is, the domains that your visitors are visiting just before they come to your site)

✔ The top ten referring URLs (the addresses of the Web pages that visitors are at just before they visit your site)

✔ The ten most common search phrases (or *strings*) entered into search engines to find your site

✔ The ten most frequent visitors to your site

✔ The ten most popular operating systems that your visitors use

✔ The ten most popular browsers that your visitors use (great information when you're deciding which browser-specific effects to use in your site)

The Top 10 List component works by culling information from the host server's logs. When you insert a Top 10 List component into a page in your site, the list that the component creates is automatically updated as the server log changes.

To use this Web component, you must publish your site on a host server that supports FrontPage Server Extensions (version 2002 or later).

To insert a Top 10 List, follow these steps:

1. **Place the cursor in the page where you want the list to appear, and then choose Insert⇨Web Component (or click the Web Component button on the Standard toolbar).**

   The Insert Web Component dialog box appears.

2. **In the dialog box's Component Type list box, click Top 10 List.**

   A list of Top 10 List types appears on the right side of the dialog box.

3. **In the Choose a Usage List, double-click the list type that you want.**

   The Insert Web Component dialog box closes, and the Top 10 List Properties dialog box appears.

4. **In the dialog box's Title Text box, type a list title.**

   Or, if you're happy with FrontPage's default choice, skip this step.

5. **Mark the Include Date Usage Processing Was Last Run check box if you want the date when the list was last updated to appear inside your page.**

6. **In the List Style area of the dialog box, click the box that represents the way you want the list to look, and then click OK.**

   The dialog box closes, and a placeholder for the Top 10 List appears in your page.

To see the Top 10 List component in action, you must publish your site and then view the page with a Web browser.

Part IV
Taking Your Web Site to a New Level

The 5th Wave   By Rich Tennant

Principal

"I found these two in the multimedia lab, morphing faculty members into farm animals."

In this part . . .

Web publishing can be a solitary task or can happen as part of a team, with many authors creating different chunks of the Web site. In this part, you discover how FrontPage helps you collaborate with a workgroup. You find out how to control who can access your Web site. You also discover how to publish your site on the World Wide Web.

Chapter 14

Web Site Management 101

*U*sing FrontPage, you can do just about anything to change, update, or repair your Web site (assuming something needs repairing).

In this chapter, you delve into the site-management capabilities of FrontPage. You become familiar with FrontPage's six views. You also discover how to use FrontPage to manage the files that make up your Web site.

Taking In the Views

FrontPage's charm lies in its *views,* or ways of displaying information about your Web site. FrontPage contains six views, each of which illuminates your site in a different way.

To switch between views, click the appropriate button on the Views bar (see Figure 14-1), or choose the name of the view you want to see from the View menu.

Figure 14-1:
The Views
bar.

Page View

You use the Page View to look at and add stuff to the individual Web pages that make up the Web site.

You spend most of your time in the Page View, so I devote most of this book to the Page View's many talents. In the chapters in Parts II and III, you find out how to put the Page View's tools to work.

Folders View

The Folders View displays your Web site as a group of files and folders to help you manage and organize your Web site's file system (see Figure 14-2). This view serves the same purpose for your Web site as Windows Explorer serves for the files stored on your hard drive and local network.

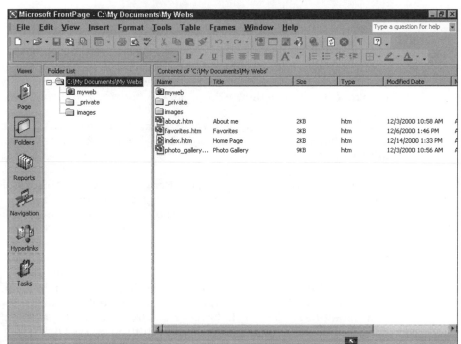

Figure 14-2:
The Folders
View.

The Folders View looks and works much like Windows Explorer:

- ✔ Click a folder in the Folder List to display its contents in the Contents area.

- ✔ To sort the list of files and folders in the Contents area, click the header label of your choice. You can sort the file list by filename, page title, and the date the page was last modified.

- ✔ To move a page into a folder, click the page icon, drag it on top of the folder, and then release the mouse button. FrontPage updates the page's hyperlinks to reflect the page's new location. (I talk more about how hyperlinks work in Chapter 5.)

Folders with globe icons on top denote *subwebs,* which are complete Web sites that live inside a folder of the main or *parent* Web site. To view the contents of a subweb in the Folders View, double-click the subweb's folder to open the subweb in a new FrontPage window. For more information about subwebs, see Chapter 1.

Reports View

The Reports View contains various reports which tell you something useful about your Web site (see Figure 14-3). For example, the Slow Pages report helps you monitor your site's estimated download speed, and the Recently Changed Files report gives you the lowdown on who updated the site and when.

The Reports View is especially handy if you're using FrontPage as part of a site-building team. I talk more about using FrontPage as a collaborative tool in Chapter 15.

To switch between the reports in the Reports View, choose View⇨Reports, and then select the name of the report you want to see. Or avail yourself of the Reporting toolbar: It contains a drop-down menu of reports, plus a couple other handy tools. If it's not already visible when you switch to the Reports View, show the Reporting toolbar by choosing View⇨Toolbars⇨Reporting.

When you first display the Reports View, you're greeted by the Site Summary report. This report rounds up interesting tidbits of information, including how many hyperlinks and pictures the site contains, how many pages can and cannot be reached by following a link from the home page, and how many pages contain broken hyperlinks. This report contains much more information than I've listed here — see for yourself!

Figure 14-3:
The Site Summary report in the Reports View.

Name	Count	Size	Description
All files	23	1,920KB	All files in the current Web
Pictures	17	862KB	Picture files in the current Web (GIF, JPG, BMP, etc.)
Unlinked files	22	1,918KB	Files in the current Web that cannot be reached by starting from your home page
Linked files	1	2KB	Files in the current Web that can be reached by starting from your home page
Slow pages	1	1,083KB	Pages in the current Web exceeding an estimated download time of 30 seconds at 28.8
Older files	0	0KB	Files in the current Web that have not been modified in over 72 days
Recently added fi...	11	1,533KB	Files in the current Web that have been created in the last 30 days
Hyperlinks	15		All hyperlinks in the current Web
Unverified hyperli...	1		Hyperlinks pointing to unconfirmed target files
Broken hyperlinks	2		Hyperlinks pointing to unavailable target files
External hyperlinks	1		Hyperlinks pointing to files outside of the current Web
Internal hyperlinks	14		Hyperlinks pointing to other files within the current Web
Component errors	0		Files in the current Web with components reporting an error
Uncompleted tasks	0		Tasks in the current Web that are not yet marked completed
Unused themes	2		Themes in the current Web that are not applied to any file

Weird FrontPage folders

When you switch to the Folders View, no doubt you notice some unfamiliar folders lurking in your Web site. All FrontPage Web sites contain a standard set of folders, and each folder has its own role:

✔ **_private:** Documents stored in this folder remain hidden from Web browsers and from the Web Search component (Chapter 13

gives you the details about this Web component).

✔ **images:** The images folder is where FrontPage stores images that appear inside Web pages. I recommend keeping all your images in that folder, too, just so your Web site remains neat.

Any of the Site Summary report titles that appear blue and underlined can be clicked to perform a relevant task or to display a more detailed report (all of which I explain in the sections that follow).

To open a page or file listed in any of the reports, double-click the file's icon. Read on for details about each of the FrontPage reports.

File-related reports

The reports in this category give you information about the files in your Web site.

✔ **All Files:** The All Files report lets you peruse a complete list of the files in your Web site. Use this report when you want details about your Web site files, such as the files' sizes or authors.

✔ **Recently Added or Changed Files:** These reports list files that were added to the site or that have been edited or changed in the last 30 days.

To change the number of days FrontPage thinks of as "recent," select a different time frame from the Reporting toolbar, or choose Tools⇨ Options to display the Options dialog box. In the dialog box, click the Reports View tab, and then type a new number in the "Recent" Files Are Less Than X Days Old text box. Click OK to close the dialog box.

✔ **Older Files:** Turn to this report for a list of aging pages (that is, pages that haven't changed for at least 72 days). If a bunch of your site's pages appear in this report, it's time to spruce up your site with some new and exciting content.

To change the number of days FrontPage thinks of as "older," select a different time frame from the Reporting toolbar, or choose Tools⇨ Options to display the Options dialog box. In the dialog box, click the Reports View tab, and then type a new number in the "Older" Files Are More Than X Days Old text box. Click OK to close the dialog box.

Problem reports

If a file in your Web site has something wrong with it, one of these reports should ferret out the problem.

- ✔ **Unlinked Files:** This report lists files that fit all of the following criteria: they do not contain hyperlinks, they cannot be reached by following hyperlinks from the site's home page, and they are not "included" inside other pages using one of the Included Content components (see Chapter 13 for details).

    Pages that appear in this report can safely be deleted, because they are effectively cut off from the rest of the site. I show you how to delete pages later in this chapter (although you can probably guess how to do it . . . select the page and then press the Delete key).

    If you delete a page using FrontPage, you can't later change your mind. FrontPage-deleted pages don't end up in the Recycle Bin — they go to Web page heaven. If in doubt, leave the page alone, or delete the page using the Windows Explorer — that way, deleted pages are placed in the Recycle Bin and can be retrieved in a pinch.

- ✔ **Slow Pages:** Web surfers hate to wait for pages to download. This report helps you keep track of the potential slowpokes in your site. The report lists pages that take more than an estimated 30 seconds to load over a 28.8 modem. I say *estimated* because download speed depends on several factors, only one of which is page content. (Other factors include the speed of the host Web server, the amount of network traffic at that given moment, and the state of the phone and data lines that make up the Internet, to name a few.)

    To change this report's assumptions about download time and speed, select a new time frame from the Reporting toolbar, or choose Tools➪ Options to display the Options dialog box. In the dialog box, click the Reports View tab, and then type a new number in the "Slow Pages" Take At Least X Seconds to Download text box. Next, select a connection speed from the Assume Connection Speed Of list box. Click OK to close the dialog box.

- ✔ **Broken Hyperlinks:** This report lists hyperlinks that are broken or that FrontPage hasn't verified yet. In Chapter 5, I show you how to find and fix broken hyperlinks.

- ✔ **Component Errors:** If you use FrontPage Web components in your site and one or more of those components runs into a problem, FrontPage lists the ailing page and a description of the problem in this report. See Chapter 13 for details about Web components.

Workflow reports

These reports give you information about the various stages of the editing and Web publishing process.

✔ **Review Status and Assigned To:** If you're part of a Web design team, these reports list the review status and assignments for each page in the Web site. In Chapter 15, I go into detail about how these reports and other FrontPage workgroup and collaboration features work.

✔ **Categories:** In FrontPage, you can create general groupings of information called *categories,* and then assign each page to a specific category. (I talk about how and when this feature can be useful in Chapter 15.) This report lists each page and the category to which it's assigned. To show only those pages assigned to a specific category, choose a category name from the Reporting toolbar.

✔ **Publish Status:** This report keeps track of when pages were last modified and which pages are ready to be published. I show you how to publish your Web site (and how to exclude unfinished pages from publishing) in Chapter 16.

✔ **Checkout Status:** If you collaborate with a team of people to build a FrontPage Web site, FrontPage's *source control* feature can help rein in the process. When you enable source control, each Web site author must check pages out before he or she can work on the pages, and only one author at a time can check out a page. (I talk in detail about source control in Chapter 15.)

This report lists the checkout status for each page in your site. A green dot signifies that the page is checked in, and a red check mark signifies that the page is checked out and can't be accessed. The report also lists the name of the person who has checked out the page, the most recent version of the page that has been checked out, and the *locked date,* or the date the page was checked out.

Usage reports

If you publish your Web site on a host server that supports the 2002 version of the FrontPage Server Extensions, you can use these reports to find out about who's visiting your Web site and how it's being used.

Because usage reports track information about how your visitors use your site, these reports are relevant only *after* the site has been live and accepting visitors for a while. So, to view usage reports, you must first publish your Web site (see Chapter 16 for directions), and then wait a few days or weeks for the server to collect usage information in its logs. When you can no longer stand the suspense, open the *live* version of the site directly from the host server (see Chapter 1 for directions), choose View➪Reports, and then choose the name of the usage report that you want to see. Here are your options:

✔ **Usage Summary:** This report provides you with an overview of your site's usage, including links to more detailed reports.

✔ **Monthly, Weekly, and Daily Summary:** These reports break usage data into time-oriented chunks. Check these reports for total numbers of visits (visits to your site overall), hits (visits to each page or file in your site), and the amount of data downloaded from your site.

- **Monthly, Weekly, and Daily Page Hits:** Which files in your site are the most popular? These reports answer that question by displaying how many hits each page or file in your site receives each month, week, or day.

- **Visiting Users:** This report lists visitors to your site by user name (if your site is hosted by a server that requires users to log into a network) or *IP address*. An IP address is a unique number that identifies a computer connected to the Internet.

- **Operating Systems:** This report settles bets about whether your Web site visitors prefer Mac or Windows (or other operating systems).

- **Browsers:** View this report to see which browsers your visitors use.

- **Referring Domains:** This report lists the domains your users visit right before coming to your Web site. For example, if lots of visitors find your Web site by searching Yahoo!, the `www.yahoo.com` domain will appear prominently in this report.

- **Referring URLs:** This report lists the full address of the page users are at just before they visit your site. So, sticking with the Yahoo! example, this report would display the address of the specific page at Yahoo! visitors use to jump to your site.

- **Search Strings:** This report displays the search phrases (or *strings*) that visitors type into search engines to find your site.

Notice a similarity between the available usage reports and the available Top 10 Lists? (If you don't know what a Top 10 List is, see Chapter 13.) FrontPage gathers the data for both features from the same source: the host server's logs. Usage reports and Top 10 Lists are simply different ways of displaying the same information.

Navigation View

You may think that I started writing this book on Page 1, right? Wrong. I spent many hours putting together a table of contents before jotting down a single word. When it was time to write, my words flowed relatively easily because the information was already organized.

I relate this anecdote because building a Web site is not unlike writing a book. You have information to present to an audience, and you want that information to be clear and well-organized. Here's where the Navigation View comes in handy. Using this view, you can map out a *navigation structure* for your Web site. A navigation structure is a graphic representation of the "levels" of pages in your site. Similar to a company's organization chart, which provides a picture of the leadership hierarchy within the company, a navigation structure illustrates the organization of the information in your site.

Building a navigation structure is optional unless you want to take advantage of FrontPage *link bars* and *page banners,* because both features make use of information in the site's navigation structure. A link bar is a row of text or graphic hyperlinks that lead to other pages, allowing your visitors to get around easily. (I show you how to create link bars in Chapter 5.) Page banners are decorative banner graphics that add spice to your pages (see Chapter 13 for details).

Designing a navigation structure

Creating a navigation structure is easy. Just think about how you want your site to be structured, and then drag the site's pages from the Folder List into place in the blue area of the Navigation View. Here's how:

1. **In FrontPage, open your Web site.**

   If you can't remember how, refer to Chapter 1.

2. **If the Navigation View isn't already visible, click the Navigation button on the Views bar.**

   The Navigation View becomes visible. The home page is already represented in the Navigation View. You construct a navigation structure by dragging pages from the Folder List and dropping them into the Navigation View. In this example, I illustrate creating a navigation structure for a simple personal Web site containing a home page, three second-level pages, and two third-level pages.

   If the Folder List isn't visible, click the Toggle Pane button on the Standard toolbar, or choose View⇨Folder List.

   Note: Web sites based on FrontPage site templates already have a navigation structure in place. Read on to find out how to add more pages to or change the setup of the navigation structure.

3. **In the Folder List, click the page you want to add to the navigation structure and then, while holding down the mouse button, drag the page into the blue area of the Navigation View.**

   As you drag the page into place, a line appears that connects the page you're dragging to the home page.

4. **Release the mouse button.**

   An icon representing that page appears in the navigation structure.

5. **Continue adding pages to the navigation structure until you've added all the pages to be represented in the site's link bars or page banners.**

   Figure 14-4 illustrates a complete navigation structure.

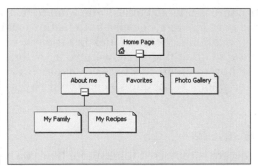

Figure 14-4:
A complete
navigation
structure.

You don't have to add every page in your site to the navigation structure —
only add those pages you want to appear in the site's link bars or page banners. If you're not sure how you should arrange the pages, skim the information about link bars in Chapter 5. Understanding how link bars work may help
you visualize the best way to lay out your Web site's navigation structure.

After you finish the navigation structure, you can easily rearrange it by clicking any icon and dragging it to a new spot. As you add new pages to your site,
you can drag them into the navigation structure as well. The navigation structure can accommodate many different organizational schemes, including
more than one top-level page. Try experimenting to figure out a structure that
works for your site.

To remove a page from the navigation structure, click a rectangle in the map
and then press the Delete key. The Delete Page dialog box appears, asking if
you want to remove the page from the navigation structure, or if you want to
delete the page entirely. Be sure the Remove Page from Navigation Structure
option button is selected, and then click OK. The dialog box closes, and the
page disappears from the navigation structure. However, the page remains
safely nestled in the Web site.

 You can print the navigation structure by clicking the Print button on the
Standard toolbar. To preview the printed page before you set it on paper,
choose File⇨Print Preview.

 FrontPage keeps a condensed, outline-like display of the navigation structure in
the Navigation Pane (visible in the Page View if you click the Navigation button
at the bottom of the Folder List). This display is handy when you're building
link bars because you don't have to keep switching back and forth between the
Page and Navigation Views to be able to see the site's navigation structure.

Changing the display

The Navigation toolbar contains a few gizmos that let you adjust the navigation structure display (see Figure 14-5). If the toolbar isn't already visible,
choose View⇨Toolbars⇨Navigation.

Here's what you can do with tools on the Navigation toolbar:

✔ **Contract and expand the map:** In the navigation structure, each page leading to another page is called a *parent page.* Each parent page icon has a minus sign icon attached to it. By clicking the minus sign, you contract the level of pages attached to the parent page (and the minus sign turns into a plus sign), making the site's basic framework easier to see. To expand the pages again, click the plus sign. To view a portion of the navigation structure (also known as a *subtree*), click the subtree's parent page, and then click the View Subtree Only button.

✔ **Portrait/Landscape:** If the Navigation View is packed with pages, you can change the orientation of the display to make it more compact. To rotate the navigation structure, click the Portrait/Landscape button.

✔ **Zoom:** You can change the magnification of the navigation structure by choosing a percentage from the Zoom list box. To smoosh the entire navigation structure into the view, choose Size to Fit.

The Navigation toolbar contains two more buttons: Add Existing Page and Included in Navigation Bars. I show you how and when to use these buttons when I show you how to create link bars in Chapter 5.

Hyperlinks View

The links between the pages in your Web site create a path that visitors follow when they explore the site. The Hyperlinks View is like a road map; it illustrates the Web site's navigational path so that you can make sure your Web site is easy to get around.

The left side of the Hyperlinks View contains the Folder List (the same list that appears in the Page and Navigation Views). When you click a page in the Folder List, an icon representing that page appears in the Hyperlinks area of the view. Figure 14-6 shows how a Web site looks in the Hyperlinks View.

Small icons with blue arrows pointing to the central page icon illustrate *incoming hyperlinks,* or pages that contain hyperlinks leading to the selected page. Small icons to the right of the central page icon illustrate *outgoing hyperlinks,* or the destinations of hyperlinks inside the selected page. If the selected page contains no hyperlinks and isn't linked to from any other page in the site, the page icon appears in the Hyperlinks area all by itself.

Broken hyperlinks appear as broken gray lines instead of blue arrows. I show you how to find and repair broken hyperlinks in your site in Chapter 5.

You can modify the Hyperlinks View diagram by right-clicking anywhere inside the yellow area of the view and then choosing one of the following options from the pop-up menu that appears:

- ✔ **Show Page Titles:** By default, the Hyperlinks View displays the page's filenames. Choose this option to display the page's titles instead.

- ✔ **Hyperlinks to Pictures:** Choose this option to display links to picture files.

- ✔ **Repeated Hyperlinks:** If the page contains more than one hyperlink to the same destination, the Hyperlinks View displays only one instance of the link. Choose this option to make repeated hyperlinks visible.

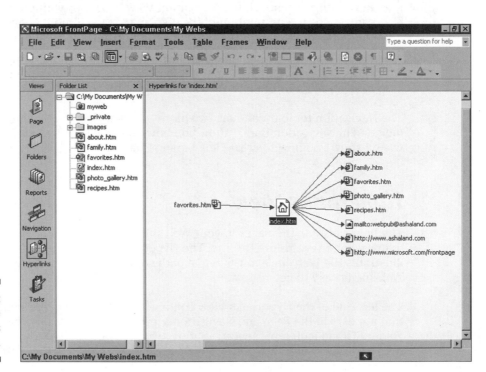

Figure 14-6:
The
Hyperlinks
View.

Tasks View

The Tasks View helps you keep track of the thousand-and-one details involved in putting together a flawless Web site. I talk about the workings of the Tasks View along with other FrontPage workgroup features in Chapter 15.

Working with Web Site Files and Folders

FrontPage gives you easy access to the files that make up your Web site. Use FrontPage whenever you want to import, move, or delete files and folders in your Web site.

Adding existing files and folders to a Web site

The easiest way to add an existing file or folder to a FrontPage Web site is to move, copy, or save that file or folder inside the Web site's folder.

 For example, say you have a document stored inside your C:\My Documents folder that you want to add to the Web site stored in the C:\My Documents\ My Webs folder. Using Windows Explorer, simply copy or move the file from the My Documents folder to the My Webs folder. The next time you open the Web site in FrontPage, the new file appears in the Folder List. (If the Web site is currently open in FrontPage, click the Refresh button on the Standard toolbar to update the Folder List.)

Another option is to save a document directly inside a FrontPage Web site folder. For example, if you're currently working on a Microsoft Word document and you want to add that document to the Web site stored in the C:\My Documents\My Webs folder, save the document in Microsoft Word in the location C:\My Documents\My Webs.

If you prefer to do all your Web site work from within FrontPage, you can *import* files into your Web site instead. You can import files that are currently stored on your computer, local network, or the World Wide Web. When you import a file, FrontPage places a copy of the file inside the currently open Web site, and the original file sits unchanged in its original location.

 In this section, I show you how to add existing files to the Web site that's currently open in FrontPage. To import an entire Web site into FrontPage, take the Import Web Wizard for a spin (see Chapter 1 for details).

In the following steps, I show you how to import single files from your computer or local network into the current FrontPage Web site. At the end of this set of steps, I tell you how to import entire folders, and I also talk about how to import material that's currently stored on the World Wide Web.

1. **With a Web site open in FrontPage, choose File⇨Import.**

   The Import dialog box appears.

   (If you choose File⇨Import when no Web site is currently open, FrontPage thinks that you want to import an entire site and displays the New dialog box with the Import Web Wizard selected.)

2. **In the dialog box, click the Add File button.**

   The Add File to Import List dialog box appears. You use this dialog box to poke around your hard drive or local network to find the files that you want to import.

3. **Navigate your hard drive or local network and select the files that you want to import.**

   To select multiple files, press and hold down the Ctrl key while clicking file icons in the Add File to Import List dialog box. To select a range of files, press and hold down the Shift key while clicking the first and last file icons. If you don't see the file that you want to import, choose All files (*.*) from the Files of Type list box.

4. **Click the Open button.**

   The Add File to Import List dialog box closes, and the file appears in the import list in the Import dialog box.

5. **To add another file to the import list, repeat Steps 2 through 4. When you're finished, click OK to close the dialog box and import the file(s).**

   If you would rather put off importing the files, click the Close button in the Import dialog box. FrontPage saves the import list and closes the dialog box, which you can later access by choosing File⇨Import.

To import a folder to your Web site, in Step 2 of the previous list, click the Add Folder button. The Browse for Folder dialog box appears, enabling you to choose the folder that you want to import. Click the folder and then click the OK button. The Browse for Folder dialog box closes, and the folder's contents appear in the import list.

To import a single file or folder, you can also resort to the quick-and-dirty approach: Simply drag the file or folder from your desktop or Windows Explorer and drop it into the contents area of the Folders View.

To import a file or folder that's currently stored on the World Wide Web, in Step 2 of the previous list click the From Web button. The Import Web Wizard launches. Refer to Chapter 1 for directions on how to use the Import Web Wizard.

Creating new folders

You can add new folders to your Web site using the Folders View. If your site contains lots of files and pages, folders help you keep the files organized.

Say, for example, your company's Web site contains four main sections — About Acme Consulting Company, Acme Services, Acme Staff, and Contact Acme — and each section contains several files. You can store each section's files in its own folder to keep your file system spic-and-span.

Don't confuse storing files inside folders to keep the files organized with creating a subweb. Although a subweb is indeed a group of files stored inside a folder in the current Web site, it is actually a distinct and fully functional Web site in its own right. I explain how to convert a folder into a subweb later in this chapter. For more information on what a subweb is, see Chapter 1.

To create new folders, follow these steps:

1. **In the Folders View, choose File⊅New⊅Folder.**

   A new folder appears. The folder name (New_Folder) is highlighted.

2. **Type a new folder name and then press Enter.**

   FrontPage renames the folder.

Renaming files and folders

I admit it. After all these years of using FrontPage, the power of the renaming feature still makes me weak in the knees. If, for any reason, you need to change the name of a file or folder in your Web site, FrontPage automatically updates all the file's associated hyperlinks.

Renaming the home page filename involves some extra considerations. I tell you about these considerations in Chapter 2.

You can rename a file or folder several ways, but the easiest is by following these steps:

1. **In any view except the Tasks View, click the icon for the file or folder you want to rename, wait a moment, and then click its filename.**

   A box appears around the filename, and the filename is highlighted. (If you don't wait a beat between clicks, FrontPage thinks you are double-clicking the file icon and opens the file, which you don't want. If this happens and the files opens, close the file and try again.)

2. **Type a new name.**

Be sure to maintain the same filename extension so that FrontPage knows what kind of file you're renaming.

3. Press Enter.

If the file contains associated links, the Rename dialog box appears, asking if you'd like to update the links to reflect the new name. (The power! Be still my beating heart!)

4. In the dialog box, click Yes.

The dialog box closes, FrontPage updates the links, and all is well.

Converting a folder into a subweb (and vice-versa)

As your site grows and you find your site filling up with lots of folders, you may want to convert one or more of the folders into subwebs.

The advantages to this arrangement are as follows:

- ✔ A subweb is a complete FrontPage Web site in its own right. You can therefore open a subweb into its own FrontPage window and manage the Web site as you see fit. This is a great way to break an overwhelmingly big Web site into easy-to-manage chunks.

- ✔ If you're working in a collaborative environment, subwebs can have different *permissions* from the parent Web site (handy when different groups of people are contributing to different parts of the Web site). I talk about permissions in Chapter 15.

- ✔ Because a subweb is distinct from the parent Web site, the subweb can have its own theme, keyword search capability, link bars, and shared borders. (You find out about all these features in Part II of this book.)

The parent Web site/subweb arrangement has its caveats, as follows:

- ✔ If you intend to nest subwebs (that is, create a subweb inside a subweb), you must publish your Web site on a host Web server that has FrontPage Server Extensions installed (for details, see Chapter 16).

- ✔ If the pages inside the folder that you are about to convert contain FrontPage link bars or the Include Page component, these features may be affected by the conversion. (More about link bars in Chapter 5 and components in Chapter 13.)

Should you decide the parent Web site/subweb setup is for you, follow these steps to convert a folder into a subweb:

1. **With the parent Web site open in FrontPage, right-click the folder you want to convert into a subweb, and choose Convert to Web from the pop-up menu that appears.**

   The Microsoft FrontPage dialog box appears, warning you that pages inside the folder will be affected by the conversion. If you change your mind and decide to maintain the status quo, click No. Otherwise . . .

2. **In the dialog box, click Yes.**

   The dialog box closes, and FrontPage converts the folder into a subweb. If the folder contains lots of files, the conversion may take a few moments. You can tell the conversion has taken place because a little globe appears on top of the folder icon.

If, later, you change your mind and want to consolidate a parent Web site and its subwebs back into a single Web site, you can convert subwebs into regular folders.

Keep in mind that the conversion comes with a few consequences:

- If the parent Web site is decorated with a theme, the subweb's pages will take on that theme (presumably this is a good thing).

- The subweb's files will take on the permission settings of the parent Web site.

- Link bar hyperlinks leading from the parent Web site to the subweb will no longer work properly.

- The subweb's task list will be lost. (For more about task lists, see Chapter 15.)

To convert a subweb into a folder, with the parent Web site open in FrontPage, right-click the subweb's folder, and choose Convert to Folder from the pop-up menu that appears. The Microsoft FrontPage dialog box appears, listing the changes that will occur in the subweb's pages as a result of the conversion. If the changes are okay with you, click Yes to close the dialog box and convert the subweb into a folder.

Converting folders isn't the only way to create subwebs. You can also use FrontPage templates and wizards to create new subwebs; for details, see Chapter 1.

Deleting files and folders

If your Web site contains a file that has outlived its usefulness or is otherwise cluttering your Web site, you can boot the file out with one swift click. To delete a file or folder, do the following:

1. **In any view except the Tasks View, click the file or folder you want to delete.**

2. **Press the Delete key.**

   The Confirm Delete dialog box appears, making sure that you want to delete the file or folder.

3. **Click Yes.**

   If you are deleting more than one file, click Yes to All to delete them all in one step (instead of having the Confirm Delete dialog box pop up before deleting each file). If you change your mind, click No or Cancel to close the dialog box without deleting the file.

Be careful, because after you delete a page or folder using FrontPage, you can't later change your mind.

Also, if you delete a file that's the destination of a link from elsewhere in your Web site, the link breaks. The damage isn't irreparable; you can always use FrontPage to find and fix broken hyperlinks. You should be aware of the problem all the same. The best way to avoid broken links caused by deleted files is to do your file cleanup using the Unlinked Files report (available by choosing View➪Reports➪Problems➪Unlinked Files). The pages listed in this report can safely be axed.

Backing up and moving Web sites

FrontPage enables you to copy your Web site to other locations such as floppy disks or other backup media. By backing up your Web site, you not only have a clean copy in the event of a computer glitch, but can also maintain a working copy to use as a scratch pad so that you avoid making permanent changes to the original. You can also use this method transfer your Web site from one computer to another should the need arise.

To back up your Web site, you follow similar steps to the ones you would follow if you were publishing your Web site:

1. **With the Web site open in FrontPage, choose File➪Publish Web.**

   The Publish Web dialog box appears.

2. **If the location visible in the Publish To box isn't the location to which you want to copy or back up your Web site, click Change.**

   The Publish Destination dialog box appears.

3. **In the dialog box's Enter Publish Destination list box, type the path to the location to which you want to back up the Web site.**

   Or click Browse to select a location on your computer or network.

4. In the Publish Destination dialog box, click OK.

If the path you entered into the Publish Destination dialog box doesn't yet exist, FrontPage first prompts you to create a Web at that location. Click OK.

The Publish Destination dialog box closes, and the Publish Web dialog box becomes visible again with the contents of the currently open Web site displayed on the left side of the dialog box, and the contents of the publish destination displayed on the right side (see Figure 14-7).

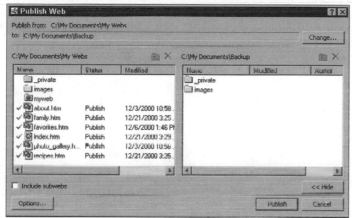

Figure 14-7:
Backing up a Web site.

5. If the Web site contains subwebs, and you want to back up the subwebs at the same time, mark the Include Subwebs check box.

6. Click Publish.

The Publish Web dialog box closes, and the Microsoft FrontPage dialog box appears and gives you a status indication about what's going on. If any of the pages in the Web site contain features that require FrontPage Server Extensions to work properly (and the location to which you're copying the site doesn't support FrontPage Server Extensions), the Publishing FrontPage Components dialog box will appear warning you that the components won't work properly. That's okay, because you're simply backing up the Web site. If this dialog box appears, click Continue to make it go away.

After the work is done, the Microsoft FrontPage dialog box appears, saying your Web site was published successfully. Don't be misled — your Web site isn't live. This is just the way FrontPage lets you know the copy process went smoothly.

7. Click Done to close the dialog box.

To move your Web site to a different computer, follow the steps in this section to copy the Web site to a floppy disk or other archive media (popular examples include Iomega Zip disks or Jaz drives). From the destination computer, launch FrontPage and then run the Import Web Wizard to copy the Web site from the disk or drive to the destination computer's hard drive. Chapter 1 explains how to import Web sites.

When you import a FrontPage Web site using the Import Web Wizard, the site's navigation structure is lost (and with it, the site's link bars and page banners). An article in the Microsoft Knowledge Base explains how to get around this problem. For help, go to support.microsoft.com and search for article number Q198229. Furthermore, if the site originally was decorated with a theme, you may need to reapply the theme to the imported version of the site.

Chapter 15

Sharing Access to Your Web Site

● ●

In This Chapter

▶ Streamlining teamwork with FrontPage collaboration features

▶ Controlling Web site access with permissions

▶ Changing access passwords

● ●

*F*rontPage gives you the power to control who can access your Web site. In this area of your life, at least, you can think of yourself as all-knowing and all-seeing.

By using FrontPage, you can regulate authoring access and site administration privileges by members of your Web site-building team, and browsing access by potential Web site visitors. FrontPage also contains a host of tools to make the collaboration process run smoothly. In this chapter, I show you how to use FrontPage workgroup and security features.

Working with a Web-Building Team

Few Web sites are one-person operations. Even if you're the lucky staff member who got tapped to put together the company Web or intranet site, you probably need input and cooperation from other members of the team. If those team members are sitting in an office 50 miles away, collaboration can be tricky.

Fortunately, FrontPage is equipped to handle the job. Because FrontPage is able to work in conjunction with a Web server on which FrontPage Server Extensions are installed, any team member with access to an internal network or Internet connection and a computer outfitted with FrontPage 2002 can work on the company Web site. The process goes like this:

1. **You work with the team to plan the site's content and design.**

2. **You create a core version of the site, which you then publish on a host Web server (either an ISP's Web server or a central company network server that's not accessible to the outside world).**

3. **All team members, using FrontPage on their individual workstations, log on to the central server to access the "live" site to add and change pages.**

By using FrontPage to connect to a site stored on a central Web server, more than one person can work on the site simultaneously, making collaboration among far-flung team members possible.

Of course, keeping track of the team's workflow is potential chaos. Fortunately, FrontPage comes with several features that help rein in the production process so everyone knows what's going on and what needs to happen next.

To use the collaboration features I talk about in this chapter, you must first publish your Web site on a Web server that has FrontPage Server Extensions installed, and then open the *live* version of the site in FrontPage. I talk more about FrontPage Server Extensions in Chapter 16. If you're not sure how to open the live version of a Web site directly from the host server, see Chapter 1.

Creating an online meeting place with SharePoint

Microsoft SharePoint is a new server-based technology that works hand-in-hand with Office XP and FrontPage 2002. With SharePoint installed on the host Web server, you can create a special type of team collaboration Web site that team members can use as a meeting place, document library, bulletin board, calendar, contact resource, and more. The beauty of the resulting SharePoint Team Web site is its incredible simplicity: Although you must use FrontPage to create and publish the site initially, the rest of the team needs only to use a browser to visit and contribute to the site.

SharePoint-powered sites can contain special interactive features called *lists*, *document libraries*, and *surveys*. A SharePoint list is an interactive list of any kind of information that your team uses, such as contact lists, product

lists, and lists of favorite hyperlinks. A document library is a special folder in the Web site earmarked as a repository for documents and files that your team wants to share. A survey enables you to poll your Web site visitors and then display the results in different ways.

The easiest way to create a SharePoint site is to use the SharePoint Team Web Site template. Chapter 1 explains how to create a new Web site based on a template.

SharePoint has specific server requirements and is also a complex enough topic that I can't do it justice in a sidebar (or even a full chapter). I've only skimmed the surface here, but if you want to learn more, start with the FrontPage Help System (choose Help⇨Microsoft FrontPage Help).

Using the Tasks View to keep track of workflow

The most challenging task for a Web publisher is, ironically, the most mundane: remembering all the details associated with creating and updating the Web site. If a team of authors maintains the site, keeping track of what needs to be done becomes even more complicated.

The creators of FrontPage understand this dilemma and thoughtfully included the Tasks View. The Tasks View helps you and the rest of the team keep track of unfinished tasks and is almost as easy to use as that pad of sticky notes sitting on your desk.

 To see the Tasks View, click the Tasks button on the Views bar or choose View➪Tasks.

Creating tasks

You can create two types of tasks: tasks associated with specific pages and independent tasks (tasks that need to be done but aren't pertinent to a particular page in the Web site, such as writing a press release or phoning a consultant).

To create an associated task, first open the live version of your Web site. Then, select the page with which you want to associate a task. (For example, open the page in the Page View, or click a page icon in the Folder List.) Then choose File➪New➪Task.

To create an independent task, without first selecting a page, follow the same steps as you would for creating an associated task.

When you create a new task, the New Task dialog box appears (see Figure 15-1).

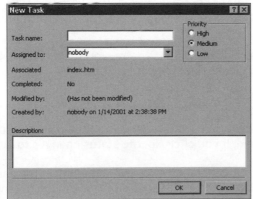

Figure 15-1:
The New
Task dialog
box.

To specify the task's details, follow these steps:

1. **In the Task Name text box, type a brief, descriptive title.**

2. **In the Assigned To text box, type the name of the person responsible for completing the task or choose a name from the list.**

   You set up the master list of names visible in the Assigned To text box by creating a user name master list. I talk about how to do this later in this chapter.

3. **In the Priority area, click the option button next to the task's priority level.**

4. **If necessary, type details or instructions in the Description box.**

5. **Click OK.**

   The dialog box closes, and the task appears in the Tasks View.

To modify a task, in the Tasks View, double-click the task. In the Task Details dialog box that appears, make any changes you want and then click OK to close the dialog box.

Starting and completing tasks

When you are ready to work on an associated task listed in the Tasks View, FrontPage helps track your progress. When you're finished, FrontPage marks the task as completed, enabling you to maintain a work history. (If you simply want to mark a task as complete, I explain how at the end of this section.)

To start working on an *associated task*, follow these steps:

1. **In the Tasks View, right-click the associated task you want to complete and then choose Start Task from the pop-up menu that appears.**

   The page associated with the task opens in the Page View. In the page, make whatever changes you want.

 2. **After you finish working on the page, click the Save button to save your work.**

   Because FrontPage remembers that you're working on a task, the Microsoft FrontPage dialog box appears asking if you want to mark the task as completed.

3. **If the task is complete, click Yes; otherwise, click No.**

   If you click Yes, in the Tasks View, the task's status changes from Not Started to Completed. If you click No, the status changes to In Progress.

To mark an associated *or* independent task as completed, in the Tasks View, right-click the task and then choose Mark Complete from the pop-up menu.

Checking documents in and out

By turning on FrontPage *source control,* you ensure that only one person at a time can edit a file — a crucial detail when several people are working on the Web site at the same time. With source control turned on, authors must check out files before they can edit them. While a file is checked out, other authors can open and read the file, but only the author who checked out the file can edit it. After the author is finished working on the file, she can save the changes and check the file back in, making the newly edited file available to the group again.

To turn on FrontPage source control, follow these steps:

1. **Open the live version of the Web site directly from the central Web server.**

   I explain how to open Web sites on remote Web servers in Chapter 1.

2. **Choose Tools➪Web Settings.**

   The Web Settings dialog box appears, with the General tab visible.

3. **In the dialog box, mark the Use Document Check-In and Check-Out box and then click OK.**

   The dialog box closes and another dialog box appears, prompting you to recalculate the Web site.

4. **In the dialog box, click Yes.**

   The dialog box closes, and FrontPage turns on source control.

With source control activated, little green dots appear next to the Web site's page icons in the Folder List, (see Figure 15-2). Green dots indicate the files are available to be checked out.

Figure 15-2:
With source control turned on, icons appear in the Folder List letting you know each file's checkout status.

To check out a file, proceed as if you are opening the file; FrontPage pops open a dialog box that asks if you want to check out the file. Click Yes. From there, the file opens as usual, and you can edit as you like. When you check out a file, a red check mark replaces the green dot in your FrontPage display. Any other authors who are logged on at the same time see a small padlock icon, indicating that the file is currently checked out by another author and cannot be edited.

You can also check out files without opening them. By doing so, you "lock out" other potential authors while you're working on a group of files. To check out a page without opening the page, right-click a file (or selected group of files) in the Folder List or in the Contents area of the Folders View, and choose Check Out from the pop-up menu that appears. After the files are checked out, you can open and close the files without having to worry about another author accessing the files.

When you are finished editing a file, save the changes and close the page. To check the page back in (making it available to the rest of the team), right-click the page's icon in the Folder List, and choose Check In from the pop-up menu that appears. In the Folder List, a green dot replaces the red check mark, and all is well.

You *must* manually check a file back in when you're finished with it — saving and/or closing the file does not automatically check in the file.

Assigning pages to specific authors and setting review status

FrontPage enables you (and other site authors) to designate who is responsible for each page in the site and to specify the page's review status. To do so, follow these steps:

1. **Open the live version of the Web site directly from the central Web server.**

   I explain how to open Web sites on remote Web servers in Chapter 1.

2. **In the Folder List, right-click the page and then choose Properties from the pop-up menu that appears.**

   (You can set the same author and status for more than one page at a time. While pressing the Ctrl key, first click each page that has the same author and status. Then right-click any of the selected pages and choose Properties from the pop-up menu.)

   The Properties dialog box for the selected file appears (the name of the dialog box depends on the page's filename).

3. **In the dialog box, click the Workgroup tab.**

   The Workgroup tab becomes visible (see Figure 15-3).

4. **In the Assigned To list box, type the name of the person responsible for the page, or choose a name from the list.**

   If the list is empty, add names by clicking the Names button. The User Names Master List dialog box appears. In the dialog box's New User Name text box, type a new name and then click Add. When you're finished, click OK to close the dialog box and return to the Properties dialog box.

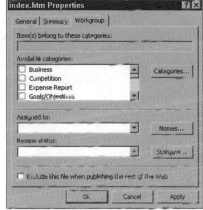

Figure 15-3:
The Workgroup tab of the Properties dialog box.

5. **In the Review Status list box, type the page's status, or choose a status from the list.**

   The list box contains three preset status listings: Approved, Denied, and Pending Review. To change or add to the list, click the Statuses button. The Review Status Master List dialog box appears. To add an item to the list, in the dialog box's New Review Status text box, enter a status and then click Add. To delete an item from the list, click the item and then click Delete. When you're finished, click OK to close the dialog box and return to the Properties dialog box.

6. **Click OK to close the Properties dialog box.**

Each time an author updates a page, he can update the page's review status (for example, changing the status from *In process* to *Finished*), keeping the rest of the team abreast of the site's progress.

For a quick overview of who is responsible for each page and of your site's overall review status, take a look at the Assigned To and Review Status reports (choose View⟹Reports⟹Workflow⟹Assigned To or choose View⟹Reports⟹Workflow⟹Review Status).

Automating site updates with the help of categories

When lots of people work on a Web site at the same time, keeping the site updated can be a major pain. After all, updating a site means more than just adding new pages. Those new pages need to be accessible from the rest of the site, so throughout the site, you must also scatter hyperlinks that lead to the new pages.

Two FrontPage features, *categories* and the *Table of Contents Web component*, can automate this process for you. First, you assign categories to the pages in your site, based on your site's organization. Then, you insert the Table of Contents component, which creates links that can help visitors move around your site. When you insert the component, you need to set it up so that it updates its list of hyperlinks to pages based on their categories. Then, each time someone in your workgroup adds a page to a category, the Table of Contents component adds a link to the new page among other links to related pages.

In FrontPage parlance, a *category* describes a subset of the information in your Web site. Depending on how your site is organized, you can set up whatever categories you like. For example, say your Web site contains three main sections: What's New, Company Services, and Technical Support. You can set up three corresponding categories for your Web site, and then assign each page in the site to one of the categories.

You can insert the Table of Contents component into any page in your Web site (a good example would be on a "site map" page users could access if they want to see complete list of the hyperlinks in your site). From then on, each time you add a new page to a category, a hyperlink leading to that page appears in the page containing the Table of Contents component.

 If more than one person logs onto a central server to edit the site, that server must have FrontPage Server Extensions installed. If, however, you're creating your Web site on your own computer with no other authors involved, you can assign pages to categories and use the Table of Contents component whether or not your host Web server has FrontPage Server Extensions installed.

Setting up and assigning pages to categories

To set up categories, follow these steps:

1. **With your Web site open, right-click a page in the Folder List and choose Properties from the pop-up menu that appears.**

   (You can choose any page, because the categories you define apply to the entire Web site.)

The Properties dialog box appears.

2. **In the dialog box, click the Workgroup tab.**

   The Workgroup tab becomes visible.

3. **To create a list of categories, click the Categories button.**

   The Master Category List dialog box appears.

4. **In the New Category text box, type a new category name and then click Add.**

   The category appears in the category list.

5. **To add more categories, repeat Step 4.**

   To delete categories, click a category in the list and then click Delete.

6. **When you're finished, click OK to close the dialog box and return to the Properties dialog box.**

   The categories you created appear in the dialog box's Available Categories list.

7. **Click OK to close the Properties dialog box.**

To assign a category to a page, follow these steps:

1. **In the Folder List, right-click the page and then choose Properties from the pop-up menu that appears.**

   (To assign the same category to more than one page at a time, while holding down the Ctrl key, first click each page to select it, and then right-click any of the selected pages and choose Properties from the pop-up menu.)

   The Properties dialog box appears.

2. **In the dialog box, click the Workgroup tab.**

3. **In the Available Categories box, click the category name(s) to which you want the page to belong.**

   You can choose more than one category.

4. **Click OK to close the Properties dialog box.**

To see a list of the categories to which your pages are assigned, choose View⇨Reports⇨Workflow⇨Categories.

Inserting the Table of Contents Based on Page Category component

Now that you have assigned your site's pages to different categories, you are ready to insert the Table of Contents component into a page. When viewed with a Web browser, the Web component replaces itself with a list of hyperlinks that lead to pages in the category (or categories) you specify. To insert the Web component, follow these steps:

1. **Place the cursor in the page where you want the table of contents to appear, and then choose Insert⇨Web Component or click the Web Component button on the Standard toolbar.**

   The Insert Web Component dialog box appears.

2. **In the Component Type list box, click Table of Contents.**

   A list of available effects appears on the right side of the dialog box.

3. **In the Choose a Table of Contents list box, double-click Based on Page Category.**

   The Insert Web Component dialog box closes, and the Categories Properties dialog box appears (see Figure 15-4).

Figure 15-4:
The
Categories
Properties
dialog box.

4. **In the dialog box's Choose Categories to List Files By box, mark the category or categories for which you want the table of contents to list hyperlinks.**

   If you choose more than one category, the Web component will list hyperlinks to pages in each category but won't distinguish between the different categories.

   If you want the page to display links to separate categories in the same page, and you want those categories to remain distinct, you're better off inserting a separate table of contents for each category.

5. **Choose an option from the Sort Files By list box.**

   The Web component can list pages alphabetically by title or sequentially according to the date the page was last modified.

6. **If you want the table of contents to list the date the page was last modified or the comments added to the page, mark the appropriate check box.**

I explain how to add comments to a file at the end of this section.

7. **Click OK.**

   The dialog box closes, and a placeholder for the table of contents appears in the page.

To see the Web component at work, use a Web browser to preview the page. (The Preview tab doesn't do the trick in this case.) When viewed with a browser, the Web component is replaced by a list of links to the pages in the specified categories. FrontPage uses the page's title as the hyperlink text.

You can attach descriptive comments to any page in your Web site. To do so, right-click the page's icon in the Folder List and then choose Properties from the pop-up menu that appears. The Page Properties dialog box appears, with the General tab visible. In the dialog box, click the Summary tab. In the dialog box's Comments box, type your comments, and then click OK to close the dialog box.

Keeping Your Web Site Secure

When I was a kid, I knew I'd pushed my parents too far if they said, "You live in our house; you live by our rules!" To this statement, I could offer no rebuttal — just resigned acceptance and a few minutes of serious pouting.

Well, this Web site is *your* home page, which means that *you* get to make the rules. You control who can update or change your Web site and even who can view it. The process is called *adjusting permissions*, and with FrontPage, you can perform the task with ease.

Permissions are different levels of Web site access. The Web site's host Web server contains a list of user names and associated passwords along with corresponding levels of Web site access. By using FrontPage, you can access the Web server's permission settings to add and change users and specify levels of access.

This feature is a blessing in a workgroup setting, because you can control who has authoring privileges. When each team member logs onto the central server to access the site, a FrontPage dialog box appears prompting them to enter a user name and password, and FrontPage grants access based on the permissions you've specified.

Permissions also enable you to create a private Web site. When visitors try to access a private Web site, their Web browser pops open a dialog box requesting a user name and password. Unless they enter the name and password you specify, they are unable to browse the Web site.

To use FrontPage to access a server's permissions, the server must have FrontPage Server Extensions installed. What's more, the *version* of the FrontPage Server Extensions installed, the Web server program that your ISP uses, as well as your own computer's network setup, affect permissions settings. The instructions in this chapter illustrate how permissions work for the 2002 version of the FrontPage Server Extensions installed with the Apache Web server, a popular UNIX-based Web server program that many ISPs use. If your host Web server uses a different Web server program or runs a different operating system, the steps are slightly different (I discuss one difference in the sidebar "Defining user roles," later in the chapter). If in doubt about any of this information, check with your ISP or system administrator and refer to the FrontPage Help system by choosing Help➪Microsoft FrontPage Help.

Setting permissions

To control who may edit your Web site, you use FrontPage to specify administrators and authors. If you want your Web site to appear only to authorized visitors, you can also create a list of people with browsing access.

FrontPage provides for the following three levels of access:

- **Administer:** Giving someone Administer access makes them an *administrator,* and an administrator can create, edit, and delete Web sites and pages and adjust a Web site's permissions. Every Web site must have at least one administrator.

- **Author:** An author can create, edit, or delete pages but cannot create or delete Web sites or adjust the Web site's permissions.

- **Browse:** A person with Browse access can only view a Web site with a Web browser; that person can't edit the Web site or even open the site in FrontPage.

If the Web site for which you're setting permissions contains a subweb, the steps are slightly more complex. By default, all subwebs have the same permissions as their *parent Web site* (the top-level Web site) and are visible to anyone with a Web browser. Therefore, if you adjust the parent Web site's permissions, you automatically change the permissions of all its subwebs as well. (If you're not sure what a subweb is, refer to Chapter 1.) In the following steps, I show you how to change the parent Web site's permission settings, as well as how to give your parent Web site and subwebs independent permission settings.

Defining user roles

On SharePoint-powered sites, and on sites hosted on Windows-based Web servers running FrontPage 2002 Server Extensions, you have more sophisticated control over permissions. These server setups support the creation of *user roles* in which you can pick and choose the various access rights users have. For example, you can designate users with browse access (those who can view the Web site, but can not edit it) and contributor access (those who can view the Web site *and* participate in discussion groups, but can not edit the site). The Help system details all of the FrontPage permission capabilities.

To set your Web site's permissions, follow these steps:

1. **Publish the Web site.**

   I explain how to publish in Chapter 16.

2. **Open the live version of the Web site directly from the host Web server.**

   In Chapter 1, I explain how to open Web sites stored on remote servers.

3. **Choose Tools➪Server➪Permissions.**

   The Permissions dialog box appears.

   - If the Web site is a parent Web site, you see one tab at the top of the dialog box: Users. Skip ahead to Step 5.

   - If the Web site is a subweb, the dialog box contains a second tab: Settings. The Settings panel enables you to change the permission setting so that the subweb uses its own set of permissions instead of inheriting the parent Web site's permission settings.

4. **If you want the subweb to have its own permission settings, click the Use Unique Permissions for This Web option button and then click Apply.**

   FrontPage adjusts the Web site's permissions.

5. **Click the Users tab.**

   The Users tab becomes visible.

6. **To add a user, click the Add button.**

   The Add Users dialog box appears.

7. **In the Name text box, type a user name.**

User names and passwords are case sensitive, which means that FrontPage sees *gonzo* and *Gonzo* as two different names.

8. **In the Password text box, type a password.**

9. **Type the password again in the Confirm Password text box.**

10. **In the Allow Users To area of the dialog box, click the option button for the level of access you want the individual to have.**

11. **Click OK.**

    The Add Users dialog box closes, returning you to the Users tab of the Permissions dialog box.

12. **To restrict browsing access to authorized users only, click the Valid Username and Password Required to Browse This Web check box.**

    If you don't mark this check box, anyone with an Internet connection and a Web browser can browse your Web site.

13. **Click Apply to activate changes and continue adjusting permissions, or click OK to activate changes and close the Permissions dialog box.**

Changing permissions

You can easily adjust your Web site's permissions. You can, for example, upgrade an author's access to administrator, or you can remove a user from the list of people authorized to browse the site. To edit a user's permissions, follow these steps:

1. **Open the Web site, and then choose Tools➪Server➪Permissions.**

    The Permissions dialog box opens.

2. **If it's not already visible, click the Users tab.**

3. **In the user list, click the name of the user whose permissions you want to change and then click Edit.**

    The Edit Users dialog box appears.

4. **In the Allow Users To area of the dialog box, click the option button for the user's new permission setting, and then click OK.**

    The Edit Users dialog box closes, returning you to the Users panel of the Permissions dialog box.

5. **Click Apply to activate changes and continue adjusting permissions, or click OK to activate changes and close the Permissions dialog box.**

To remove a user from the permission list, follow the same instructions, but in Step 3, click the Remove button rather than the Edit button.

Chapter 16

Making Your Worldwide Debut

Drumroll, please! It's the moment of truth . . . time to unveil your painstakingly prepared, lovingly built Web site and make the site visible to the world.

In this chapter, I show you how to publish your Web site, and I give you tips on how to update your site to keep it fresh and interesting.

What "Publishing Your Web Site" Means

Publishing your Web site means making the site visible on the World Wide Web for all to see (or, in the case of an intranet site, visible to members of the intranet). For your site to be accessible to visitors, you must store all the site's files and folders on a computer called a Web server. A Web server is a computer running special Web server software that maintains a high-speed, round-the-clock connection to the Internet or internal network. (In Chapter 3, I give you an overview of how the Internet's client-server setup works.)

Most people gain access to a host Web server by getting an account with an Internet Service Provider (ISP). Having an account at an ISP enables your computer and modem to establish a connection to the Internet. After you're connected, you can then use the Internet to send and receive e-mail, browse the Web, and transfer files between computers.

A typical ISP also provides a limited amount of publishing space on its Web server as part of your regular monthly fee. The amount of storage space varies. (Some ISPs provide as little as 5MB; mine provides 50MB.) Check with your ISP for details.

Not sure how much file space your Web site takes up? Try this: In the Folder List, right-click the site's top-level folder and then choose Properties. The dialog box that appears displays the Web site's total file size. (The file size shown here doesn't including the size of any subwebs; you must open sub-webs separately to check their sizes.)

Several companies provide Web server space for free. All you have to do is register at the company's Web site. Popular choices include Tripod (`www.tripod.lycos.com`) and Yahoo! Geocities (`geocities.yahoo.com`).

If you're building an intranet site, your company maintains its own Web server and network connection. Speak to your company's system administrator for details about your network setup.

The Skinny on FrontPage Server Extensions

Having access to a host Web server is only part of the publishing picture. For certain FrontPage-created features to work, the Web server must have a set of auxiliary programs called *FrontPage Server Extensions* installed. FrontPage Server Extensions are a special set of programs that act as translators between FrontPage and the Web server program.

Installing FrontPage Server Extensions on a Web server is a big job, which is why many ISPs and system administrators have yet to fully support FrontPage. The number of FrontPage-friendly ISPs is growing every day, however, and the number is sure to increase. (I give you tips on finding an ISP to host your FrontPage Web site in the sidebar, "Finding a FrontPage ISP.")

Finding a FrontPage ISP

The benefits of publishing your Web site with a FrontPage-friendly ISP are clear. But how do you find a FrontPage ISP? Check local computer magazines and newspapers, ask friends for recommendations, and lean on Microsoft for assistance. The Publish Destination dialog box (available the first time you attempt to publish a Web site) contains a link that leads your Web browser straight to the Microsoft Web site, where you find an index of registered FrontPage Web presence providers (most of whom offer full Internet access as well).

If you're happy with your current ISP, consider publishing your Web site at Tripod (`www.tripod.lycos.com`). Tripod provides free Web space to anyone who registers . . . and, best of all, Tripod supports FrontPage Server Extensions.

The good news is that you can publish a FrontPage Web site on *any* Web server — including servers without FrontPage Server Extensions installed — with certain caveats. Repeat: you do *not* have to run out and sign up for a different Web hosting service if yours doesn't support FrontPage Server Extensions, as long as you're aware of some limitations. You can use all FrontPage features except for the following, which rely on FrontPage Server Extensions:

- ✔ The _private folder (you can use this folder, but it doesn't have any password protection)
- ✔ Nested subwebs (that is, subwebs within subwebs)
- ✔ The following Web components: Confirmation Field, Web Search, Hit Counter, Table of Contents based on categories, and Top 10 List
- ✔ FrontPage workgroup features, including source control
- ✔ FrontPage discussion groups
- ✔ FrontPage user registration systems
- ✔ The Database Interface Wizard and the Send To Database form handler
- ✔ Usage reports
- ✔ File upload form field
- ✔ Custom link bars
- ✔ Shared border background properties
- ✔ Permissions and security

Additionally, if you want to open or create a Web site on a remote Web server, that server must have FrontPage Server Extensions installed.

The built-in FrontPage form handler works hand-in-hand with FrontPage Server Extensions, but you can adjust the form handler to work on any Web server with a form handler installed. See Chapter 9 for details.

If you attempt to publish a site that contains FrontPage Server Extensions-related features on a host Web server that doesn't have FrontPage Server Extensions installed, FrontPage pops open a dialog box that lists the pages that won't work properly and prompts you to change or remove the pages. FrontPage also lists these pages in the Component Errors report. To see the report, after publishing (or after canceling a publishing attempt), choose View⇨Reports⇨Problems⇨Component Errors).

If you intend to publish your site on a server that doesn't support FrontPage Server Extensions, you can customize FrontPage to make available only those options that will work properly (see Chapter 4 for instructions). You must do this *before* you create your Web site. Changing FrontPage compatibility options does not remove features from your site; it simply instructs FrontPage to dim those commands and menu items that require FrontPage Server Extensions to be able to work.

One final hurdle: With the release of FrontPage 2002 comes a new release of FrontPage Server Extensions, which means that every ISP that supports FrontPage must upgrade from the older versions to the new 2002 version of the FrontPage Server Extensions. If you publish a FrontPage 2002-authored site on a host server running an older version of the FrontPage Server Extensions, the following features won't work properly:

- ✔ Usage reports
- ✔ File upload form field
- ✔ Custom link bars
- ✔ Shared border background properties
- ✔ The Top 10 List Web component
- ✔ Certain permissions options

An ISP or company that still uses an older version of the FrontPage Server Extensions is probably in the process of upgrading. (Contact your system administrator or ISP to make sure.)

Going Public

Time to take your show on the road. In this section, I show you how to publish your Web site.

Excluding unfinished pages from publishing

Before the curtain goes up, give your Web site the white glove test so that the site makes its debut with style and polish. Rev up the FrontPage spell checker (choose Tools⇨Spelling), make sure that your hyperlinks work properly (choose View⇨Reports⇨Problems⇨Broken Hyperlinks), and go through every inch of your site using a Web browser — preferably more than one browser model.

If your site contains files (Web pages, graphics, or any other files) that aren't yet ready for public viewing, you can tell FrontPage to hold those files back while publishing the rest of the site. To do so, in the Folder List, right-click the file you want to hold back (or select multiple files by pressing the Ctrl key while clicking icons, and then right-click the selection), and choose Don't Publish from the pop-up menu that appears. A red X appears next to the file icon letting you know that file won't be published the next time you publish the site.

For an overview of your site's publish status, take a look at the Publish Status report by choosing View⇨Reports⇨Workflow⇨Publish Status.

If you exclude a page from being published that is linked to another page in the site, that link will not work properly in the live version of the site. Therefore, before you publish, be sure to dismantle any hyperlinks that lead to unfinished pages. For instructions on how to do this, see Chapter 5.

Publishing your Web site

After you've given your Web site a thorough once-over, the next step is to find out your publishing address. This address tells FrontPage where in the host Web server's file system to store your Web site's files. On servers that have FrontPage Server Extensions installed, the address may look something like `http://www.mydomain.com` or `http://www.server.com/~username`. On servers that don't have FrontPage Server Extensions installed, the address may instead begin with `ftp://`. (The difference has to do with the method or *protocol* that FrontPage uses to connect to the Web server and transfer the files.) If in doubt, your ISP or system administrator can tell you your publishing address.

You must have the correct publishing address in hand to publish your Web site.

To publish your Web site for the first time, follow these steps:

1. **In FrontPage, open the Web site you want to publish.**

   If the site is already open in FrontPage, be sure to save any changes you have made to the site's pages.

2. **Activate your Internet connection.**

3. **Choose File⇨Publish Web.**

   The Publish Destination dialog box appears (see Figure 16-1).

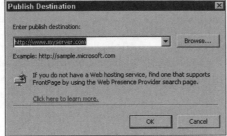

Figure 16-1:
The Publish
Destination
dialog box.

4. **In the dialog box's Enter Publish Destination list box, type the Web site's publishing address.**

   The address you enter in this dialog box is specific to your Web server and is different from what is pictured in Figure 16-1.

5. **Click OK.**

   The Publish Destination dialog box closes, and FrontPage contacts the host Web server at the address you specified. If the Web server contains security features (most do), the Name and Password Required dialog box appears.

6. **In the Name and Password text boxes, enter the user name and password that you chose when you established your account, and then click OK.**

   The dialog box closes. If you've never published a FrontPage Web site to that location before, a Microsoft FrontPage dialog box appears asking if you'd like FrontPage to create a Web there.

7. **Click OK.**

   The dialog box closes, and the Publish Web dialog box appears (see Figure 16-2).

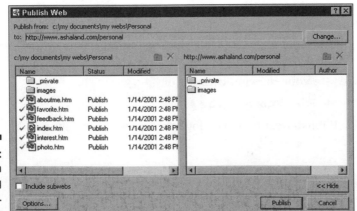

Figure 16-2:
The Publish
Web dialog
box.

This dialog box contains all sorts of useful information. The file system for the Web site you're about to publish appears in the left half of the dialog box, and the file system of the publishing destination — where the Web site's files eventually end up on the host Web server — appears on the right.

8. **If your Web site contains subwebs and you want to publish the parent Web site and subwebs together, mark the Include Subwebs check box, which is at the bottom of the dialog box.**

    Double-check the address in the To list box at the top of the Publish Web dialog box; make sure this address is indeed the location to which you want to publish. (If you notice a typo, click Change to display the Publish Destination dialog box again, enter the proper publishing address, and click OK.) If everything looks good, take a breath and. . .

9. **Click OK.**

    The Publish Web dialog box closes, and FrontPage copies all your Web site files to the host Web server. Depending on the size of your Web site and the speed of your Internet connection, this process may take a few minutes. (Watch your screen for messages that explain what's happening.)

    On servers that have FrontPage Server Extensions installed, FrontPage takes care of file management and cleanup duties as it publishes your site. For example, if the host Web server contains files at the publishing address that are not part of the Web site you're publishing, FrontPage gives you the option of deleting those files from the host Web server.

    If the host server has FrontPage Server Extensions installed and the host Web server recognizes a default home page filename other than index.htm, FrontPage changes the home page filename on the host Web server and updates any associated hyperlinks.

    If the host server recognizes a home page filename other than index.htm and *does not* have FrontPage Server Extensions installed, you must change the home page filename in the local copy of your Web site and then publish the site again. (I explain how to rename files in Chapter 14.) If you're not sure which home page filename your host server recognizes, ask your ISP or system administrator.

    After the work is done, the Microsoft FrontPage dialog box pops up to tell you the publishing process was a success.

10. **In the dialog box, click Done.**

    The dialog box closes.

Congratulations — your site is now visible to the world!

You're Live!

Pass the bubbly! Your Web site has joined the Internet community, and you can now call yourself a true-blue Web publisher. Using your Web browser, visit your live Web site at its new URL and, just to be safe, give the site one last check. If all is well, heave a sigh of relief and enjoy a moment of satisfaction.

You might even want to line up a group of sympathetic testers who use different types of computers and browsers and ask them to give your site a run-through. Even if everything works perfectly when viewed with your computer and browser, a glitch might pop up when viewed from a different platform.

If something doesn't work properly, fix the problem on the *local* copy of your Web site — the copy stored on your computer — and publish your Web site again. I show you how in the following section.

Now that your Web site is open to the public, you need to let everyone know you're entertaining visitors. Every site can benefit from publicity. How do you invite the world to your home page? Here are a few suggestions:

✔ **Search services:** List the page with popular search services, such as Yahoo! (`www.yahoo.com`), Excite (`www.excite.com`), and AltaVista (`www.altavista.com`). Each search service posts listing instructions on its Web site. (Be sure to check out some of the programs included on the CD at the back of the book; several assist in the process of getting your site listed with search engines.)

✔ **E-mail signature:** Include your Web site URL in the signature line of your e-mail messages. Most e-mail programs enable you to append a few lines of text to the bottom of every message.

✔ **Newsgroups:** Post a discreet announcement to newsgroups that discuss related topics. Keep your announcement low-key and respectful. If you blanket a newsgroup with advertising hype, not only will you irk the other newsgroup participants (hence, bad word-of-mouth), your publicity campaign may well backfire.

✔ **Traditional print advertising:** Add your Web site URL to business cards, letterhead, and print advertising.

✔ **Word-of-mouth:** Invite your friends and colleagues to visit your Web site and encourage them to spread the word.

For more promotion inspiration, check out the links in the Publicity Corner of my Web site, the Web Publishing Online Resource, at `www.ashaland.com/webpub`.

Keeping Your Web Site Fresh

Stagnant Web sites are as appealing as day-old pastry. On the World Wide Web, freshness counts, so keep your site vital by changing its content, updating its graphics, and adding new features regularly.

To update your site (or to correct any mistakes you find), you make changes on the local copy of your Web site and then publish the Web site again. To update the site's changed pages, a single button-click does the trick, as follows:

1. **In FrontPage, open the Web site you want to update and make (and save) whatever changes you want.**

2. **Activate your Internet connection.**

 3. **Click the Publish Web button on the Standard toolbar.**

   If the host server supports security features, the Name and Password Required dialog box appears.

   Note: If you update your site several times during a single FrontPage session, this dialog box only appears the first time you publish or update the site.

4. **In the Name and Password text boxes, type your user name and password and then click OK.**

   The dialog box closes, and FrontPage copies the changed pages to the host Web server. Your site is now fresh as a daisy.

If you prefer to choose which pages and files to update (as opposed to letting FrontPage simply publish all files that have changed), in the Folder List, right-click the file or folder you wish to publish (or select multiple files and folders by pressing the Ctrl key while clicking icons, and then right-click the selection), and choose Publish Selected Files from the pop-up menu appears. The Publish Destination dialog box appears with the site's publishing address visible in the Publish Selected Files To list box. Click OK to close the dialog box and publish the selected file(s).

To republish the entire Web site (not just the changed pages) or to publish the Web site to a different location, follow the steps in the previous section.

Part V
The Part of Tens

The 5th Wave   By Rich Tennant

LARRY KING LIVE

"OK LARRY, ENOUGH ABOUT THE ELECTION. LET'S TALK INTERNET BROWSERS. NEITHER ONE OF THE TWO BIG ONES ADEQUATELY REPRESENTS THE USER, WHICH IS WHY I PLAN TO LAUNCH A THIRD ALTERNATIVE—THE 'REFORM BROWSER.'"

In this part . . .

*I*n the following chapters, I give FrontPage a rest and share some tips that help you expand your Web-publishing consciousness. I list ten things you can do with your Web site and ten Web sites you should plan to visit.

Chapter 17

Ten Things You Can Do with Your Web Site

● ●

In This Chapter

▶ Making money with your Web site

▶ Setting up a site just for friends and family

▶ Using your site for business purposes

▶ Spreading your world view

● ●

*W*eb sites are like rubber bands — if you put your mind to the task, you can think of a million ways to use them. To get you started, here are ten of my favorite ways to use a Web site.

Make a Million Bucks

The Internet Gold Rush may be over, but some folks still see flashing dollar signs as they think of the millions of potential customers surfing the Web. Secure credit card transactions and electronic commerce technology make online shopping more and more popular every year. So fire up FrontPage and create a slick Web site. Who knows — maybe you're destined to become the next Net Rockefeller. (If you're interested in ecommerce, be sure to check out the commerce-related bCentral Web Components and the commerce-related extras included on the book's CD. I talk about Web Components in Chapter 13, and I tell you all about the book's CD in Appendix B.)

Keep in Touch

Your parents settled down in Miami. Your best friend is pursuing her dreams in Paris. Your brother works all the time and has no energy for phone calls. No problem! Use your Web site as a meeting place for friends and family. They can log on and share news 24 hours a day. Set up a password-protected discussion group that only registered loved ones can enter. (See the bonus chapter on the CD for details on setting up a discussion group; Chapter 15 has information about password-protecting your Web site.) Post a family tree online with hyperlinks to the home pages of other wired relatives. Devote a page to people's birthdays and anniversaries. Scan snapshots from the last family reunion and put them online for all to see.

Impress Potential Employers

A Web site is the perfect place to toot your own horn. Post your résumé online. List your accomplishments, talk about your goals, and point to the Web sites of past workplaces and your alma mater. Add your Web site address to your business card and present the card, along with a firm handshake, to people you want to impress.

Impress Geeky Friends

If you like to play "my hard drive is bigger than your hard drive" with your friends, use your Web site to become king or queen of the high-tech hill. Create a list of favorite Web destinations and include links to the home pages of Slashdot (www.slashdot.com), News.com (www.news.com), and the Official Star Trek Fan Club. Cultivate a vocabulary full of techie buzzwords and use them often. ("Yeah, I added a JavaScript to my IMG tags, but it wonked out after my friend ran it with Netscape 7.4026b and her box crashed.")

"Wire" Your Company

If your employees have Web access or are part of a company intranet, use a Web site as a central information hub. Publish company policies and the employee handbook. (Think of all the paper you save by updating these documents online.) Set up discussion groups for each of your departments. Start a Web-based company newsletter. Use the Guest Book page template to create an employee suggestion box. (See Chapter 2 for instructions on how to create a new Web page by using a page template.)

Spread the Word about a Good Cause

Can you think of something you want the world to know? A Web site is potentially visible to millions of people, making your site one of the most effective ways to spread the word about an important cause. Create that Web site, publicize the site far and wide, and watch interested visitors start pouring in. (See Chapter 16 for promotion tips.) Create a feedback form or a discussion group so that visitors can ask questions. (For more information about forms, see Chapter 9, and for details about discussion groups, see the bonus chapter on the CD.) Offer to send more information to those who are interested. Keep your site up-to-date so it becomes a well-respected resource for information and news. Insert a hit counter in your home page so that everyone knows just how many other people care about the issue you support (see Chapter 13 for information on hit counters).

Indulge Your Artistic Side

If you're a poet, artist, or musician, publishing a Web site could be the next best thing to a local reading, a gallery showing, or a concert. Use your Web site to showcase your creativity. Transform your favorite poems into Web pages and invite feedback. Include sample clips of your music (I explain how in Chapter 12). If your work is on display somewhere else, tell visitors where to go to experience your talent.

Incite World Revolution

The photocopy machine put the power of the press into everyone's hands. Social activists produce reams of flyers and leaflets to help spread the word about important issues. The Web makes broadcasting information even easier. A Web page is visible to millions, and you don't need to staple it to telephone poles or hand it to passersby. So use your Web site to make a difference. Get on your virtual soapbox and issue a call to action.

Share Your Expertise

You may not consider yourself an expert on anything, but I would venture to say that most of us know a lot about *something*. Perhaps you're passionate about Australian Ridgebacks, or you're up on all the newest electronic gadgets, or you make a delectable tiramisu. Whatever the topic, consider using your Web site to share your knowledge. I can almost guarantee that someone, somewhere in the world, will find the information helpful.

Erect a Personal Monument

Seeing your name in print or engraved on a plaque is inherently thrilling. Perhaps the permanence is the key — the idea that your words or ideas will always be there. A Web site can be the electronic equivalent of a personal monument — a place where you can immortalize the things most important to you. Scan your favorite vacation snapshots and create an online travel diary. Start an unofficial fan club for someone you admire; the number of celebrities who have e-mail addresses and participate in online chats may surprise you. Use your Web site as a place to pay tribute to the things that inspire you.

Chapter 18

Ten Web Sites You Don't Want to Miss

In This Chapter

▶ Finding out about FrontPage, HTML, and Web design on the Internet

▶ Searching the Web with Google

▶ Downloading stuff from Download.com

*T*hroughout this book, I point you to Web sites that I find particularly helpful. In this chapter, I highlight ten must-see spots you really shouldn't miss.

Microsoft FrontPage Home Page

www.microsoft.com/frontpage

This site is the place to go for all things FrontPage. Here you find FrontPage tips and information, free accessory downloads, and links to related resources. You can also access online support and FrontPage help, including FrontPage newsgroups, a list of frequently asked questions, and much more.

Microsoft Knowledge Base

support.microsoft.com

Got a question? This mammoth online database contains thousands of articles that answer common software questions or explain annoying bugs. The Knowledge Base contains articles pertaining to all Microsoft products, including FrontPage.

HTML for Beginners

```
www.builder.com/Authoring/Basics/?tag=st.bl.3881.dir1.bl_Basics
```

The surest way to beef up your Web publishing savvy is to learn HTML, the language behind every Web page. Plenty of good books on the subject are out there, but if you're ready to get started *now*, check out this straightforward, easy-to-take introduction to HTML basics.

Builder.com

```
www.builder.com
```

If you like to keep on top of Web publishing happenings, make this Web site one of your regular stops. Builder.com contains practical how-to articles for all sorts of Web tricks.

Webmonkey

```
hotwired.lycos.com/webmonkey
```

The attitude-filled folks at Webmonkey offer advice about all things Web design. Enthusiastic Web publishers can spend hours here; the site contains information on everything from basic Web page creation to advanced design and programming tips.

Learn the Net

```
www.learnthenet.com
```

If you just want to know how the Internet works, visit this well-organized Web site. You can find tons of good, well-written information, but not so much that you'll be overwhelmed. Be sure to check out the excellent section devoted Web site building.

Google

`www.google.com`

The Web contains information about the current political climate, pictures of African wild dogs, and several online dating services — the trick is finding these sites. I've tried most of the search engines out there, and I keep coming back to Google. This engine always chug-a-chugs me in the right direction.

Download.com

`www.download.com`

Everyone keeps talking about the gigabytes of free software available on the Net, but where do you get all that stuff? This site groups shareware offerings into categories such as Business and Finance, Multimedia and Design, and Internet. Or you can look at a list of top picks or the most-popular titles.

Dummies.com

`www.dummies.com`

If you can't wait to get your hands on your next good read, check out the Dummies.com Web site. Find out which new books are about to hit the shelves, pick up some savvy tips, or order a title online.

Web Publishing Online Resource

`www.ashaland.com/webpub`

In closing, I invite you to my little corner of the Web. I maintain this repository of interesting and useful Web publishing resources so that you can have a single place to visit when you're not sure where else to find the Web publishing answer that you're looking for.

By the way, I maintain the Web site using FrontPage. I don't know how I ever got along without it. Really.

Part VI
Appendixes

The 5th Wave   By Rich Tennant

"He found a dog site over an hour ago and has been in a staring contest ever since."

In this part . . .

The two appendixes contain extra info you may find helpful. If you want help with installing FrontPage on your computer, read Appendix A. After you pull the CD out of the plastic cover on the back of this book, Appendix B helps you easily install all the CD goodies on your computer.

Appendix A

Installing FrontPage

· ·

*I*f installing FrontPage on your computer seems like a gargantuan task, you have help. In this appendix, I take you step-by-step through the FrontPage installation process.

Microsoft FrontPage 2002 is not included on the CD that comes with this book. You need to buy FrontPage at a software or computer store. See www.microsoft.com/frontpage for details. For information about the book's CD, refer to Appendix B.

FrontPage 2002 comes in two versions: the version bundled with Microsoft Office XP and the stand-alone version. I wrote the following steps using the stand-alone version of FrontPage 2002, but the Setup programs for both versions are very similar.

If not, remember that your licensed copy of Office or FrontPage gives you access to real, live Microsoft technical support engineers, either by telephone (it's a long-distance call, but you get real-time help) or via e-mail (no long-distance charges, but you must wait one business day for an answer). For details about your support options, see www.microsoft.com/support.

To install FrontPage, follow these steps:

1. **Turn on your computer and CD-ROM drive.**

   If your computer is already on, exit any programs that are currently open.

2. **Insert the Microsoft FrontPage 2002 CD (or the Microsoft Office CD 1), with the label facing up, into your CD-ROM drive.**

   In a moment, the opening screen of the Setup program appears. The Setup program takes you step-by-step through the installation process.

   If no opening screen appears, on your Windows desktop, double-click the My Computer icon to open a window that contains icons for each of your computer's drives. To launch the Setup program, double-click the CD-ROM icon.

3. **In the opening screen, type your user information.**

   Enter your name, initials, organization, and the 25-digit CD key. (You can find the CD key on a sticker affixed to the CD case.)

4. **Click the Next button.**

   The next dialog box appears.

5. **Read the License Agreement. When you're finished, mark the check box next to I Accept the Terms in the License Agreement, and then click Next.**

   The next dialog box appears.

   You can, at any time, return to a previous dialog box to change your settings by clicking the Back button. To exit the Setup program, click the Cancel button.

6. **Select the Install Now option button, and then click Next.**

   By clicking Install Now, you're telling the Setup program to perform a typical installation (this option works fine for most folks). If you want more control over the installation process and don't mind a few extra steps, select the Custom option button, click Next, and then follow the Setup program's directions.

   After you click Next, the next dialog box appears. This dialog box lists all the installation tasks that the Setup program is about to perform.

7. **Click Install.**

   After you click Install, the Installing dialog box appears. This dialog box stays in view as the Setup program installs Office (or the stand-alone version of FrontPage) on your computer. The setup process takes a few minutes, so sit back and relax. When installation is complete, a dialog box appears letting you know.

8. **Click OK to close the dialog box.**

   You're ready to begin using FrontPage.

9. **To launch FrontPage, click the Start button, and then choose Programs⇨Microsoft FrontPage.**

   FrontPage launches, and you're ready to roll.

Appendix B

About the CD

● ●

*T*he CD-ROM included with this book contains goodies that make Web publishing with FrontPage easier and more fun.

Even better, the CD comes with its own interface that helps you easily install the programs onto your hard drive. In this appendix, I show you how to work with the CD-ROM.

Microsoft FrontPage 2002 is *not* included on the CD that comes with this book. You need to buy FrontPage 2002 at a software or computer store. See www.microsoft.com/frontpage for details.

System Requirements

Make sure your computer meets the minimum system requirements listed below. If your computer doesn't match up to most of these requirements, you may have problems using the contents of the CD.

- ✔ A PC with a Pentium or faster processor.
- ✔ Microsoft Windows 98 or later.
- ✔ At least 16MB of total RAM installed on your computer. For best performance, we recommend at least 32MB of RAM installed.
- ✔ At least 100 MB of hard drive space available to install all the software from this CD. (You'll need less space if you don't install every program.)
- ✔ A CD-ROM drive — double-speed (2x) or faster.
- ✔ A sound card for PCs.
- ✔ A monitor capable of displaying at least 256 colors or grayscale.
- ✔ A modem with a speed of at least 14,400 bps.

If you need more information on the basics, check out *PCs For Dummies,* 7th Edition, by Dan Gookin; *Windows 98 For Dummies*; or *Microsoft Windows Me Millennium Edition For Dummies,* both by Andy Rathbone (all published by IDG Books Worldwide, Inc.).

Using the CD with Microsoft Windows

To start using the stuff on the CD, follow these steps:

1. **Insert the CD into your computer's CD-ROM drive.**

2. **Open your Web browser.**

   It doesn't matter which Web browser you use — any browser will do.

3. **Choose Start⇨Run.**

4. **In the dialog box that appears, type** D:\START.HTM

   Replace *D* with the proper drive letter if your CD-ROM drive uses a different letter. (If you don't know the letter, on your Windows desktop, double-click My Computer; the window that opens displays the CD-ROM's drive letter.)

5. **Read through the license agreement, nod your head, and then click the Accept button if you want to use the CD. After you click Accept, you'll jump to the Main Menu.**

   This action displays the file that walks you through the content of the CD.

6. **To navigate within the interface, click any topic of interest for an explanation of the files on the CD and how to use or install them.**

7. **To install the software from the CD, click the software name.**

   You see two options — the option to run or open the file from the current location and the option to save the file to your hard drive. Choose to run or open the file from its current location, and the installation procedure continues. After you are done with the interface, close your browser as usual.

 To run some of the programs, you may need to keep the CD inside your CD-ROM drive. This is a Good Thing. Otherwise, the installed program would have required you to copy a very large chunk of the program onto your hard drive, eating up lots of drive space.

What You'll Find

Shareware programs are fully functional, free trial versions of copyrighted programs. If you like particular programs, register with their authors for a nominal fee and receive licenses, enhanced versions, and technical support. *Freeware programs* are free, copyrighted games, applications, and utilities. You can copy them to as many PCs as you like — free — but they have no technical support. Trial, demo, or evaluation versions are usually limited either by time or functionality (such as being unable to save projects).

Here's a summary of the software on this CD.

Adobe Acrobat Reader, from Adobe Systems, Inc.

This freeware program enables you to view and print PDF files. (In fact, the bonus chapter on the CD is stored as a PDF file, so you have a use for this program right away.) Many Web designers use PDF files to preserve the design of a particular document and also to make the document available across platforms and over the Web.

To find out more about Adobe Acrobat Reader, see www.adobe.com/products/ acrobat/readermain.html.

Bonus chapter: Can We Talk?

Turn to this chapter if you want to add a FrontPage discussion group to your Web site. This chapter explains the ins-and-outs of the Discussion Web Wizard, plus all the other details you need to know to customize and set up an interactive discussion group.

Paint Shop Pro 7, from JASC Software Inc.

If you're itching to try your hand at Web graphics creation, but you lack a graphic editing program, be sure to give this well-regarded program a try (I've included the evaluation version on the CD). Paint Shop Pro contains drawing, cropping, screen capture, and painting tools, plus special effects such as drop shadows, chiseling, and tiling. Paint Shop Pro can also save just about any image format as GIF or JPEG, allowing you to use those graphics in your Web site.

For more information about Paint Shop Pro, see www.paintshoppro.com.

Third-party FrontPage add-ins

Plenty of savvy programmers have taken advantage of FrontPage's popularity by writing add-in programs that add bits of functionality to FrontPage. I've collected a few such programs for you to try.

If you like what you see here, be sure to visit officeupdate.microsoft.com/ welcome/frontpage.asp for more downloadable goodies that work with FrontPage.

JustAddCommerce, from Rich Media Technologies, Inc.

Install this application, and you can add a shopping cart to your FrontPage Web site quickly and easily. The trial version on the CD is fully functional, except that it blocks out customers' credit card and phone numbers.

(FrontPage also has built-in support for ecommerce; be sure to check out the ecommerce-related Web Components. I talk about Web Components in Chapter 13.)

For more information about JustAddCommerce, see www.richmediatech.com/msportal.html

El Scripto Lite, from A Big Lime

This collection of JavaScript-based components enables you to drop extra bits of functionality into your Web pages. El Scripto Lite (the trial version of El Scripto) comes with three components: Last Modified, Text Scroll, and Pop-Up Window. The full version (which you must pay for) comes with fifteen components.

For more information about El Scripto Lite, see www.elscripto.com/info/index.htm

Programs that intergrate with FrontPage

The following programs can be used with FrontPage. They will need to be started from the start menu.

Hi-Visibility for FrontPage, from Hiawatha Island Software, Inc.

This time-limited trial version of the program streamlines the long process of submitting your site information to search engines. The program not only suggests changes you can make to your site's content to make the site more "attractive" to search engines, but also does the submission work for you.

For more information about Hi-Visibility, see www.hisoftware.com/hivisfpam.htm

TagGen for FrontPage, from Hiawatha Island Software, Inc.

This program helps you create *metadata* for your site — that is, descriptive information that search engines, catalog services, and other automated information services can use to index your site. Effective, meaningful metadata increases your site's chances of showing up more frequently in search engines, potentially making your site easier for visitors to find. I've included a trial version on the CD.

For more information about TagGen, see www.hisoftware.com/tgfp.htm

Hi-Position for FrontPage, from Hiawatha Island Software, Inc.

This program helps you see how your site stacks up against its competitors inside search engines. Using Hi-Position, you can enter search phrases, and then see the "rank" of your site's pages, which is based on the results in various search engines. You can also see if other sites score higher and why. I've included a trial version on the CD.

For more information about Hi-Position, see www.hisoftware.com/hiposfp.htm

metaContents Builder, from Hiawatha Island Software, Inc.

This add-in builds portal-style index pages using your pages' metadata (which you can create using TagGen, described earlier), so visitors can easily browse the contents of your site. I've included a trial version on the CD.

For more information about metaContents Builder, see www.hisoftware.com/metaContents.htm

If You've Got Problems (Of the CD Kind)

I tried my best to compile programs that work on most computers with the minimum system requirements. Alas, your computer may differ, and some programs may not work properly for some reason.

The two likeliest problems are that you don't have enough memory (RAM) for the programs you want to use, or you have other programs running that are affecting installation or running of a program. If you get error messages like Not enough memory or Setup cannot continue, try one or more of these methods and then try using the software again:

- Turn off any antivirus software that you have on your computer. Installers sometimes mimic virus activity and may make your computer incorrectly believe that a virus is infecting it.

- Close all running programs. The more programs you're running, the less memory is available to other programs. Installers also typically update files and programs. So if you keep other programs running, installation may not work properly.

- Have your local computer store add more RAM to your computer. This is, admittedly, a drastic and somewhat expensive step. However, if you have a Windows PC, adding more memory can really help the speed of your computer and allow more programs to run at the same time. This may include closing the CD interface and running a product's installation program from Windows Explorer.

If you still have trouble with installing the items from the CD, please call the Hungry Minds Customer Service phone number: 800-762-2974 (outside the U.S.: 317-572-3993).

Index

Hungry Minds, Inc.
End-User License Agreement

5. **Limited Warranty.**

    (a) HMI warrants that the Software and Software Media are free from defects in materials and workmanship under normal use for a period of sixty (60) days from the date of purchase of this Book. If HMI receives notification within the warranty period of defects in materials or workmanship, HMI will replace the defective Software Media.

    (b) HMI AND THE AUTHOR OF THE BOOK DISCLAIM ALL OTHER WARRANTIES, EXPRESS OR IMPLIED, INCLUDING WITHOUT LIMITATION IMPLIED WARRANTIES OF MERCHANTABILITY AND FITNESS FOR A PARTICULAR PURPOSE, WITH RESPECT TO THE SOFTWARE, THE PROGRAMS, THE SOURCE CODE CONTAINED THEREIN, AND/OR THE TECHNIQUES DESCRIBED IN THIS BOOK. HMI DOES NOT WARRANT THAT THE FUNCTIONS CONTAINED IN THE SOFTWARE WILL MEET YOUR REQUIRE-MENTS OR THAT THE OPERATION OF THE SOFTWARE WILL BE ERROR FREE.

    (c) This limited warranty gives you specific legal rights, and you may have other rights that vary from jurisdiction to jurisdiction.

6. **Remedies.**

    (a) HMI's entire liability and your exclusive remedy for defects in materials and workman-ship shall be limited to replacement of the Software Media, which may be returned to HMI with a copy of your receipt at the following address: Software Media Fulfillment Department, Attn.: *FrontPage 2002 For Dummies*, Hungry Minds, Inc., 10475 Crosspoint Blvd., Indianapolis, IN 46256, or call 1-800-762-2974. Please allow four to six weeks for delivery. This Limited Warranty is void if failure of the Software Media has resulted from accident, abuse, or misapplication. Any replacement Software Media will be warranted for the remainder of the original warranty period or thirty (30) days, whichever is longer.

    (b) In no event shall HMI or the author be liable for any damages whatsoever (including without limitation damages for loss of business profits, business interruption, loss of business information, or any other pecuniary loss) arising from the use of or inability to use the Book or the Software, even if HMI has been advised of the possibility of such damages.

    (c) Because some jurisdictions do not allow the exclusion or limitation of liability for conse-quential or incidental damages, the above limitation or exclusion may not apply to you.

7. **U.S. Government Restricted Rights.** Use, duplication, or disclosure of the Software for or on behalf of the United States of America, its agencies and/or instrumentalities (the "U.S. Government") is subject to restrictions as stated in paragraph (c)(1)(ii) of the Rights in Technical Data and Computer Software clause of DFARS 252.227-7013, or subparagraphs (c) (1) and (2) of the Commercial Computer Software – Restricted Rights clause at FAR 52.227-19, and in similar clauses in the NASA FAR supplement, as applicable.

8. **General.** This Agreement constitutes the entire understanding of the parties and revokes and supersedes all prior agreements, oral or written, between them and may not be modified or amended except in a writing signed by both parties hereto that specifically refers to this Agreement. This Agreement shall take precedence over any other documents that may be in conflict herewith. If any one or more provisions contained in this Agreement are held by any court or tribunal to be invalid, illegal, or otherwise unenforceable, each and every other pro-vision shall remain in full force and effect.

Installation Instructions

The *FrontPage 2002 For Dummies* CD offers valuable information that you won't want to miss. To install the items from the CD to your hard drive, follow these steps.

For Microsoft Windows Users

1. **Insert the CD into your computer's CD-ROM drive.**

2. **Click Start↷Run.**

   In the dialog box that appears, type D:\Start.HTM.

   Your browser opens and displays the license agreement.

4. **Read through the license agreement, nod your head, and click the Agree button; the Main menu appears.**

5. **To navigate within the interface, click any topic of interest to take you to an explanation of the files on the CD and how to use or install them.**

6. **To install the software from the CD, click the software name and choose to run or open the file from its current location.**

For more complete information, please see the "About the CD" appendix.

FOR DUMMIES
BOOK REGISTRATION

We want to hear from you!

Visit **dummies.com** to register this book and tell us how you liked it!

✔ Get entered in our monthly prize giveaway.

✔ Give us feedback about this book — tell us what you like best, what you like least, or maybe what you'd like to ask the author and us to change!

✔ Let us know any other *For Dummies* topics that interest you.

Your feedback helps us determine what books to publish, tells us what coverage to add as we revise our books, and lets us know whether we're meeting your needs as a *For Dummies* reader. You're our most valuable resource, and what you have to say is important to us!

Not on the Web yet? It's easy to get started with *Dummies 101: The Internet For Windows 98* or *The Internet For Dummies* at local retailers everywhere.

Or let us know what you think by sending us a letter at the following address:

For Dummies Book Registration
Dummies Press
10475 Crosspoint Blvd.
Indianapolis, IN 46256

BESTSELLING
BOOK SERIES